Katharine Mendelsohn

Judy Garton-Sprenger • Philip Prowse

Macmillan Education
Between Towns Road, Oxford OX4 3PP
A division of Macmillan Publishers Limited
Companies and representatives throughout the world

ISBN 978 0 435 25559 6

First published 2000

Designed by James Evoy

Printed and bound in Great Britain by Martins the Printers, Berwick upon Tweed

2010 2009 2008 2007
10 9 8 7

CONTENTS

INTRODUCTION

Who is Shine for?
It's a three-level course for teenagers starting from beginner or false beginner level in English.

What are the components of Shine?
- Student's Book
- Activity Book
- Teacher's Book
- Two Cassettes

Student's Book

What's in the Student's Book?
- Welcome Unit
- Units 1-9, each with four lessons and a Review
- Story: Super Suzy
- Pairwork Activities
- Projects
- Grammar Summary
- Word List
- Irregular Verb List

How is the Student's Book organised?
The Welcome Unit provides an introduction to the course, and includes a review of some Shine 1 and 2 language such as the present continuous, introductions, countries and leisure activities. It also reintroduces the students to the concept of a vocabulary notebook.

Units 1-9 are topic-based and follow the adventures of a group of young people at an adventure holiday centre. Lessons 1-3 of each unit introduce, practise and personalise the new language. The language is introduced in a dialogue or text which is followed by a number of comprehension and practice activities. Students typically use the new language to talk about themselves and their world, and lessons usually end with a writing activity. All these lessons contain a Grammar File and either a Sound File or a Word File, and many lessons have Look! boxes, Games and Fact Files. The lesson material can be exploited flexibly according to the size and kind of class you have. The Teacher's Book suggests warmers for the beginning of each lesson, optional activities throughout each lesson, consolidation, extension, end-of-class activities and homework. Lesson 4 of each unit has five sections covering Reading, Listening, Speaking, Writing and Study Skills. The Study Skills help the students develop as independent learners. The Review revises the language of the unit and ends with a song.

What about grammar?
Lessons 1-3 in each unit focus on particular grammatical points. These are highlighted in the lesson heading, in Grammar Files which students complete, and in Look! boxes. There is a comprehensive Grammar Summary at the back of the book, organised by unit, which students and teachers can consult during lessons or for homework.

What about pronunciation?
Sound Files in Lessons 1-3 of each unit give integrated practice in pronunciation, stress and intonation. These activities are recorded and provide models for repetition and discrimination. Phonemic symbols are given as support where relevant; these are intended for recognition only. The Word List includes phonemic transcriptions of all items.

What about vocabulary?
Word Files in Lesson 1–3 of each unit highlight aspects such as lexical categories and phrasal verbs, while the Word Building sections focus on prefixes and suffixes. The Word List gives lesson-by-lesson coverage of all new words. Students are encouraged to develop their own vocabulary notebooks in the Study Skills sections.

What about the story?
The story, Super Suzy, follows the grammatical syllabus of the book and is designed to be done on completion of each unit.

What about pairwork?
As with projects, the Pairwork Activities are a flexible resource which can be exploited during or at the end of a unit, with the whole or part of the class.

What about projects?
There are nine projects at the back of the Student's Book, one for each unit. The projects are intended to be used flexibly. Some teachers may wish to do a project with the whole class after completing a unit while others may wish to integrate the project as they progress through the unit. Other options include using the projects for homework, or with the more confident students in mixed ability classes. Projects provide a valuable resource for student creativity and self-expression.

Activity Book

What's in the Activity Book?

Lessons 1-3 of each unit contain Grammar, Vocabulary and Pronunciation activities. Lesson 4 develops Reading, Writing and Study Skills, and includes a crossword for vocabulary consolidation. The Review contains more formal exercises in the style of the Cambridge Exams to revise the unit language, and ends with a 'How good are you?' section inviting students to review their progress in the unit. The Round-Up, at the end of the book, is an informal quiz covering every aspect of grammar and topic in the book.

How do I use the Activity Book?

The Activity Book offers many options. It can be used for homework or in class after completing a lesson in the Student's Book. Alternatively you may wish to do some or all of the activities as you proceed through the lesson; the Teacher's Book indicates which activities may be done at each stage of the lesson. You may like to use the Review as a test. The Activity Book Answers are at the back of the Teacher's Book.

Teacher's Book

What's in the Teacher's Book?

- Introduction
- Lesson notes including word lists, tapescripts and answers
- Story: Super Suzy
- Activity Book Answers

How do I use the lesson notes?

The lessons in the Student's Book are designed to be taught as they stand. All you need is the Student's Book and the cassette. The lesson notes in the Teacher's Book offer you extra options: warmers to start the lesson, optional activities throughout the lesson, and consolidation, extension, end-of-class and homework suggestions. The tapescript and answers for each lesson are also provided. So a quick look at the lesson notes before class will enable you to tailor your lesson to the particular group you are teaching without having to spend a long time on preparation. Similarly the answers to activities in the Student's Book and Activity Book can be given to students on the board if desired, cutting down on your time spent marking after class.

Cassettes

What's recorded on the cassettes?

The cassettes contain all the recorded listening material in the Student's Book, including Sound Files, Review activities and the songs. Recorded items are indicated by a cassette symbol in both the Student's and Teacher's Book.

Meet Everyone!

p4

Target language

Present continuous
Present simple

Vocabulary

Indoor and outdoor leisure activities
Holidays
Interests

Optional Aids

- World map showing Greece, Italy, Spain, England, USA - California
- Holiday brochures with pictures of activities.

Warmer

- Introduce yourself to the class. Say: *Hello! My name's ... I'm from ...*
- Walk around the class introducing yourself to individual students, using *I'm (called) ...* and *I'm from ...* . The students reply in the same way.
- Students introduce themselves to each other.
- Use the maps to show the different places.
- Ask students to look at the ACE advertisement on page 4 and show them that ACE is an adventure holiday centre for young people situated on the south-west coast of England.
- Play the cassette to introduce the characters while students follow pages 4 and 5 of their books.

Tapescript

Alison *Hi! I'm Alison. Welcome to ACE Adventure Holiday Centre, your home for the next two weeks!*

Manuel *My name's Manuel. I'm from Barcelona in Spain.*

Aliki *Hi - I'm Aliki. I'm from Hania in Greece.*

Lucy *Hi! I'm Lucy, and I come from London.*

Holly *Hi, there! I'm called Holly. I'm from the United States, from California.*

Paolo *Hello! My name's Paolo. I'm from Milan in Italy.*

Mark *My name's Mark. I'm from Bristol - in the west of England.*

Optional activities

- Point to different characters and ask *What's his/her name? Where's he/she from?*
- Ask *Who's Alison? How long do people stay at ACE? Where is ACE?*

1 Read and Speak

Aim: to revise present continuous and present simple and to introduce vocabulary of holiday activities.

- Look at the ACE brochure on pages 6 and 7. Ask about the activities in the photos, e.g., *Is he/she climbing/swimming?* Students answer, e.g., *Yes, he/she is. No, he/she isn't. He/She's skydiving.*
- Students ask and answer round the class.
- They can also use the photos on page 4.

Activity Book p2 Exercise 1

Optional activities

- In pairs, students ask each other further questions about the characters, e.g., *Who's abseiling? Is Alison dancing?* etc.
- Use the brochures you have brought for students to talk about available holiday activities.

2 Speak

Aim: to revise superlative adjectives and to personalise the vocabulary of holiday activities; to practise superlative adjectives with *most.*

- Ask students one or two of the questions.
- Encourage students to ask your opinion.
- In pairs or small groups students discuss the four questions.
- They can summarise their answers and report back to the class, e.g., *Two of us think that water-skiing is the most exciting, but the others think windsurfing or abseiling is more exciting. Everyone thinks that skydiving is the most dangerous, and no one thinks it's the most fun.*
- Ask two or three students what they would most like to do at ACE.
- Say what you would like to do, and why.
- In pairs or small groups students discuss the question.
- As before, they can report back to the class.

Optional activities

- Students write statements about the four activities they think are the most exciting, etc.
- They write a short paragraph about what they would most like to do at ACE and why. This is also suitable for homework.
- Do a class survey on holiday activities. Students can find out what people have done and would or would not like to do, and why.

3 Read and Write

Aim: to find out about the people at ACE and to practise question words.

- Books closed, ask students *Who is Alison?*
- They read *Who's who at ACE?* and write questions.
- Check orally.

Answers

2 How old is she/Alison?
3 What is she writing?
4 What does she love doing?
5 What languages does she speak?
6 Who is helping Alison?
7 Where is Rick from?
8 How long are they staying at the Centre?

Optional activity

- Books closed, ask questions about Alison, Rick and Tara.

4 Grammar File

Aim: to practise the present simple compared with the present continuous.

- Students complete the chart in their notebooks.
- Check orally.
- Then ask the questions.

Answers

Present continuous

*She's abseiling. She **isn't** climbing.*
*Alison **is** writing a book.*
*Rick and Tara **are** staying at ACE.*

Present simple

*Alison **is** a qualified sports instructor.*
*She **loves** watersports.*
*Rick **comes** from Australia.*

*We use the present **simple** to talk about states and routines. We use the present **continuous** to talk about temporary events and what is happening at the moment.*

Optional activity

- Students make statements using the two tenses in contrast, e.g., *My aunt lives in the city, but just now she's staying in the country on holiday.*

Activity Book p2 Exercise 2

5 Listen and Write

Aim: to use the present simple and continuous to talk about people's interests and activities.

- Students first read the chart and note where the gaps are.
- Play the cassette. Students listen and complete the chart.
- Play it again if necessary.
- Check orally.
- Using the paragraph about Alison as a model, students write about Rick and Tara.
- This is also suitable for homework.

Tapescript 

Rick *Hi everyone, I'm Rick, and I'm 21. I teach sport and technology, and this summer I'm having a great time designing computer games. You can help me! But I really like watersports more than anything. And I speak Italian.*

Tara *And I'm Tara. I'm 20 and I teach sport, drama and music. This summer, I'm learning to scuba dive, which is fun! I love dancing, and I speak Spanish and French.*

Answers

	Rick	*Tara*
Age	***21***	***20***
Teaches	*Sport and technology*	***Sport**, drama and **music***
This summer	*Designing **computer games***	*Learning to **scuba dive***
Loves	*Watersports*	***Dancing***
Speaks	***Italian***	*Spanish and **French***

Optional activity

- Students work in pairs, taking turns to ask about Alison, Rick and Tara. The student answering has his/her book closed.

Activity Book p3 Exercise 3

6 STUDY SKILLS

Aim: to help students to learn vocabulary systematically.

- Encourage students to bring vocabulary notebooks to class.
- Copy the word map on to the board. Students add other words.
- They suggest other topics for word maps, e.g., food.

Activity Book p3 Exercise 4

Consolidation and Extension activities

- Use the word map areas as the basis for a vocabulary quiz. With books closed, and in a given time, students think of as many activities as they can in one category, e.g., *outdoor sports*.
- Character quiz. Give students a short time to look again at pages 5-7. Then ask questions about the characters. This could be organised in teams.
- Students each make a chart like the one on page 7, with an alternative for Teaches, e.g., Studies. Then they work in pairs, asking questions to complete the chart about their partner. They can report back to the class.

Homework

- Students complete the word map in their notebooks.
- They review the form and use of the present simple and continuous.
- They complete a chart, like that on page 7, for themselves. Then they write a paragraph about themselves and one about their partner, in the form of an entry for *Who's who at ACE?*

Activity Book Welcome Unit, p2-3
Grammar Summary p118

1 WATERSPORTS

Lesson 1 *It's a fabulous day, isn't it?* p8

Target language
Question tags
Gerund
Vocabulary
Leisure activities

Warmer

- Quickly check what activities students remember from the Welcome Unit.
- Then ask about their likes, e.g., *Do you like windsurfing/abseiling?* or *Have you tried canoeing/riding a horse?*

1 READ

Aim: to present question tags and gerunds.
- Point to each person in turn and ask *What is he/she doing?*
- Then ask who the people are.
- Play the cassette. Students listen and follow in their books.
- Play it again, sentence by sentence, for students to repeat. This is best done with the class divided into three groups, each taking one part.
- In groups of three, students read the dialogue.
- Then they complete the true or false exercise in their notebooks.
- Check orally.

Tapescript

Lucy *Hi, Mark. It's a fabulous day, isn't it?*
Mark *It's OK.*
Lucy *You arrived yesterday, didn't you? Where are you from?*
Mark *I live in Bristol.*
Lucy *Oh, that isn't far from here, is it? I'm from London. What are you going to do today?*
Mark *I don't feel like doing anything.*
Lucy *Why not? What's the matter?*
Mark *You ask a lot of questions, don't you?*
Lucy *I'm only being friendly! Why don't you go windsurfing? It'll be a laugh.*
Mark *I'm really not keen on watersports. I can't stand getting wet.*
Holly *Hi, Mark - can I borrow your pen?*
Mark *Sure, here you are.*
Holly *Thanks. I love canoeing - so I'm going with Tara. What about you guys?*
Mark *Oh, well ... perhaps I'll go canoeing too.*
Lucy *I see. Well, I'm going windsurfing with Rick. And I'm really looking forward to it.*

Answers

1 *True.*
2 *True.*
3 *False. He doesn't feel like doing anything.*
4 *False. He's really not keen on watersports.*
5 *True.*
6 *False. Mark lends Holly a pen./Holly borrows Mark's pen.*
7 *True.*
8 *False. She's looking forward to going windsurfing.*

Optional activities

- Ask questions about the text, e.g., *Who's from London? Who doesn't like watersports?*
- Students act out the dialogue.
- Students imagine they are at ACE and decide which watersport they would sign up for, if any, giving reasons.

Activity Book p4 Exercise 1

2 GRAMMAR FILE

Aim: to present and practise question tags.
- Students copy and complete the sentences in their notebooks.
- Check orally.

Tapescript and answers 

Question tags
It's a fabulous day, ***isn't it?***
It isn't far from here, ***is it?***
You ask a lot of questions, ***don't you?***
She hasn't got a pen, ***has she?***
He arrived yesterday, ***didn't he?***
They can swim, ***can't they?***

Activity Book p4 Exercise 2

3 Sound File

Aim: to practise question tags with falling intonation.
• Play the cassette again, sentence by sentence, pausing for students to repeat.
• Pay particular attention to the falling intonation on the tag.

Optional activity

• Students read the passage again, picking out question tags.
• They read the sentences with question tags, focusing on the falling intonation.

4 Write and Speak

Aim: to practise question tags in speaking and writing.
• Point to the picture of Mark and say *This is Mark. Mark lives in Bristol, doesn't he?*
• Students complete the exercise in their notebooks.
• Check orally. Pay attention to the falling intonation.
• Make similar statements with tag questions about students e.g., *You come to school by bus, don't you? You can't speak Russian, can you?*
• Students work in pairs or small groups. They talk about the topics given, using statements with questions tags.
• If there is space, they can move round the room asking different people.

Answers

1 ***Lucy*** *lives in London,* ***doesn't she?***
2 ***Holly*** *is American,* ***isn't she?***
3 ***Mark*** *doesn't like watersports,* ***does he?***
4 ***Lucy*** *has got blonde hair,* ***hasn't she?***
5 ***Holly*** *hasn't got a bag,* ***has she?***
6 ***Mark*** *lent Holly a pen,* ***didn't he?***

Optional activity

• Students note the answers they are given and report back to the class.
• Students write up a short dialogue between themselves and one partner.

Activity Book p4 Exercise 3

5 Speak and Write

Aim: to practise gerunds by finding out about people's interests.
• First choose two or three items in the chart and ask students their views.
• Students move round the room asking questions to complete the chart. If there isn't room, they work in groups of about eight.
• When their charts are complete, they use the information to write sentences in their notebooks.
• Check the work.
• Students may report back to the class.

LOOK! box
• Check students understand that we use the gerund form of the verb after certain verbs and after all prepositions.
• Several students make sentences round the class. These may be based on their charts in Activity 5, about themselves or about characters in the book.

Activity Book p5 Exercise 4

6 Write

Aim: to personalise the use of gerunds after certain verbs and prepositions.
• Students write sentences about themselves and their likes and dislikes.

Activity Book p5 Exercises 5 and 6

Consolidation and Extension activities

• Conversation chain. You start by saying to a student, e.g., *You like football, don't you?* He/She answers *Yes, I do* then turns to the next student and says, e.g., *You're good at English, aren't you?*
• Memory chain. You start again, saying, e.g., *I'm keen on reading.* A student says, e.g., (*Your name*) *is keen on reading and I'm keen on playing tennis.* Continue in this way round the class. Anyone who forgets is 'out' and a new round starts.
• The game can be adapted with other verbs/ prepositions.

Homework

• Students use the chart in Activity 5 to find out about their family's likes and dislikes. Then they write sentences.
• Students research a pop, film or sports star and write about the person's likes, dislikes and hopes.

Activity Book Unit 1 Lesson 1, p4-5
Grammar Summary p118

Lesson 2 *I didn't mean to laugh*

Target language
Verb + infinitive
Vocabulary
Feelings

Optional Aids

Magazine pictures, e.g., from films or photo stories, showing people with obvious emotions, e.g., fear, shame, etc.

Warmer

- Tell students how you are feeling, e.g., *Today I'm feeling happy, because I had a letter from a friend. I'm also feeling tired, because I was working late last night.*
- Students make similar comments about themselves and people they know.
- Pin up or pass round the pictures you brought. Students choose two or three to speak about, saying, e.g., *She looks miserable. And he looks angry.*

1 Read

Aim: to present verbs with infinitives and adjectives for feelings.

- Students look at the picture and focus on specific characters asking, e.g., *How's Holly/Mark/Tara feeling?*
- Use the cassette to present and practise the passage.
- Students answer the questions. This may be done orally or they may write the answers in their notebooks.
- Check the answers orally.

Tapescript

'First,' said Tara, 'we're going to practise capsizing.'

'What?!' exclaimed Mark. 'I'm not going to capsize - I don't want to get wet!'

'You need to know how to capsize safely,' explained Tara. 'So listen carefully. I want you to hold the sides of the canoe with your arms and lean over. The canoe will then capsize.'

Everyone laughed - except Mark. He seemed to be a bit nervous.

'Keep calm. Wait until you are completely upside down in the water before you try to get out. Then you push yourself out of the canoe and swim to the surface. OK. Are you ready? Take a deep breath, everyone - and go!'

One by one the canoes turned over. Mark was the last to capsize. And one by one the heads came up - except for Mark.

'Hey, what's happened to Mark?' asked Tara.

Holly laughed. 'He's pretending to be in trouble.'

Tara was worried. 'Perhaps he really is in trouble!'

Holly swam to Mark's canoe and dived underwater. She reappeared with Mark and managed to pull him to the side. Tara couldn't help laughing because he looked so miserable.

'What happened, Mark?' she asked. 'Did you get stuck?'

'He's swallowed a lot of water,' said Holly. 'I think he panicked.'

Then Tara understood. 'Oh, Mark! You can't swim, can you?'

Mark shook his head. He looked very ashamed.

'Oh, Mark, I didn't mean to laugh,' said Tara. 'I'll teach you to swim,' she offered. 'Would you like to learn?'

Answers

1 *He refused to capsize.*
2 *He felt nervous.*
3 *No, he really was in trouble.*
4 *She managed to pull him to the side.*
5 *Because Mark looked so miserable.*
6 *He shook his head.*
7 *'I didn't mean to laugh.'*
8 *'I'll teach you to swim.'*

Optional activities

- Books closed, students retell the story. This can be done sentence by sentence round the class.
- In groups of three, students act out the story, using the direct speech from the text.
- In groups of four, one student narrates while the others act.

2 LISTEN AND SPEAK

Aim: to listen for specific information to complete sentences using verbs with infinitive.

- Students first look quickly through the sentence parts.
- Play the cassette. They listen and match the sentences.
- Play it again for them to check.
- Check orally. Different students read complete sentences.

Tapescript

Rick	*Alison - I need to go to the shops after lunch. Can I borrow your bike?*
Alison	*OK, but I need it later this afternoon.*
Rick	*Oh, no problem. I'll be back in an hour.*
Alison	*Do you want me to give you a lift in my car?*
Rick	*No, I'd like to cycle. But thanks for the offer.*
Tara	*Alison, did you hear what happened this morning?*
Alison	*Yes, Tara, I know. Mark can't swim.*
Tara	*I'm a bit worried about him. Could you talk to him?*
Alison	*Yes, I promise I'll have a word with him this evening. And please will you teach him to swim?*
Tara	*Sure. We're going down to the beach for a swim now. Do you want to come with us?*
Alison	*No, I'm not going to go swimming today! It's much too cold!*
Tara	*OK - see you later.*
Alison	*Wait a minute - I wanted to talk to you about the barbecue at the weekend. Do you think we should have it on Saturday or on Sunday?*
Tara	*Well, we're going on a boat trip on Sunday so...*
Alison	*OK. Let's have the barbecue on Saturday.*

Ask and answer

- Ask the first question and elicit the answers.
- Students continue asking and answering, taking the questions in any order.
- This can be done in pairs or round the class.

Answers

1c Alison agreed to lend Rick her bike.

2e She offered to give Rick a lift.

3f She promised to talk to Mark.

4b She asked Tara to teach Mark to swim.

5a She refused to go swimming.

6d She decided to have the barbecue on Saturday.

Optional activity

- Guessing game. This can be played in pairs or teams. Student A thinks of something he/she has promised/refused/decided, etc. to do. Student B must guess by asking a set number of questions, e.g., *Have you decided to do something? Have you decided to do something at school? Have you decided to work harder?* etc. Then they change roles.

Activity Book p 6 Exercise 1

3 GRAMMAR FILE

Aim: to present and practise verbs followed by the infinitive.

- Students copy the chart into their notebooks and complete it.
- Check orally.
- Students now find and list other examples of verbs used with infinitives from the first two activities.

Answers

Verb + infinitive

Holly and Mark decided to go canoeing.

Tara told everyone ***to take*** *a deep breath.*

Tara offered ***to teach*** *Mark to swim.*

Activity 1

going to practise going to capsize want to get wet need to know want (someone) to hold seemed to be try to get out pretending to be managed to pull mean to laugh teach (someone) to swim like to learn

Activity 2

agreed to go offered to give promised to talk asked to teach refused to go decided to have

Activity Book p6 Exercise 2

4 WRITE

Aim: to practise verbs followed by the infinitive or gerund.

- Students complete the exercise.
- Check orally.
- Give extra practice if there are problems.

Answers

1 *Mark didn't enjoy* ***canoeing*** *very much.*
2 *He tried* ***to get*** *out of his canoe.*
3 *He wasn't pretending* ***to be*** *in trouble.*
4 *He couldn't help* ***swallowing*** *water.*
5 *Holly managed* ***to rescue*** *Mark.*
6 *Now Mark wants* ***to learn*** *to swim.*
7 *Tara decided* ***to give*** *Mark some lessons.*
8 *He can practise* ***swimming*** *in the sea.*
9 *He needs* ***to know*** *how to float.*

Optional activity

• Team game. Each team prepares a list of about six verbs which are followed by either the gerund or the infinitive. They take turns to challenge the other team to make a correct sentence when given a verb.

Activity Book p7 Exercise 3 and 4

5 WORD FILE

Aim: to present and practise adjectives describing feelings.
• Students write the adjectives in the correct columns. They may refer to the text for meanings.
• Now they look for adjectives in the text.
• Check orally, or let different students write the words on the board in two columns.
• Ask two or three students questions.
• Students continue, working either in pairs or small groups.
• They may report back to the class, or summarise, e.g., *All of us feel nervous when we're going to take an exam. Two of us feel scared when we watch a horror film, one person feels excited, but the other one feels bored.*

Answers

calm	*angry*
excited	*ashamed*
happy	*bored*
pleased	*miserable*
relaxed	*nervous*
relieved	*sad*
	scared
	tired
	worried

In the text
nervous, calm, worried, miserable, ashamed

Optional activity

• Students write sentences about their own and their partner's feelings.

Activity Book p7 Exercise 5

6 WRITE

Aim: to personalise the target language by writing about a past event.
• Prepare this by class discussion and sharing ideas.
• Students then write about the incident, using the prompts given.
• Check the work. Students may exchange paragraphs and read each other's.
• This is also suitable for homework.

Consolidation and Extension activities

• Group or pair game. Students find the opposites of the adjectives in Exercise 5 e.g., bored-interested.
• Mime game. This can be played in teams. Students think of an adjective, or you can whisper one to them. Then one mimes doing things in that way, e.g., smiling for *happy*, etc. The others guess the adjective.

Homework

• Students write the adjectives in their vocabulary notebooks, grouping them by meaning.
• Students interview a friend or a member of their family about the first time they did something new, e.g., first day at work or school, first time in a plane, first swim, etc. and ask how they felt. If they use L1 they should write notes in English.
• Then they use their notes to write a short report.

Activity Book Unit 1 Lesson 2, p6-7
Grammar Summary p118

Lesson 3 *Try harder!*

Target language
Comparison of adverbs
Adverbs of degree
Vocabulary
Watersports and outdoor activities

Warmer

• Play 'Hangman' to revise vocabulary for watersports and outdoor activities.

1 READ

Aim: to present sports vocabulary and superlative adverbs.

• Go round the class quickly to find how many people regularly do any kind of sport, and how many enjoy watching sport, either live or on TV.
• Ask the students to look at the photos and play the cassette. Ask which sport goes with with which picture.
• Students answer the questions. Check orally.

Tapescript 

SPLASH

Parascending

This looks really exciting. You have a parachute which is attached to a speedboat. The parachute fills with air and lifts you higher and higher into the sky. But when you're up in the air, it's quite boring because all you can do is hang there and enjoy the view! At the end, you splash down gently into the water.

Snorkelling

The best place to do this is along a rocky coastline. You don't have to be a strong swimmer - all you have to do is float and pull yourself along the rocks. This is a good sport for people who are extremely lazy! You'll see some amazing things underwater - empty drink cans, old shoes - and you may even see some fish!

Windsurfing

This is very hard work when you're a beginner! When you first stand on the board and try to pull up the sail, it seems impossible. You need to practise keeping your balance on the board, and you mustn't be afraid of falling off. If you don't get wet, try harder! After a couple of lessons, you'll find that you can stay up longer and travel further.

Water-skiing

The hardest part is getting up onto your feet. You sit in the water holding the rope and wait for the boat to pull you up. Suddenly the rope tightens and your arms are almost pulled off. Then if you're lucky, you speed across the water. When you can stay up longer than a few seconds, you'll start to enjoy it! But it's an incredibly expensive sport.

Answers

A Water-skiing.
B Windsurfing.
C Snorkelling.
D Parascending.

1 Snorkelling.
2 Windsurfing.
3 Water-skiing.
4 Parascending.

Optional activities

• Students work in pairs or small groups. They choose a sport and write a similar short paragraph about it. Then they present their sport to the class.

Activity Book p8 Exercise 1

2 GRAMMAR FILE

Aim: to present and practise the comparison of adverbs.

• Students copy and complete the chart.
• Check orally or ask different students to complete the chart on the board.

Answers

Comparison of adverbs

Comparative	*Superlative*
more + adverb	***most + adverb***
more easily	*(the) **most** easily*
***more** slowly*	*(the) **most** slowly*
***more** quickly*	*(the) **most quickly***

Irregular forms

well	*better*	*(the) best*
badly	*worse*	*(the) worst*
hard	***harder***	*(the) hardest*
fast	*faster*	*(the) **fastest***
high	***higher***	*(the) highest*
far	***further***	*(the) furthest*
long	*longer*	*(the) **longest***
late	***later***	*(the) latest*
early	*earlier*	*(the) **earliest***

Optional activities

- Students find examples of such adverbs in the text.
- They make sentences using adverbs from the chart.
- Chain comparisons. Student 1 says, e.g., *A bird flies high*. Student 2 says, e.g., An *aeroplane flies higher than a bird*. Student 3 says, e.g., *A space ship flies the highest*. Student 4 starts with a new adverb.
- This can also be played in groups.

Activity Book p8 Exercises 2

3 LISTEN AND SPEAK

Aim: to listen for specific information; to practise comparison of adverbs.

- Students look at the chart to see what kind of information they are listening for.
- Play the cassette. They listen and complete the chart.
- Check orally.
- Read the speech bubbles.
- Students then make more sentences. This can be done round the class or in groups or pairs.

Tapescript and answers 

Lucy *Hi. Holly.*

Holly *Hi, everyone. Did you have fun windsurfing?*

Lucy *Yes, it was great.*

Paolo *Aliki was brilliant!*

Aliki *Well, it was quite easy for me - I've done windsurfing before.*

Holly *How long did you stay up, Aliki?*

Aliki *I stayed up for **about 10 minutes**.*

Holly *Great - and how far did you go?*

Aliki *I went **about 500 metres**.*

Holly *Wow! And how many times did you fall off the board?*

Aliki *I suppose I fell off **five times**.*

Holly *How about you, Lucy?*

Lucy *Not too bad. I stayed up for **five minutes** and I went about **100 metres**.*

Holly *How many times did you fall off?*

Lucy *Oh, I fell off the board **at least 10 times**! But Paolo fell off more than me.*

Holly *How many times did you fall off, Paolo?*

Paolo *I don't know - I lost count! **At least 20 times**.*

Holly *And how long did you stay up?*

Paolo *I stayed up for **about thirty seconds** - and I only I went **about ten metres**. And now I'm extremely tired.*

Holly *Poor Paolo!*

	Aliki	*Lucy*	*Paolo*
How long did they stay up?	***10 mins***	***5 mins***	***30 seconds***
How far did they go?	***500m***	***100m***	***10m***
How many times did they fall off the board?	***5***	***10***	***20***

Answers

1 *Aliki.*
2 *Aliki.*
3 *Paolo.*

Activity Book p9, Exercise 3

4 SPEAK

Aim: to present and practise adverbs of degree.

- Students find the adverbs from the Look! box in the text.
- Check they understand the strength of the adverbs, e.g., *quite* (moderate)to *incredibly* (strong).
- Read the two statements. You may give one or two more.
- Students then think of more statements.
- They talk in groups about sports and games.
- Monitor the activity and check use of adverbs.

Optional activity

- Groups make notes on their discussion and present it to the class as a short report.

Activity Book p9 Exercise 4

5 SOUND FILE

Aim: to practise initial /s/ + consonant.

- Play the cassette. Students listen and repeat.
- Give extra practice if there are problems. Make sure students do not insert an /ɪ/ between consonants.

Tapescript

sky *skiing* *snorkel* *speed* *sport*
stay *start* *swimmer* *splash* *strong*

Optional activities

- Students think of other words beginning with /s/ + consonant, e.g., *school, student, small,* etc.
- They use the words in sentences.

6 SPEAK

Aim: to practise making comparisons about personal achievements.

- You may tell students your own answers to the questions.
- Students work in groups of three, noting down their own and the other answers.
- They make comparisons.
- Monitor activity and check use of comparisons.
- Groups may report back to the class.

7 WRITE

Aim: to use superlative adverbs in writing.

- Students write sentences based on their notes.
- Check their writing. You may also check orally.
- This is also suitable for homework.

Consolidation and Extension activities

- Choose a letter of the alphabet. Give students a limited time to see how many adverbs they can think of beginning with that letter.
- This can also be done with sports-related words.
- Give the class a simple task, e.g., say or write the alphabet, say or write their own address, etc. Time them and see who finishes first, last, etc. This is probably better done in small groups, with the groups making the comparisons and reporting back to the class.
- Confident students could try making up tongue twisters using words with /s/ + consonant, e.g., *The strong swimmer swam swiftly and started splashing.* They write them on the board for others to say.

Homework

- Students learn the comparison of adverbs chart.
- They look for reports of sporting events in the papers or on TV and make a short summary report in English, using adverbs of comparison and degree. They can read the report in class and then hand it in.

Activity Book Unit 1 Lesson 3, p8-9
Grammar Summary p118

Lesson 4 *Penpals!*

Vocabulary
Personal information
Linking words *so* and *but.*
Prefixes *dis-* and *un-*.

Optional Aids

Bring in magazines which arrange penpals or addresses of penpal organisations.

Warmer

- Find out if any students have penpals. Invite them to tell the class about them.
- Ask what kind of information one would put in a first letter to a penpal.

READING

1 Aim: to read a letter for gist and to note structure and layout.

- Students read through the letter, matching topics and paragraphs.
- Check orally.
- You may comment on the structure of the letter, starting with the reason for writing, then describing the writer herself, her family, school, and interests, and ending with questions to the penpal.
- Draw the students' attention to the layout of the letter.

Answers

1 Why she is writing
2 Where she lives
3 Her family
4 Her school
5 Free time
6 Two questions

Optional activity

- Books closed, students answer questions about Aliki. This could be done in pairs, with the questioner's book open.

2 Aim: to focus on linking words *so* and *but.*

- Students re-read the letter and underline the words.
- Then they complete the rule.
- Check that they have found all the examples.

Answers

We use ***but*** *to talk about two contrasting ideas.*
We use ***so*** *to talk about consequence or result.*

Activity Book p10 Exercise 1

LISTENING

3 Aim: to listen to a conversation for specific information.

- Students first look through the penpal details and may guess at how to fill the blanks.
- Play the cassette. They listen and complete the coupons.
- Check orally. Then ask which person Aliki has written to.
- If students have problems, play the cassette again, pausing after useful information is given.

Tapescript and answers 

Manuel *Is this your magazine?*
Aliki *Yes - it's not bad at all. It's got lots of penpals in it and I've just written to one.*
Manuel *Which one?*
Aliki *Which one do you think?*
Manuel *The one who likes watersports?*
Aliki *That's right! He's* ***16****, which is great. And he can write in French and* ***Spanish*** *too, so why don't you write to him?*
Manuel *You must be joking! I want to practise my English, not my Spanish! And anyway he only wants to write to* ***girls****.*
Aliki *Oh yes. I missed that. How about this one? She looks pretty.*
Manuel *Mm , but she's only 14.*
Aliki *So what? She says she wants to write to people who are* ***older*** *than her.*
Manuel *Yes, but look here. She hates computers and* ***football****. No thanks. I quite like the sound of this girl though. She's 15 and she likes computers and* ***dogs.***
Aliki *Yes. And she says she hopes to* ***meet*** *you one day. And there's another one here called Rachel - she's* ***16*** *years old.*
Manuel *Yes, and it says she likes clothes, and* ***music****. I wonder what kind of music?*
Aliki *Why don't you write and ask her?*
Manuel *OK. I think I will. What's her address?*
Aliki *It doesn't say - you have to write to the magazine and then they send your letter on.*
Manuel *Oh, I see. Right.*

Answers

1 16	*2 music*	*3 dogs*
4 meet	*5 16*	*6 girls*
7 Spanish	*8 football*	*9 older*

Aliki has written to ***Dave Fairbrook.***

Optional activities

- Students choose which person they would write to, and say why.
- Give students addresses of penfriend organisations. Show students the magazines you have brought in. Encourage students to choose and write to someone.
- If you have access to e-mail, students could find electronic penpals.

SPEAKING

4 Aim: to give personal details.

- Students first complete the coupon for themselves.
- Ask a few students to read their coupons to the class.
- Students ask each other about their interests and find a penpal. This can either be done in groups of 6-8 or, if space, by moving around the room.
- They report back.

WRITING

5 Aim: to focus on the structure and layout of personal letters.

- Students re-read the letter on p14, referring to the explanatory notes.
- If you have not already done so, draw attention to the order of the topics in the letter.
- Students use the completed coupons to write a letter.
- This task is suitable for homework.

Activity Book p10 Exercise 2.

WORD BUILDING

6 Aim: to present and practise negative prefixes *dis-* and *un-*.

- You may first check that students use the prefixes correctly and understand the meaning of the words with and without the prefix.
- Then they complete the sentences.
- Check orally.

Answers

2 unpopular	*3 unnecessary*	*4 disagree*
5 unusual	*6 Unfortunately*	*7 unlucky*
8 disappeared	*9 unconscious*	

Optional activities

- Students think of other words that make an opposite by adding a prefix, e.g., *unhappy, displeased.*
- Learning tip: there is no easy way to remember which words take which prefix, although those derived from verbs often take *dis-*, e.g., *disagree, disagreeable,* while adjectives and nouns tend to take *un-*, as in *unpopular, unpopularity.*

STUDY SKILLS

7 Aim: to encourage students to increase their knowledge of English by reading.

- Ask students to bring in and share any English language magazines or books.
- If you can, start a class library of English books. Graded readers are a good way to start. Another possibility is to bring in local English language newspapers or pop and sports magazines.
- Another option is to subscribe to an English teaching magazine.

Activity Book p11 Exercises 3 and 4

Consolidation and Extension activities

- If anyone is reading an English book or subscribes to an English magazine, encourage them to tell the class about it.
- Adjective chain. This may be played in large groups or round the class. Students write a list of words that use negative prefixes. Then round the class/group, one says a word. The next student says the negative, then turns to the third and says a new word. Those who get a word wrong or repeat one are 'out'.
- Guessing game. Play this in groups or teams. Students think of an activity they like and one they hate. The others have to guess what it is, and whether they like or hate it, in a limited number of guesses, e.g., ten. To make it more challenging, they may not ask a direct question until they have asked a correct indirect question, e.g., *Is this an outdoor activity?* If the answer is *Yes*, they may ask e.g., *Is it cycling?* If *No*, they should ask e.g., *Is it a team activity?*

Homework

- Students start a section in their vocabulary notebooks for words with negative prefixes.
- Students think of a famous person, living or dead, they would like as a penfriend and write their first letter to that person. They also add a note saying why they chose that person.
- Students pretend to be a famous person, or cartoon character, and write their first letter to a penfriend.

Pairwork

Pairwork Activity p107 and 115
Aim: to use the target language to carry out an information gap activity.

- Remind students that the activity will only be successful if they do not look at each other's material.
- They each look at their chart and work out the questions they need to ask.
- Student A asks first, and fills in the spaces.
- Then they change roles.
- Monitor the activity for correct use of verb forms in particular.

Answers

	Mark	*Holly*	*Manuel*	*Lucy*	*Paolo*
Mother	***teacher***	***model***	*travel agent*	***doctor***	***works in a bank***
Father	***unemployed***	*film director*	***cartoon artist***	***journalist***	***engineer***
Loves	***playing chess***	***going to the movies***	***computer games, football***	***playing the guitar, dancing***	***taking photos***
Hates	***bossy people***	***being alone***	***snakes***	***people who are late***	***flying***
Doing at the moment	***looking for a girlfriend***	***trying to get into drama school***	***saving up for a computer***	***writing a new song***	***learning karate***

Activity Book Unit 1 Lesson 4, p10-11
Grammar Summary p118.

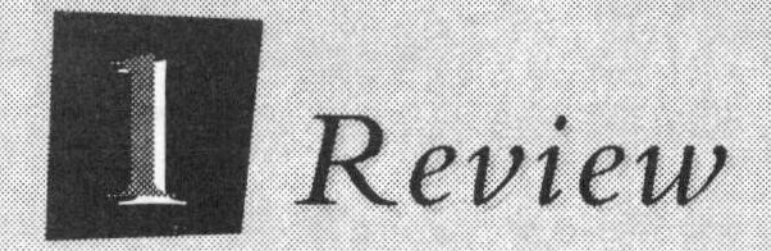

1 Review

1 Read and choose

Answers

1 so *2 is making* *3 to* *4 pleased*
5 to improve *6 to send* *7 nervous* *8 to be*
9 are working *10 help* *11 aren't* *12 excited*
13 meeting *14 to try* *15 to send* *16 because*
17 to leave *18 are visiting*

2 Read and complete

Answers

1 am having *2 am making* *3 are looking*
4 are *5 teach* *6 take*
7 organise *8 watch* *9 have*
10 am writing *11 want* *12 is starting*

3 Listen and add

- Students may first write the tags.
- Pay attention to intonation on the tags.

Tapescript and answers

Listen and add question tags to show that you are sure, like this:

Rick comes from Australia.
Rick comes from Australia, doesn't he?

Now you.

1 *Rick comes from Australia.*
Rick comes from Australia, doesn't he?
2 *Manuel is Spanish.*
Manuel is Spanish, isn't he?
3 *Lucy and Mark are English.*
Lucy and Mark are English, aren't they?
4 *Aliki hasn't got a sister.*
Aliki hasn't got a sister, has she?
5 *Mark can't swim.*
Mark can't swim, can he?
6 *Paolo went windsurfing.*
Paolo went windsurfing, didn't he?
7 *He wasn't very good at it.*
He wasn't very good at it, was he?
8 *He fell off the board a lot.*
He fell off the board a lot, didn't he?

4 Complete

Answers

1 to go, dancing *2 playing* *3 swimming* *4 to break*
5 to send *6 falling* *7 going* *8 to give*

5 Write

- You may go through this orally first.

Answers

1 *Paolo can run faster than Mark, but Manuel can run the fastest.*
2 *Rick gets up earlier than Tara, but Alison gets up the earliest.*
3 *Aliki goes to bed later than Holly, but Lucy goes to bed the latest.*
4 *Paolo sleeps longer than Manuel, but Mark sleeps the longest.*

Optional activity

- In groups of three students write similar information about themselves. They then compare each other's habits in the same way as in the exercise.

6 Rewrite

- You may need to do one or two sentences with the class to make sure they get the transformation right.

Answers

1 *Mark can't swim, so he doesn't like watersports.*
2 *Aliki lives by the sea, so she is a good swimmer.*
3 *Paolo hasn't been abroad before, so he is nervous.*
4 *Manuel's mother is a travel agent, so he travels a lot.*
5 *Holly's father makes movies, so she loves going to the cinema.*

7 Game: Adverb Tennis

- In word tennis, the aim is to respond quickly to a word offered. In this case students must give the comparative and superlative forms of adverbs.
- This can be played in pairs or two teams.
- Students should prepare by making a list of adverbs.

Song

- Students read the song.
- They decide what the correct words may be.
- Play the cassette. Students listen and check.
- Check orally.

Tapescript and answers

Chorus
Good Day Sunshine
Good Day Sunshine
Good Day Sunshine

I need to ***laugh*** *and when the sun is* ***out***
I've got ***something*** *I can* ***laugh*** *about,*
I feel ***good*** *in a special way.*
I'm in love and it's a ***sunny*** *day*

Chorus

We take a walk the ***sun*** *is shining* ***down,***
Burns my feet as they touch the ground

Chorus

And then we lie beneath a shady tree
I ***love*** *her and she's loving me*
She feels ***good****, she knows she's looking fine,*
I'm so ***proud*** *to know that she is mine.*

Chorus

Optional activities

- Listen to the song. Students sing along.
- Ask students what the song is about.
- Ask students to think of three adjectives to describe (a) how they feel when the sun is shining, (b) how they feel when they sing.
- In pairs students compare adjectives.

Activity Book Unit 1 Review, p12-13

Poster p110

- In this unit students will make a poster asking for penfriends.
- For group work you may wish to group students yourself so as to balance abilities and interests, or you may let them choose their own groups.
- Students should start their work in class, but may do some writing at home.
- They check their work carefully, and show it to you for correction.
- Then they write their details neatly and stick them to the poster.
- They should add photos or drawings of the group members.
- If possible, show the poster to another English class in your school or in another school where you know people. Encourage students to write to each other in English.

2 STARS

Lesson 1 *She won't talk to you* p18

Target language

Future review: *will* and *going to*

Vocabulary

Phrasal verbs with *out*
Hopes and plans

Warmer

- Revise vocabulary from Unit 1 by drawing a word map about one of the unit topics on the board and asking the class to fill it in as a class.
- Ask students about what they do at weekends. Ask them if they have different plans for each weekend or if every weekend is the same. Students write down their plans for next weekend. (To be used after Activity 2).

1 READ

Aim: to present future with *will* contrasted with future with *going to*

- Use the cassette to present and practise the dialogue.
- Students read the dialogue in groups.
- They complete the questions.
- Check orally.
- Next students choose the correct answers to the questions.
- Check orally by having pairs of students read the question and answer.

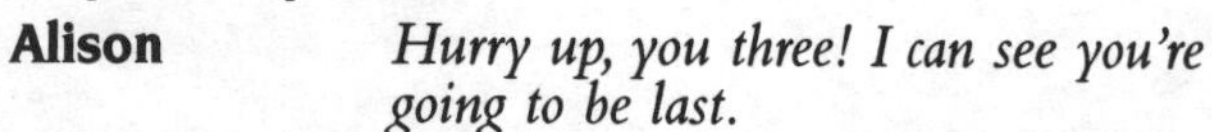

Tapescript

Alison	*Hurry up, you three! I can see you're going to be last.*
Lucy	*OK, Alison. Sorry. We'll catch up. Promise!*
Mark	*Oh no, we won't! I'm worn out. I'm going to have a rest.*
Lucy	*Then you won't have lunch. We're going to eat at one o'clock. Come on, Holly.*
Holly	*I think I'll stay with Mark. See you later.*
Mark	*Mm. It's lovely and quiet, isn't it?*
Holly	*What's that? Oh no!*
Photographer	*Look out, you two! Get out of the way! You're going to spoil the picture!*
Mark	*It's a hot air balloon! And look who's in it. It's, you know, whatshername.*
Holly	*Who?*
Mark	*You know. The model who's in the jeans advert on TV. It's her! I'm going to say hello to her.*
Holly	*I bet she won't talk to you!*
Mark	*I bet she will! Let's find out!*

Answers

1 *What can Alison see they **are going** to be?*
2 *What does Lucy say they **will** do?*
3 *What **is** Mark **going** to do?*
4 *What **won't** Mark have?*
5 *When **are** they **going** to eat?*
6 *What **are** Mark and Holly **going** to spoil?*
7 *Does Holly think the model **will** talk to Mark?*

Answers

1B 2E 3G 4D 5C 6A 7F

Optional activities

- In groups, students act out the dialogue.
- Students speculate about what will happen next.

2 GRAMMAR FILE

Aim: to review the future with *will* and *going to*.

- Students copy and complete the chart.
- Check orally.

Answers

Future review: will and going to

*Then you **won't** have any lunch.*
*I bet she **won't** talk to you.*
*We'**ll** catch up.*
*I think I'**ll** stay with Mark.*
*We'**re going** to eat at one o'clock.*
*I'**m going** to say hello to her.*
*I can see you'**re going** to be last.*
*You'**re going** to spoil the picture!*

Optional activities

- Students look through the text for the two kinds of future.
- In pairs or small groups they make predictions and talk about plans using the notes they made in the warmer.

Activity Book p14 Exercise 1

3 Listen and Speak

Aim: to make predictions according to sounds heard.

- Students look through the activity. They may try completing some of the sentences.
- Play the cassette. Students listen. Then they complete the sentences.
- Play the cassette again for them to check.
- Check the sentences orally.

Tapescript

1 *Sound of a car skidding.*
2 *Sound of a plane about to take off.*
3 *Sound of footsteps running towards a ringing phone.*
4 *A woman saying 'On your marks, get set ...'.*
5 *Sound of clapping dying away as Alison says 'Good evening, everybody ...'.*
6 *Sound of restaurant noises, with a waiter saying 'That's £23.75. I hope you enjoyed your meal.'*

Answers

1 *The car* ***is going to crash.***
2 *The plane* ***is going to take off.***
3 *Alison* ***is going to answer the phone.***
4 *The race* ***is going to start.***
5 *Alison* ***is going to make a speech.***
6 *Alison* ***is going to pay the bill.***

Optional activity

- Game. This can be played in groups or teams. A student mimes something that is about to happen, e.g., riding a motorbike (going to fall off); running (going to be late); arranges a pile of books too near the edge of the desk (going to fall); etc. The others must guess what is going to happen and make correct sentences.

4 Speak and Listen

Aim: to practise future with *will*, and to listen for specific information.

- Students read and choose their answers.
- You may discuss answers and ask for reasons.
- Play the cassette. They listen and check their answers.

Tapescript 

1	**Mark**	*Would you like to go to the cinema with me tonight?*
	Holly	*I'm sorry. I can't. I'm going to wash my hair.*
2	**Rick**	*Could you lend me £25 until Saturday?*
	Alison	*I'm sorry. I haven't got any money either.*
3	**Tara**	*Could you turn your music down? It's too loud.*
	Manuel	*Oh, sorry. Yes. of course I will.*
4	**Lucy**	*I wonder if I could borrow your jacket tonight. It's really great.*
	Aliki	*Sure. Look after it, won't you? It's almost new.*
5	**Alison**	*Could you help with the swimming this afternoon, please?*
	Tara	*I'd like to but I'm afraid I can't. I've hurt my wrist.*

Answers

1A 2A 3B 4B 5C

Optional activities

- Play the cassette again for students to listen to the language of polite refusals.
- In pairs or small groups students ask each other favours and either refuse politely, make an excuse, or agree, but with a caution (like Aliki's answer to Lucy). If they are in groups, they ask different people in turn, and they give different answers.

Activity Book p14 Exercise 2

5 Speak and Write

Aim: to contrast the two forms of the future.
- Students complete the dialogue with the correct verbs.
- Check orally by letting pairs of students read aloud.

Answers

1 She's going to | *2 they'll* | *3 I'll*
4 We're going to | *5 they'll* | *6 They'll*
7 it's going to

Optional activity

- Students make predictions about what's going to happen to Holly and Mark.

Activity Book p15 Exercise 3

6 Word File

Aim: to present phrasal verbs with *out*.
- Students work alone or in pairs to match the phrasal verbs and their meanings.
- They should work out some meanings from their use in the dialogue. *Wear out, get out* and *look out* are in the dialogue.
- This is suitable for homework or study time, to give students a chance to use dictionaries.
- Check orally.

Answers

1 c 2 a 3 f 4 e 5 b 6 d

Optional activities

- Students make sentences using the phrasal verbs.
- They think of other phrasal verbs they know with *out*, e.g., *take out, leave out*.

Activity Book p15 Exercise 4

7 Write

Aim: to personalise the target language in a written passage about future plans.
- Before writing students may discuss their plans for the weekend with each other, and make notes.
- This is suitable for homework.
- Check their work and give additional practice if there are still problems.

Consolidation and Extension activities

- Team game. The teams prepare a list of sentences using phrasal verbs with *out*. Then they take turns to say them. The others must quickly and correctly rephrase the sentence without the phrasal verb, e.g., *My shoes were worn out* becomes *My shoes were old and full of holes.*
- Prediction chain. Round the class students make predictions and disagree with them, like this: Student 1: *It's going to rain tomorrow.* Student 2: *No, it isn't. It's going to snow.* Student 3: *Our team is going to win the game.* Student 4: *No, it isn't. It's going to come second.*
- Negative predictions can be countered with affirmatives.

Homework

- Students start a section in their vocabulary books for phrasal verbs and write in the phrasal verbs with *out*. These will be easier to learn if they write example sentences.
- Students choose a famous person, e.g., a sports star or a singer, and write predictions about him/her.

Activity Book Unit 2 Lesson 1, p14-15
Grammar Summary p119

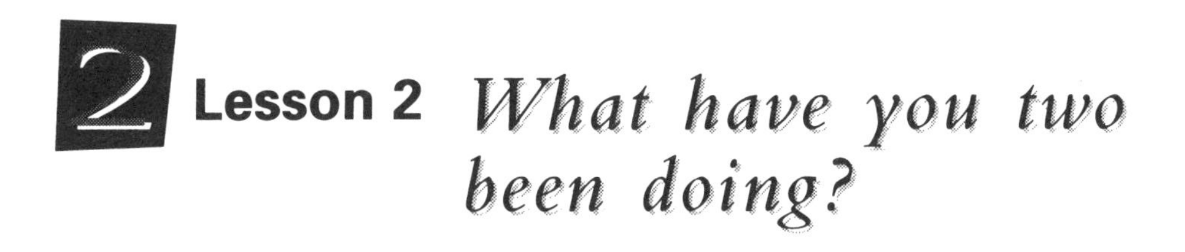

Lesson 2 *What have you two been doing?*

p20

Target language

Present perfect continuous with *for* and *since*
Present perfect continuous and present perfect simple

Vocabulary

Personal history

Warmer

- Without looking back at the previous lesson, students tell the story of Holly and Mark and the hot air balloon. Ask them if they remember what the photographer said. (*'Look out, you two! Get out of the way! You're going to spoil the picture!'*)
- Ask students to quickly write down four other phrasal verbs using *out*.
- Ask students questions with *How long*, e.g., *How long have you lived here? How long have you been in this class?*
- Then ask questions with *Have you ever?* e.g., *Have you ever been to a pop concert? Have you ever been to the USA?* etc. Some may be fantastic, e.g., *Have you ever been to the Moon?* Students answer *Yes, I have*, or *No, I haven't (but I'd like to/and I wouldn't like to)*.

1 Read

Aim: to present and practise the present perfect and present perfect continuous with *for* and *since*.

- Use the cassette to present the dialogue.
- In groups of four, students read the dialogue.
- They read and correct the sentences.
- Check orally.
- Then they make questions for the answers.
- Check orally by letting students ask each other the questions.

Tapescript

Lucy *What have you two been doing? It's two o'clock now. And you've been missing since twelve thirty. We've all had our lunch and we've been waiting for you for ages.*

Holly *I'm sorry, Lucy. I can explain...*

Lucy *And Alison's been worrying about you. She's phoned ACE three times to see if you were there.*

Mark *Never mind. We've had the most fantastic time! You'll never guess who we've been talking to.*

Lucy *Go on, try me.*

Mark *Right! We've been talking to Celeste, the model!*

Paolo *What! The one in the jeans advert! I've seen her on TV in Italy.*

Lucy *You've made this up! You haven't been talking to a top model.*

Holly *Oh yes, we have! And we've been up in a hot air balloon!*

Lucy *I don't believe it!*

Answers

1 *False. Lucy doesn't know what they've been doing.*
2 *True.*
3 *False. They've all had their lunch.*
4 *False. Alison has contacted ACE three times.*
5 *False. Holly and Mark haven't been on TV, only Celeste has.*
6 *True.*
7 *True.*

1 *How long have Holly and Mark been missing?*
2 *How long have the others been waiting for them?*
3 *Who has Alison been worrying about?*
4 *How many times has Alison phoned ACE?*
5 *Who have Holly and Mark been talking to?*
6 *Who has seen Celeste on TV (in Italy)?*
7 *Who have been up in a hot air balloon?*

Optional activity

- Ask students if anyone has seen a hot air balloon or been up in one? Or have any of them ever seen or met anybody famous?

2 GRAMMAR FILE

Aim: to present the present perfect continuous compared with the present perfect simple.

- Students copy and complete the chart.
- Check orally.

Answers

Present perfect continuous

*We **have been** waiting for you for ages.*

*Alison **has been** worrying about you.*

*What **have** you two **been** doing?*

*You **haven't been** talking to a top model.*

Present perfect simple

*We **have** all had our lunch.*

*She **has** phoned ACE three times.*

*I **have** seen her on TV.*

*We can use the present perfect **continuous** to describe a recent temporary action. The action may still be continuing or it may have finished.*

*We can use the present perfect **simple** to describe a complete action in the past which affects the present.*

Optional activity

- Students find examples of the two forms of the present perfect in the text.

Activity Book p16 Exercise 1

3 SPEAK

Aim: to practise talking about length of time with the present perfect simple and continuous and *for* and *since*.

- Introduce this by talking about yourself, e.g., *I started teaching ... years ago, so I've been teaching for ... years, since ...*
- Students read the profile of Alison.
- Ask the first question. Students read the two answers in the book.
- Now ask another question, e.g., *How long has she been (living) in Devon?* Students give both possible answers.
- Continue with questions and answers round the class or in pairs.

Answers

How long has she been living in Devon? Since she was 17./For 9 years.

How long has she been teaching climbing? For 4 years./Since she was 22.

How long has she been working at ACE? Since she was 20./For 6 years.

How long has she been skydiving? For two years./Since she was 24.

How long has she been learning German? For a year./Since she was 25.

How long has she been writing a book? For six months./Since last winter.

Optional activities

- Students write sentences about Alison, e.g., *Alison has been teaching watersports for ten years.*
- Pairs. One student pretends to be Alison and the other interviews her, asking questions beginning *How long have you...?*

Activity Book p16 Exercise 2

4 SPEAK AND WRITE

Aim: to personalise the target language by speaking and writing about oneself.

- Ask two or three students one or two of the questions.
- Students continue asking and answering the questions in small groups.
- Monitor for correct use of tenses and *for* and *since*.
- Students now write sentences about themselves.
- Check their work. This is suitable for homework.

Optional activities

- Students report back to the class about the other people in their group.
- Students write sentences about the other people in their group.

Activity Book p17 Exercise 3

5 WRITE

Aim: to practise the target language in writing.

- Students copy the passage with the correct tenses.
- Check orally.

Answers

1 come   *2 had*   *3 been*   *4 got*   *5 eaten*
6 forgotten   *7 taken*   *8 written*   *9 been*

Activity Book p17 Exercise 4

6 LISTEN

Aim: to listen for specific information about the events in a story.
- Students work alone or in pairs to re-order the events.
- Play the cassette. They listen and check.
- Check orally.

Tapescript

Alison *Where have you two been? I've been looking for you everywhere.*

Mark *Sorry, Alison. You know, we didn't mean to be so late. We just stopped for a quick rest.*

Alison *Yes, Lucy told me. But you've been missing for an hour and a half!*

Mark *Yeah, well. It's like this, see. We sat down for a rest and this huge balloon suddenly appeared. And Celeste, the model, was in the balloon! We jumped up to have a look at the balloon and then we heard lots of shouting. A photographer was really angry with us because we were in his picture.*

Alison *I'm not surprised.*

Mark *Anyway we got out of his way and he finished taking photos. Then the most amazing thing happened. The balloon landed close to us. We ran up and asked Celeste for her autograph - I didn't have anything for her to write her name on but Holly found a notebook. Then Celeste talked to us for a long time. And then, guess what?*

Alison *What?*

Mark *We went up in the balloon! It was fantastic! We could see ever so far.*

Alison *That's funny. We didn't see you - or the balloon. Are you sure you're not making this up?*

Mark *It's all true. The balloon didn't fly over you - the wind was in the other direction. Then the balloon landed again two kilometres away. We got out and we've walked back from there. That's why we were away so long.*

Alison *I'm still not sure that I believe you.*

Mark *Well, look at this then. It's Celeste's autograph!*

Answers

1f 2d 3g 4c 5e 6a 7b

Optional activity

- Pairs or small groups. Students pretend to be Holly/Mark and Alison/the others. They act out the meeting when Holly and Mark return.

7 WRITE

Aim: to personalise the target language by writing a letter to a penpal.
- Brainstorm some ideas in class first.
- Students make notes.
- Then they write a letter to a penpal.
- Check their writing. This is suitable for homework.

Consolidation and Extension activities

- Boasting chain. Teams or groups. Student 1 says, e.g., *I've been learning English for a year.* Student 2 says *Well, I've been learning English for two years.* Student 3 says *I've been learning Russian for two years.* In each case the student must say something longer or more difficult.
- This can also be used with the present perfect simple, e.g., *I've visited three foreign countries. Well, I've visited six foreign countries*, etc. Keep the pace up. Anyone who gets the wrong tense or isn't boastful enough is 'out'.
- Spelling game. Play hangman or another spelling game with words from the lesson, e.g., *medicine, exhausted, worried,* etc.
- Verb tennis. Students play this with verbs and their past participles, e.g., *be - been, go - gone, eat - eaten.*
- Students role-play an interview with a famous person, asking them how long they have done/been doing various things, e.g., singing with a group, working in films, playing for a team. They can make notes.

Homework

- Students revise irregular past participles.
- Students write up their notes from the role-play interview in the form of a short article for a magazine, using the present perfect.

Activity Book Unit 2 Lesson 2, p16-17
Grammar Summary p119

Lesson 3 *Believe in yourself*

Target language

Reflexive pronouns
How often ...? and adverbial phrases of frequency

Vocabulary

Adjectives - opposites
Routines

Optional Aids

Bring fashion magazines and/or pictures of models, male and female, from magazines.

Warmer

- Introduce the topic of fashion. Find out what students like and dislike in the way of clothes.
- Show the pictures/magazines you have brought and ask students to comment on the clothes and models.
- Finally ask if they know what the life of a fashion model is like. (Very hard work and not as glamorous as it appears in the pictures.)

1 READ

Aim: to read for specific information; to present reflexive pronouns, *how often?* and adverbial phrases of frequency

- Use the cassette to introduce the passage.
- Students read through the text.
- You may wish to go through it paragraph by paragraph, checking for gist. One way to do this is to ask them to tell you one fact about each paragraph, e.g., a pretty face is not enough; always behave well; you have to change a lot; it's very hard work; get a good education as well.
- Or ask spot questions, e.g., *In which paragraph does she advise you to behave well?*
- Students then complete the questions, and match the answers.
- Check orally, with students asking and answering.

Tapescript

CATWALK STAR!

Super model Celeste tells us about the fashion scene.

Believe in yourself

If you want to be a model, you've got to believe in yourself. Millions of girls (and boys!) dream about a career as a model but few succeed. It's the hardest career in the world to break into, and having a pretty face is only the start.

Always look good, be on time and smile

You're paid to look good even if you've just got off a twelve-hour flight. So look after yourself properly: no late nights (think of the bags under your eyes!) and no junk food (think of your waist and skin). Behave yourself (no bad temper) and be punctual. Models who are bad-tempered or late don't get asked again and can only blame themselves. Most importantly, smile. It's hard to smile as if you mean it a hundred times a day, but that's the way to the top.

Ten times a show!

Doing a big fashion show can be exhausting. You'll have to change clothes as many as ten times a show. The catwalk may look glamorous, but the changing rooms are always small and crowded. You don't usually do your make-up or hair yourself. However, it's important that you know how to, just in case!

It sounds fun but...

Photographic modelling sounds fun, but the pictures you see don't always tell the truth. I've just finished a session modelling ski clothes. But it wasn't in the mountains, it was in a hot studio in London. I had to stand in one position for what seemed like hours while the photographer got the lighting right. And I had to look as if I was enjoying myself in the lovely cold mountain air. But in fact I was exhausted and boiling hot. And some mornings you can have a really early start - last week I had to get up at 4am for a picture at sunrise.

Fashion facts

It's a young person's game. Models usually start when they're teenagers and are too old by the time they're 25. You have to be at least 175cm tall and have a slim figure. The big fashion shows are held in the major capital cities every autumn and spring. You can send photographs to model agencies but it is much better to visit them yourself. Model agencies see hundreds of would-be models a year and only a few are successful. And how often do the successful ones get work? They're lucky if they work more than once or twice a month at the start. In fact most days most models are unemployed. So it's really important for a would-be model to get herself a good education to prepare for the day when she can only find work at the Ugly Model Agency (it's true - there is one!)

Answers

1 What/d	*2 Why/a*	*3 What/b*
4 What/e	*5 How/f*	*6 What/c*

Optional activities

- Ask students e.g., *Would you like to be a model?* They give reasons, based on the text.
- Students make a checklist of advice for models.
- Students list the advantages and disadvantages of being a model.

2 Word File

Aim: to focus on adjectives and their opposites.
- You can do this as a competition or set a time limit.
- Check orally.

Answers

early/late	*easy/hard*	*empty/crowded*
fat/slim	*freezing/boiling (hot)*	*relaxing/exhausting*
short/tall	*ugly/pretty*	

Optional activities

- Students pick out the other adjectives from the text. Do any of them have opposites?
- Some of the adjectives have more than one opposite. You may explain the difference between e.g., *slim* (attractive, positive) and *thin* (may be neutral but can be negative).
- Students use the pairs of adjectives in sentences.

Activity Book p18 Exercise 1

3 Write

Aim: to practise using reflexive pronouns.
- Students complete the sentences, if necessary referring to the text.
- Check orally.

Answers

Successful models behave ***themselves*** *and are punctual.*

Make sure you look after ***yourself*** *and look good.*

A good model knows how to do her make-up ***herself****.*

Visit model agencies ***yourself****.*

Models should get ***themselves*** *a good education.*

Optional activity

- Students find examples of reflexive pronouns in the text.

4 Grammar File

Aim: to present the use of reflexive pronouns.
- Students complete the chart.
- Check orally.

Activity Book p18 Exercise 2

Answers

Subject pronouns	***Object pronouns***	***Reflexive pronouns***
I	*me*	*myself*
you	*you*	***yourself***
he	*him*	***himself***
she	*her*	***herself***
it	*it*	***itself***
we	*us*	*ourselves*
you	*you*	***yourselves***
they	*them*	***themselves***

Optional activity

- Students make sentences about themselves using reflexives, e.g., *I enjoyed myself at the weekend - I went to the cinema with my friends. I try to look after myself - I play lots of sport.*

5 Write

Aim: to practise reflexive pronouns.
- Students write the correct sentences.
- Check orally.

Answers

1 herself	*2 -*	*3 me*	*4 -*
5 yourselves	*6 myself*	*7 -*	*8 yourselves*

6 Listen and Speak

Aim: to listen for specific information and to give personal information using adverbial phrases of frequency.
- Students read through the chart.
- Play the cassette. They listen and complete it for Aliki.
- Check orally.
- They then complete the chart for themselves.
- Pairs. Students take turns to ask each other the questions and complete the chart.
- Go through the LOOK! box focusing on any new expressions.

Tapescript and answers

Manuel	*Hey, Aliki, there's a questionnaire in this magazine!*
Aliki	*What's it about?*
Manuel	*It's about how often you do things. Shall I ask you the questions?*
Aliki	*Sure, go ahead.*
Manuel	*OK, so first question: How often do you* ***watch TV****?*
Aliki	*That's easy.* ***Every day****! I always watch TV before dinner.*
Manuel	*Right - second question: How often do you* ***go shopping****?*
Aliki	*Oh, I'd say . . .* ***once a week*** *- usually on Saturdays.*
Manuel	*Do you go shopping on your own?*
Aliki	*No, I usually go with my mum.*
Manuel	*Right, now the next question is personal! How often do you* ***wash your hair****?*
Aliki	*When I have a shower - and that's* ***every day****.*
Manuel	*Well, your hair always looks lovely!*
Aliki	*Thank you! Next question?*
Manuel	*This one's interesting. How often do you* ***write letters****?*
Aliki	*Not very often I'm afraid.* ***Once a year****!*
Manuel	*Only once a year!?*
Aliki	*Yes - after my birthday, I write thank you letters!*
Manuel	*Oh, I see! Here's another personal question: how often do you* ***brush your teeth****?*
Aliki	***Twice a day*** *- every morning and every evening.*
Manuel	*So you don't* ***go to the dentist*** *very often.*
Aliki	*No. Only* ***twice a year****. And I never have any fillings!*
Manuel	*That's very good! Next question - how often do you* ***get new shoes****?*
Aliki	*Let me see - well, I suppose it's* ***twice a year*** *- I get new shoes every autumn and spring.*
Manuel	*And here's the last question. How often do you* ***play football****?*
Aliki	*I* ***never*** *play football - I prefer basketball and volleyball.*

Optional activity

- Students report back to the class about how often their partner does the things in the chart.

Activity Book p19 Exercise 3

7 WRITE

Aim: to use adverbial phrases of frequency in writing.

- Ask two or three students to compare themselves and their partner as in the example.
- Students then write sentences.
- Check their work.

Optional activity

- Pairs combine to make groups and they build up a class profile of how often people perform the various activities.

Consolidation and Extension activities

- Play adjective tennis. Students return the 'serve' with the opposite adjective.
- Play a spelling game to practise adjectives.
- Guessing game: How often? This may be played by pairs or teams. Student 1 says e.g., *I do it once a day*. The other have to guess what it is, e.g., *You help your mother*. The student answers *No, I do that three times a day*, or *Yes, but that's not it*, or *Yes, you're right*.
- In pairs, students role-play an interview with someone famous, asking them e.g., *How often do you fly every year? How often do you train/practise every day/week?* etc. They make notes about the answers.

Homework

- Students list the adjectives and their opposites in their vocabulary notebooks.
- They learn new adjectives. Learning them with their opposites is useful, but they could also arrange them in a word map.
- Students write up their notes from the role-play interview as a short passage.
- Students write a questionnaire like the one in activity 6. They use it with their friends or family.
- They write up the results of their questionnaire.

Activity Book Unit 2 Lesson 3, p18-19
Grammar Summary p119

Lesson 4 *Superstar*

Vocabulary

Biographies
Linking words: *and* and *but*, *as soon as* and *until*
Noun suffixes: *-r*, *-er*, *-ist*

Warmer

- Students work in pairs or small groups. They find out one thing about each other's past, one about something they do now, and one thing about their hopes or plans for the future. They use questions with *how long/how often*, etc. They write the three things on a sheet of paper with no name on.
- Collect all the papers in and give them out again, making sure that no one gets the notes they wrote. Students guess who the notes refer to.
- They take turns to ask people e.g., *Were you born on 6 September? How often do you play football every week? Are you going to continue playing football? Then I think these notes are about you.*

Reading

1 Aim: to read an article for gist.

- Students listen and read the article and match the topics with the paragraphs.
- Check orally.

Tapescript

Roberto Carlos has been playing for Real Madrid in Spain since 1996. As a football superstar, he lives life in the fast lane with more money than most people can dream of. But his heart is back home in Brazil. 'I hope I'll have enough money to retire as soon as I'm 40,' he says. 'Then I'm going to go back to Brazil and enjoy myself with my family. Until then, I'm going to enjoy my football.'

Roberto Carlos was born in a small village called Garça in São Paulo State in 1973. When he was seven his family moved to the city of São Paulo. 'It was a very small house and I shared a room with my three sisters,' he remembers. 'We played together and had lots of fun. I didn't always behave myself but I didn't do anything really naughty!'

Today Carlos's parents have a big house and two cars but they haven't changed. 'My father has always been a truck driver and he still works every day,' Carlos says. 'I've asked him to stop but he won't.' Carlos' father took him to watch Santos, the local football team, as soon as he was able to walk.

'I've been playing football since then,' Carlos says. 'First I played in the small street outside our house. We used stones to make the goals. When a car came along we had to stop playing until the car went by. Then we put the stones back and carried on playing.'

Carlos has always wanted to be a footballer. 'I've been lucky,' he says. 'I just did things at the right time. And now I play for my country and last year my club won the European Champions League. But football is sometimes a dangerous sport. It's easy to hurt yourself while you're playing or for someone to injure you.

Carlos is famous for his free kicks and he is able to 'bend' the ball around a wall of players. He practises most days a week and prefers to spend time at home in the evenings. Few of his friends are footballers. 'You never know who your best friends are,' he says. 'My only real friend is my father.'

Answers

1 The future	*2 Childhood*	*3 Parents*
4 Starting to play	*5 Career*	*6 Friends*

Optional activity

- Ask comprehension questions about the article.

2 Aim: to focus on the use of *and* and *but*.

- Students read the text and underline linking words.
- They complete the rule.
- Then they complete the text.
- Check orally.

Answers

We use ***and*** *to connect two similar ideas.*

We use ***but*** *to connect two contrasting ideas.*

1 and 2 but 3 and 4 and 5 and 6 but 7 but

Optional activity

- Students write four or five sentences about themselves using *and* and *but*.

Activity Book p20 Exercise 1

3 Aim: to focus on the use of *as soon as* and *until*.

- Students read through the text and underline *as soon as* and *until*.
- They complete the rule.
- Then they complete the sentences, orally or in writing.
- Check orally.

Answers

1 until *2 as soon as* *3 As soon as*
4 As soon as *5 until*

***As soon as** means immediately after something happens.*

***Until** means up to the time when something happens.*

Optional activities

- Students write four to six sentences with *as soon as* and *until*.
- Pairs. Students rewrite their sentences, omitting *as soon as* and *until*. They give their sentences to their partner to complete.

Activity Book p21 Exercise 2

Listening

4 Aim: to listen for detail and to complete written notes.

- Students first read through the notes and get an idea of what they are about.
- Play the cassette. Students listen and complete the notes.
- Check orally.

Tapescript

Mark *Hi! Can I have your autograph, please?*

Celeste *Sure! We're just waiting for the photographer to get ready.*

Holly *What's it like being a model?*

Celeste *Great - most of the time, that is.*

Holly *And how long have you been doing it?*

Celeste *I've been modelling full-time for two years now.*

Holly *And how long do you think you'll go on with it?*

Celeste *I expect I'll retire when I'm 25. There aren't many jobs for old models, you know.*

Holly *What are you going to do then?*

Celeste *I don't know. I'd like to have my own model agency.*

Holly *I know it's a personal question, but how old are you?*

Celeste *18. I was born in Manchester but I don't live there now. I moved to London when I was five. We lived in a small flat and I shared a room with my sister for ten years!*

Mark *And when did you decide to be a model?*

Celeste *While I was still at primary school. My sister and I dressed up in old clothes at the weekends and pretended to be models. Then I got my first modelling job while I was still at secondary school - I was so excited! I started full-time modelling as soon as I left school at 16.*

Balloon pilot *We're ready to go now*

Celeste *OK. Come on you two, get in. Don't you want a ride in the balloon?*

Holly/ Mark *Yes, please.*

Answers

Facts about Celeste

NOW AND THE FUTURE

*Modelling full time **for two** years.*

*Retire **when** she is **25** years old.*

CHILDHOOD

*Born in Manchester **18** years **ago**.*

*Moved to London **when** she was **five**.*

*Shared a room **for ten** years with her sister.*

CAREER

*Decided to be a model **while** she was still at primary school.*

*Got her first modelling job **while** still at secondary school.*

*Started full time modelling **as soon as** she left school.*

Optional activity

- Pairs. Students take turns to ask each other questions with *when* and *how long*, answering with *when, while, for, since, until* and *as soon as*.

Speaking

5 Aim: to read an article for specific information, make notes and then speak about the article.

- Students reread the text.
- Ask for one or two suggestions for the notes.
- Then they complete their notes.
- Groups. Students take turns to talk about the life of Roberto Carlos.

Writing

6 Aim: to write a short article, focusing on topic based paragraphs.

- Students use the notes to write three short paragraphs about Celeste.
- Check their work.

Word building

7 Aim: to present and practise different noun suffixes.

- You may do this orally.
- Note the spelling of *cyclist*.

Answers

1 -er farmer footballer photographer singer teacher

2 -r dancer driver manager miner rider

3 -ist artist cyclist motorist tourist receptionist

Optional activities

- It may help students remember the correct suffix if they work out that all the third group are nouns, all the second are verbs, and most of the first group are verbs. We often add *-(e)r* to verbs and *-ist* to nouns to create the words for jobs.
- Students think of other nouns they know with those endings. Do they fit in with the rule?

STUDY SKILLS

8 Aim: to help students vary their language learning habits.
- Learning words doesn't have to be boring. The suggestions given are fun ways to learn vocabulary in particular.
- Discuss the ideas with students and find out if anyone uses any of them.
- Does anyone have suggestions to add? For example, two students who are neighbours can talk to each other in English.

Activity Book p21 Exercises 3 and 4

Consolidation and Extension activities

- Game. Play this in teams or pairs. Students make a list of nouns ending in *-(e)r* or *-ist*. Then they list the root words. They take turns to give each other the roots. The others must make the new word correctly.
- They could also use the words in sentences.
- Memory chain. This is best played in groups of about eight. Student 1 says, e.g., *When I leave school, I'm going to study at college.* Students add one idea each time, e.g., *When I leave school, I'm going to study at college and I'm going to play football and I'm going to travel,* etc.
- Students work in pairs to interview each other about their past and their future plans. They make notes.

Homework

- In their vocabulary notebooks, students make lists of nouns with the same suffixes.
- Students interview someone they know about their past, career and future plans. They may question in L1 and write notes in English.
- They write a short article about the person, in topic based paragraphs.
- Students write a letter to a penpal about themselves, with paragraphs about their past and their future plans.

Pairwork

Pairwork Activity p107 and p115

Aim: to use the target language to carry out an information gap activity.
- Students look through the appropriate boxes and work out their questions.
- Students B ask students A their questions and complete their sentences.
- Then they change roles.
- Monitor the activity and check for correct language use.
- Check the sentences orally.

Answers

How long has Rick been teaching sport?
He's been teaching sport for 4 years.
So he's been teaching sport since... .

How long has Holly been trying to get into drama school?
She's been trying to get into drama school for six months.
So she's been trying to get into drama school since February.

How long has Manuel been saving up for a computer?
He's been saving up for a computer for six months.
So he's been saving up for a computer since February.

How long has Lucy been writing songs?
She's been writing songs for two years.
So she's been writing songs since ...

How long has Mark been looking for a girlfriend?
He's been looking for a girlfriend for three weeks.
So he's been looking for a girlfriend since 10th July.

How long has Tara been learning to scuba dive?
She's been learning to scuba dive for two months.
She's been learning to scuba dive since 1st June.

How long has Paolo been having karate lessons?
He's been having karate lessons for twelve months.
So he's been having karate lessons since last summer.

How long has Aliki been taking computer classes?
She's been taking computer classes for six months.
So she's been taking computer classes since February.

How long has Mark been living in Bristol?
He's been living in Bristol for two years.
So he's been living in Bristol since ...

How long has Alison been teaching skydiving?
She's been teaching skydiving for six months.
So she's been teaching skydiving since the end of January.

Activity Book Unit 2 Lesson 4, p20-21
Grammar Summary p119

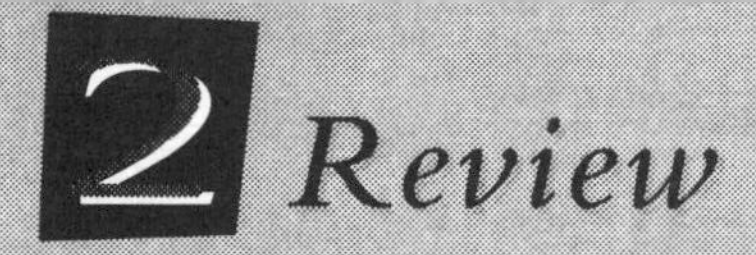

2 Review

1 Read and complete

- You may first ask students what they know about Leonardo Di Caprio, and whether they have seen any of his films.

Answers

1C	*2B*	*3A*	*4C*	*5C*	*6B*
7A	*8C*	*9B*	*10C*	*11C*	*12B*

2 Complete

Answers

1 will	*2 as soon as*	*3 I'm going to*	*4 until*
5 will	*6 will*	*7 as soon as*	*8 will*
9 is going to	*10 will*		

Optional activity

- Students discuss what they think Mark will do next.

3 Read and choose

- If students have problems, point out that if the activity is still continuing, they should use the present perfect continuous.

Answers

1 been teaching	*2 been living*	*3 has been teaching*
4 visited	*5 worked*	*6 been working*
7 been studying	*8 learnt*	

4 Complete

Answers

1 himself	*2 themselves*	*3 her*	*4 yourself*
5 themselves	*6 myself*	*7 her*	

5 Match

- This may be used as a team game.

Answers

1 actor/actress/drama	*6 journalist/news*
2 artist/paintings	*7 photographer/photos*
3 doctor/medicine	*8 travel agent/holidays*
4 farmer/fields	*9 model/clothes*
5 driver/cars	*10 teacher/students*

6 Test each other

- This can be done in pairs or as a team game.

Song

- Students read the gapped song.
- They decide which words go where.
- Play the cassette. Students listen and check.
- Check orally.

Tapescript and answers

Wednesday morning at five o'clock
As the day begins
*Silently closing her bedroom **door***
Leaving the note that she hoped would say more
She goes downstairs to the kitchen
Clutching her handkerchief
*Quietly turning the backdoor **key***
Stepping outside she is free.
She (We gave her most of our lives)
is leaving (Sacrificed most of our lives)
*home (We gave her everything money could **buy**)*
She's leaving home after living alone
For so many years. Bye bye.

Father snores as his wife
gets into her dressing gown
*Picks up the **letter** that's lying there*
Standing alone at the top of the stairs
*She breaks down, and cries to her **husband***
Daddy, our baby's gone.
Why swould she treat us so thoughtlessly?
*How could she do this to **me**?*
She (We never thought of ourselves)
is leaving (Never a thought for ourselves)
home (We struggled hard all our lives to get by)
She's leaving home after living alone
For so many years. Bye bye.

*Friday morning at **nine** o'clock*
She is far away
Waiting to keep the appointment she made
***Meeting** a man from the motor trade*
She (What did we do that was wrong?)
*is having (We didn't **know** it was wrong)*
fun (Fun is the one thing that money can't buy)
*Something **inside** that was always denied*
For so many years. Bye bye.
She's leaving home. Bye bye.

Optional activities

- Listen to the song again. Students sing along.
- Ask students what the song is about.
- Ask the students who is saying the words in brackets.
- Students choose 5 words from the song that are new to them. They can try to work out their meaning from the context and then use their dictionary. In pairs, they teach each other the words.
- Students can act out the song in various ways:

  In groups of 4, students could mime a sketch between mother, father, daughter and man as the song is being sung.

  In groups of 3, students write a dialogue between mother, father and daughter the evening before she leaves.

  In pairs, students could write a dialogue between the girl and the man planning her escape.
- Class discussion about leaving home.
- Students can write the letter to the girl's parents. What did she say that made her mother cry?

Activity Book Unit 2 Review, p22-23

Poster p111

- In this unit, students make a poster about a famous person.
- You may start by brainstorming famous people.
- Encourage groups to choose different stars to make their poster about.
- If possible, students research their star, and find news clippings or photos.
- They can do the writing for homework.
- Make sure they check it carefully before writing it up neatly.
- They add illustrations.
- Display the posters if possible.

3 TREASURE!

Lesson 1 *They must be the islands!* p28

Target language
must and *can't* for deduction
Past simple passive review
Vocabulary
History
Geographical features

Optional Aids

Bring a map of the UK showing Cornwall and the Scilly Isles; pictures from magazines showing e.g., a busy street scene, a wildlife park, agriculture.

Warmer

- Find out if any students have ever been snorkelling or scuba diving. Ask them to tell the class about it.
- Guessing game. A student thinks of something, e.g., a chair. The others must guess what it's made of, what it's used for, and then what it is.

1 READ

Aim: to present *must* and *can't* for deductions, and the past simple passive.

- Students look at the photo and talk about it.
- Use the cassette to present the dialogue.
- In groups students read the dialogue.
- Then they match the parts of the sentences.
- Check orally.

Tapescript

Aliki *Look! They must be the islands!*

Alison *That's right. The big island is called St Mary's.*

Paolo *It can't be easy to sail among the islands with so many rocks.*

Alison *No, that's why there were lots of shipwrecks on the islands. We're going to dive on a ship which was wrecked in 1740.*

Paolo *Over 250 years old! There can't be much left of the ship now.*

Alison *Yes, there is. My friend Jack says it was completely covered in sand.*

Aliki *It must be hard to find a wreck under the sand.*

Alison *Jack's a very good diver. There was a storm last week and it moved some of the sand. That's why he found the ship.*

Paolo *I'm so glad we were chosen to come with you.*

Rick *Well, you're the two most experienced divers in the group.*

Paolo *Where exactly is the wreck?*

Alison *See those two islands. I think the wreck must be between them.*

Aliki *It can't be there. There aren't any boats or divers near it.*

Alison *No. Jack hasn't told anyone where it is - except for me! It's a secret. Who knows - we might discover some treasure!*

Answers

1f 2d 3a 4e 5c 6b

Optional activities

- Show students where the Scilly Isles are on the map brought in.
- Ask students about shipwrecks or treasure in their country.

2 GRAMMAR FILE

Aim: to present *must* and *can't* for deduction.

- Students copy and complete the chart.
- Check orally.

Answers

must and can't for deduction

*They **must** be the islands!*

*There can't **be** much of the ship left now.*

*It **can't be** easy to sail among the islands.*

*We can use **must** to show that we are sure something is true.*

*We use **can't** to show that we are sure something is not true.*

Optional activities

- Students find examples of *must* and *can't* in the text.
- Guessing game. This can be played with objects or with words, in pairs or teams. One student hides something, e.g., a book in a bag. The others guess what it is, saying, e.g., *It fits in the bag, so it can't be very big. I think it must be something small, like a pencil,* etc.

Activity Book p24 Exercise 1

3 Speak and Write

Aim: to practise making deductions with *must* and *can't*.

- Go through these orally first.
- Then students write the sentences.

Answers

2 *He must be rich.*

3 *She must be a good swimmer.*

4 *She can't be afraid of heights.*

5 *She can't be well.*

6 *She must be pleased.*

7 *He must be hungry.*

Optional activity

- Working in small groups, students think of other situations, e.g., *Mark's got lost again.* The others make suitable responses, e.g., *Alison must be worried*, etc.

4 Listen

Aim: to make deductions based on comments heard and information given.

- Students first read the information in the box.
- Play the cassette. Pause after the first sentence, and elicit the answer.
- Now play the remaining sentences, pausing after each, if necessary, for students to find the answer.
- Check orally. Make sure students use correct sentences as well as getting the reason right.

Tapescript 

1 **Manuel** *Someone's eaten all my chocolate. Who is it?*

2 **Alison** *Someone's borrowed my water skis. Who is it?*

3 **Rick** *Who is this present for?*

4 **Alison** *Someone is playing loud music. Who is it?*

5 **Paolo** *Whose are these red boots?*

6 **Lucy** *Who's got the Spice Girls video?*

Answers

2 *It can't be Mark because he can't swim properly yet.*

3 *It must be for Lucy because it's her birthday.*

4 *It must be Manuel because he's just bought some CDs.*

5 *They can't be Mark's because he hasn't got any boots.*

6 *It must be Holly because she loves the Spice Girls.*

Optional activity

- Guessing game. Blindfold a student with a scarf, or let him/her close his/her eyes. He/She now has to guess the identity of another student by asking questions. The student may speak in a disguised voice. The one guessing must deduce who it is from information given, e.g., asking *Do you like football? - No. - It can't be* (name), *because he/she likes football*, etc.

Activity Book p24 Exercise 2

5 Read

Aim: to read a passage for specific information and to practise the past simple passive.

- Students read the statements.
- Then they read the text and look for differences.
- Check orally.
- Point out the past simple passive in the three sentences.
- Students now find other examples in the text.

Answers

1 *The islands were all joined together* <u>*1500*</u> *years ago.*

2 *People say that fishermen* <u>*hear*</u> *bells on quiet days.*

3 *Over a* <u>*thousand*</u> *ships were wrecked in the past. Several are wrecked every year.*

Activity Book p24-25 Exercises 3 and 4

6 Word File

Aim: to find words to match definitions.

- Students work out the answers.
- Check orally.

Answers

1 a continent *2 flooded* *3 a diver*
4 treasure *5 an island*

Optional activity

- Students think of other definitions. They give them to others to guess. This may be done in pairs or as a team game.

7 WRITE

Aim: to practise the past simple passive by writing up notes.

- This may be done orally first.
- Students then write the sentences.
- Check orally.

Answers

A new wreck ***was discovered*** *on the Isles of Scilly by Jack. Alison* ***was invited*** *to go there. Aliki and Paolo* ***were chosen*** *to go with her. Helicopter tickets* ***were bought****. Jack* ***was told*** *when they were arriving. The teenagers* ***were woken*** *early and* ***were driven*** *to the airport by Alison. They* ***were given*** *window seats in the helicopter. When they landed on St Mary's they* ***were met*** *by Jack.*

Consolidation and Extension activities

- Play Passive Tennis. One student says the verb and the other 'returns' the past simple passive.
- Show the pictures you have brought. If possible give one to each group of about eight students. They speak about the picture, saying e.g., *It must be difficult to cross the street. Yes, it can't be easy with all those cars. Those houses must be expensive*, etc.
- They can also describe them using the past simple passive, e.g., *I think those houses were built more than 50 years ago.*
- If there has been any kind of archaeological find or scientific discovery recently, students talk about it, using the past simple passive.

Homework

- Students write a story about a discovery.
- They imagine they are one of the teenagers who flew to the Scilly Isles and write a letter home about the flight.

Activity Book Unit 3 Lesson 1, p24-25
Grammar Summary p119-120

Lesson 2 *But the crab had gone*

Target language

Past perfect simple and past simple

Vocabulary

Diving
Body movements

Warmer

- Ask students what they did yesterday/last week/last summer.
- Memory chain. Start e.g., *Last summer I went on holiday. Last summer I went on holiday and I swam in the sea ...*

1 Read

Aim: to present and practise the past perfect simple and the past perfect.

- Students look at and talk about the picture.
- Use the cassette to present the dialogue.
- Students read out the dialogue.
- Then they answer the questions.
- Check orally.

Tapescript

Aliki *It's a coin! I'm sure it's silver!*

Rick *Great! Hold my hand and I'll help you out of the water.*

Aliki *Thanks. It's really cold.*

Rick *Here, don't just stand there. Put this towel around you. You're shivering.*

Aliki *It's much colder than diving in Greece!*

Rick *So, tell me what happened. Where did you find the coin?*

Aliki *We'd been in the water for ten minutes when we saw part of the wreck. After Jack had photographed the wreck, we cleared away some of the sand with our hands. Then I put my hand into a hole under a piece of wood and felt something hard.*

Rick *Was it a coin?*

Aliki *No! I got a terrible shock because the thing suddenly moved. Then I realised what had happened. I'd touched a crab!*

Rick *Oh no!*

Aliki *I put my hand into the hole again but the crab had gone. I felt some small hard things like stones and picked one up. It was a coin! I waved to Jack and he came over. I showed him what I'd found. I was so excited. My coin had been at the bottom of the sea for over 250 years. Then it was time to come up because I'd been underwater for half an hour.*

Rick *Great! Now let's have a look at that coin. I think it's a Spanish coin called a 'piece of eight'. We can ask them in the museum.*

Answers

1. *They saw part of the wreck.*
2. *After Jack had photographed the wreck.*
3. *A crab.*
4. *The coin she had found.*
5. *For over 250 years.*
6. *Because she had been underwater for half an hour.*

Optional activities

- Pairs. Students act out the story.
- Students retell the story in sequence.

Activity Book p26 Exercise 1

2 Grammar File

Aim: to present and contrast the past perfect simple and past simple.

- Students copy and complete the chart.
- Check orally.

Answers

Past perfect and past simple

*We **had been** in the water for ten minutes when we **saw** the wreck.*

*Then I **realised** what **had happened**.*

*I **had touched** a crab.*

Optional activity

- Students reread the text and find sentences using the two tenses.

Activity Book p26 Exercise 2

3 Listen and Write

Aim: to listen for specific information and to write a sequence of events using the past simple and past perfect simple.

- Students first read through the sentences and try to order them.
- Play the cassette. Students listen and order the sentences.
- They may need to listen a second time to check.
- You may wish to check the correct order now.
- Students complete the sentences. They can use this as a way of checking that their sentences were in the correct order.
- Check orally.

Tapescript

Aliki: We had a great day! Jack met us all at the airport - he was really friendly - and we caught a bus to the town. We collected our diving equipment from a place in the harbour, and went on to Jack's boat. You know, I'd love to have boat like that! OK, so the boat left St Mary's harbour and Jack told us exactly where the wreck was. It didn't take long to get there. We arrived at the wreck and er, of course, we checked our diving equipment. Then Jack told us what to do underwater, and explained everything, and we put on our diving equipment. And then we dived! Wow, but the water was freezing cold! Anyway, we searched underwater for ten minutes and then we found the wreck! Fantastic!

Answers

f k l g e h a i d b c j

1 *After Jack had met them at the airport, they caught a bus to the town.*
2 *When they had collected their diving equipment, they went on to Jack's boat.*
3 *Jack told them exactly where the wreck was after the boat had left St Mary's harbour.*
4 *After they arrived, they checked their diving equipment.*
5 *They put on their diving equipment after Jack had told them what to do underwater.*
6 *They found the wreck after they had searched underwater for ten minutes.*

Optional activity

- Books closed, students retell the story, in order, round the class.

Activity Book p27 Exercise 3

4 Listen and Speak

Aim: to sequence pairs of events according to sound cues.

- Students look through the sentences to prepare for listening.
- Play the cassette. They listen and note which events go together.
- They complete the sentences.
- Play the cassette again if necessary.
- Check orally.

Tapescript

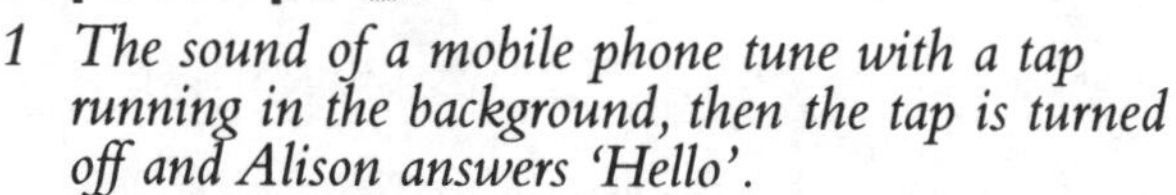

1 *The sound of a mobile phone tune with a tap running in the background, then the tap is turned off and Alison answers 'Hello'.*
2 *The sound of two people playing tennis.*
3 *The sound of a bus driving away and then someone arriving, running and panting.*
4 *Paolo finishing a phone call, saying 'Ciao Mama!' and then hanging up.*
5 *Manuel and Lucy playing table tennis.*
6 *The end of a guitar solo.*
7 *The sound of someone playing a noisy computer game.*

Answers

1 *Alison answered the phone after she had turned off the tap.*
2 *After Aliki had played tennis, she had a shower.*
3 *The bus had left when Tara got to the bus stop.*
4 *After Paolo had spoken to his mother he went for a swim.*
5 *Manuel and Lucy went for a walk after they had played table tennis.*
6 *When Rick had finished playing, he put his guitar away.*
7 *After he had played a computer game, Mark went to bed.*

5 Word File

Aim: to define words.
- Students reread the dialogue, find the words and match them with their definitions.
- Check orally.

Answers

1 shiver *2 wave* *3 hold*
4 clear *5 touch* *6 stand*

Optional activities

- Students use the words in sentences.
- They pick out up to six other words from the dialogue and write a definition for each. Then they give their partner the definition for them to find the word.

6 Write

Aim: to write a short narrative using past simple and past perfect simple to show sequence of events.
- You may go through the story orally first.
- Students write their paragraphs, paying particular attention to the correct use of tenses.
- Check their work.
- This is suitable for homework.

Consolidation and Extension activities

- Chain of events. Round the class students tell the events of a day, e.g., *I woke at seven after I had had a good night's sleep. After I had woken up, I read in bed for ten minutes. When I had finished reading ...* Each student mentions what the previous one did and adds a new event.
- Chain of events. In groups of up to eight, students tell the events of a day, but this time they must remember all the events that preceded theirs.
- The class can prepare a role-play based on the story. They imagine that Jack and the others are interviewed on local TV about their discovery. People needed are the divers, an interviewer, and an expert to look at the treasure. They prepare and act out the interview.

Homework

- Students write a story or an account of an eventful day, or a visit, or a match, paying attention to the use of tenses showing sequence of events.

Activity Book Unit 3 Lesson 2, p26-27
Grammar Summary p119-120

Lesson 3 *He had been telling the truth!* p32

Target language
Past perfect continuous
Vocabulary
Shipwrecks and treasure

Warmer

- Revise words from Activity 5 Word File in Lesson 2.
- Mime game. A student comes to the front and mimes a process, e.g., laying the table, making a cup of coffee, getting up in the morning. There should be about four to six steps. The others then describe what he or she did, e.g., *First, he got out of bed. After he had got out of bed, he brushed his teeth. After he had brushed his teeth, he washed. When he had washed, he got dressed,* etc.
- Ask students where Jack and the others dived in Unit 3 Lesson 2. (On a shipwreck.) Have they heard of any other famous shipwrecks?

1 READ

Aim: to present the past perfect continuous.
- Use the cassette to present and practise the passage.
- Students read the text. Go through it paragraph by paragraph, checking vocabulary as you go.
- They answer the questions.
- Check orally.

Tapescript

SHIPWRECK!

The Association

It was the night of October 22nd 1707 and the Isles of Scilly were covered in thick fog. The Association, a large ship carrying 800 sailors and soldiers, was on its way from southern France to England. It had been sailing for twelve days when it got close to England.

The captain was in a hurry to get home. Earlier that day, a sailor who came from the Isles of Scilly had dared to tell the captain that the ship was going in the wrong direction. The captain had refused to change direction and had told the man that he was a liar.

Suddenly in the fog The Association hit a rock and sank within minutes. Everyone on the ship was drowned. The sailor had been telling the truth!

In 1966 a diver called Roland Morris discovered the wreck, which had been lying in deep water. He brought some of the cargo to the surface, including lots of coins.

The Kyrenia wreck

There are often storms in the Mediterranean Sea and it is here that you can find some of the oldest shipwrecks. The wreck of an ancient Greek sailing ship was recently found in the sea near Kyrenia in Cyprus. It had been carrying a cargo of wine in 'amorphorae' - large jars - when it sank over 2,400 years ago. The cargo had protected the bottom of the wooden ship and much of it was not damaged at all by such a long time in the water. A copy of the Kyrenia was built from details of the wreck and sailed in the Mediterrean!

The Mary Rose

It was an afternoon in the summer of 1545. The Mary Rose was the second largest ship in the English navy and had lots of heavy guns. A gentle wind had been blowing all day, but suddenly there was a storm. The wind filled the sails and the Mary Rose leant over in the water. It leant further and further. Water poured in through the gun holes and the ship capsized.

Over 650 sailors and soldiers were drowned. The wreck of the Mary Rose was discovered in 1971. Divers raised the ship and you can now see it in a museum in Portsmouth.

Answers

1 *False. It had been sailing for twelve days.*
2 *False. He had refused to change direction.*
3 *False. It had been lying in deep water.*
4 *True.*
5 *False. Much of the ship was not damaged at all.*
6 *True.*
7 *False. Water filled the gun holes.*

Optional activities

- Books closed. Students see how much they can remember about each shipwreck.
- Give simple prompts, e.g., *near the Scilly Isles, the wind changed,* to prompt the name of a ship (the *Association*; the *Mary Rose*).

2 GRAMMAR FILE

Aim: to present the past perfect continuous.
- Students copy and complete the chart.
- Check orally.

Answers

Past perfect continuous

*The sailor had been **telling** the truth.*

*The ship **had been** carrying a valuable cargo.*

*A gentle wind **had been blowing** all day.*

Optional activities

- Students find examples of the past perfect continuous in the text.
- You may compare it with the present perfect continuous.

3 WRITE

Aim: to practise the past perfect continuous.

- Students read and match the sentence parts.
- Check orally.

Answers

1c the captain ***had been worrying*** *about being late.*
2d the sailors ***had been checking*** *the sails.*
3e the cooks ***had been making*** *supper.*
4f the ship's doctor ***had been looking*** *after a patient.*
5b everyone ***had been looking*** *forward to being home.*
6a only one man ***had been expecting*** *a shipwreck.*

4 SPEAK AND WRITE

Aim: to make deductions about activities from a picture, using the past perfect continuous.

- Students look at the picture and guess what people had been doing.
- Go through this orally first.
- Students then write the sentences.
- Check their work.

Possible answers

Alison had been shopping because she had lots of shopping bags.

Alison had been drinking tea or coffee because she had a mug in her hand.

Paolo had been playing tennis because he had a tennis racket.

Aliki had been swimming because she had wet hair, a towel and swimming costume.

Activity Book p28 Exercises 1 and 2

5 SOUND FILE

Aim: to listen to and distinguish between the sounds /eɪ/ and /eə/.

- Play the cassette, pausing for students to repeat each word.
- Now play the next section, pausing for them to write the words they hear.
- Check orally.
- You may play the second section again to give additional pronunciation practice.

Tapescript and answers 

/eɪ/	/eə/
way	*where*
day	*dare*
pay	*pair*
stay	*stair*
hey	*hair*

where day pay stair hair

6 WRITE

Aim: to use notes to write a description using the past perfect continuous.

- You may go through this orally first.
- Students write their paragraphs.
- Check their work, paying attention to correct use of tenses and sequencing.
- This is suitable for homework.

Consolidation and Extension activities

- Pairs or teams. Students list up to ten words with the sounds /eɪ/ and /eə/. They take turns to say one. The others have to spell it and use it correctly in a sentence.
- Pairs or teams. Students make up questions which can be answered with the past perfect continuous, e.g., *Why was John tired?* The others have to think of interesting answers, e.g., *Because he had been dancing all night.* Monitor for correct use of tenses and reasonable answers.
- Students choose one of the four shipwrecks they have read about and make notes like those in Activity 6. Then they make a short report to the class or to their group.

Homework

- Students write up to six sentences showing the difference in meaning between the past simple, past perfect simple and past perfect continuous.
- They write an account of an accident describing the events leading up to it.

Activity Book Unit 3 Lesson 3, p28-29
Grammar Summary p119-120

Lesson 4 *Discovery*

Vocabulary

Underwater archaeology
Linking words: *although*
Prefixes: *in-* and *im-*

Warmer

- What ancient places do you know of? How do we know about them and their uses today?
- Has anyone visited an ancient place, or a museum?

READING

1 **Aim:** to read a passage for gist.

- You may start by asking students what the purpose of a paragraph is, e.g., each paragraph usually has a new topic.
- Look at the picture and discuss what the passage is about.
- Use the cassette to present and practise the passage.
- Students read the passage and match the topics with the paragraphs.
- Check orally.

Tapescript

THE LIGHTHOUSE OF ALEXANDRIA

It was early morning in Alexandria, Egypt, one day in March 1994. Asma el-Bakri, an Egyptian film-maker, put on her diving equipment in the eastern harbour. She took her camera and dived underwater. What she found under the water was incredible. The bottom of the harbour was covered with 3000 huge ancient stones and statues. Asma had discovered the lighthouse of Alexandria, one of the seven wonders of the ancient world. It had been lying underwater since a great earthquake in 1303.

The lighthouse of Alexandria, the first, and greatest, lighthouse in the world, was built 2300 years ago. Before then, people had lit fires on hills to warn ships of dangerous rocks or to show the entrance to a harbour. The lighthouse was as tall as a modern skyscraper with 25 floors. At the top there was a fire which burned 24 hours a day. The lighthouse took twelve years to build. We know that it was well-made because it lasted for a very long time - much longer than the builders had expected. Although there were lots of earthquakes in Alexandria, the lighthouse fire continued to burn. However, the earthquakes damaged the building and it was repaired many times.

Then, on 8th August 1303, there was an extremely violent earthquake. It shook the lighthouse and stones started to fall. The lighthouse leant more and more and finally fell into the sea. The lighthouse had stood there for 1600 years, but now it had disappeared and was invisible. A hundred and seventy-five years later, a castle was built in the same place and gradually the position of the lighthouse was forgotten. Although people no longer remembered exactly where the lighthouse had been, they knew about it from old books and pictures.

Asma made her great discovery several years ago. Since then, archaeologists and divers have been working in the harbour. Although they have found a lot of things, there is still a lot to do. People hope that one day they will find the palace of Queen Cleopatra.

Answers

1 *The discovery*
2 *What it was like*
3 *The disaster*
4 *The future*

Optional activity

- Ask further questions about the passage, e.g., *How long had the lighthouse been lying underwater? What had been there before the castle was built?* etc.

2 **Aim:** to practise using *although*.

- Students find *although* in the text.
- Then they rewrite the sentences. Make sure they write a comma after the *although* clause. You may want to go through the sentences orally first.
- Check orally.

Answers

1 *Although there were lots of earthquakes, the lighthouse fire continued to burn.*
2 *Although there are over 150 islands in the Isles of Scilly, people only live on five.*
3 *Although the water was cold, Aliki stayed underwater for half an hour.*
4 *Although the sailor was telling the truth, the captain called him a liar.*
5 *Although the wreck was close to the coast, all the sailors were drowned.*

Optional activities

- Students find the sentence with *but* in the text and rewrite it with *although*.
- Students find sentences with *although* in the text and rewrite them with *but*.

Activity Book p30-31 Exercises 1 and 2

Listening

3 **Aim:** to listen for specific information.
- Students first go through the notes.
- Play the cassette. Students listen and note the correct information.
- Finally they give a heading from activity 1 to each paragraph.

Tapescript 

In 1985, an American submarine made an amazing discovery in the North Atlantic Ocean. It took photographs and made videos of a huge ship 4,000 metres underwater. The ship was lying on the bottom of the sea in two pieces. It was the most famous shipwreck in the world - the Titanic. The ship had been lying on the bottom of the sea for 73 years.

The Titanic was built in Belfast in Northern Ireland in 1911. The ship took 26 months to build. It was as big as a luxury hotel and could carry 3,511 people. The Titanic was also very fast and took only four days to cross the Atlantic. Everyone had heard of the Titanic, which was the largest and most luxurious ship in the world.

People also said it was the safest ship in the world.

The disaster came on her first crossing of the North Atlantic. On 15th April 1912, the Titanic hit an iceberg. Seawater filled the great ship and it sank in three hours. Although the ship had some lifeboats, there were not enough for everyone. More than 1,500 people were drowned.

Since then, submarines have photographed the wreck several times. In 1987, a French submarine raised hundreds of things from the ship. People will find out much more about the ship before it disappears. But it will be impossible to raise the Titanic because it is in two pieces.

Answers

1985; submarine; North Atlantic; 4000 metres; 73 years

Northern Ireland; 1911; 26 months; hotel; 3511 people; 4 days; most luxurious; safest

15 April; an iceberg; 3 hours; 1500

submarines; photographed; hundreds; impossible

1 The discovery   *2 What it was like*
3 The disaster   *4 The future*

Speaking

4 **Aim:** to tell a story based on notes.
- Play the cassette again. Students listen and check their notes.
- You may check orally first.
- Students talk about the *Titanic*. To give maximum opportunity for students to speak, let them do this in pairs while you monitor.
- Then choose two or three students to talk to the class.

Writing

5 **Aim:** to write an account focusing on topic based paragraphs.
- Students look at the note about paragraphs. They re-read the text about the Alexandria Lighthouse.
- Now they write a similar text about the Titanic, in four paragraphs, using their notes.
- Check their work.
- This is suitable for homework.

Word building

6 **Aim:** to present and practise the negative prefixes *in-* and *im-*.
- Students add the prefixes to the words. They can use their dictionaries to help.
- Check orally.
- Students complete the sentences.
- Check orally.
- Students then complete the rule.

Answers

***in**correct*   ***in**credible*   ***im**perfect*
***im**polite*   ***im**possible*   ***in**visible*

1 invisible   *2 incorrect*   *3 impossible*
4 incredible   *5 impolite*   *6 imperfect*

*We use in- before words beginning with **c** and **v**.*
*We use im- before words beginning with **p**.*

Study skills

7 **Aim:** to encourage students to work out the meaning of new words from context, cognates, etc.
- Discuss the ideas with students.
- Refer them back to the text and ask them to work out the meaning of any words they don't know.

Activity Book p31 Exercises 3 and 4

Consolidation and Extension activities

- Negative Tennis. In teams or pairs, students give the adjective and 'return' its negative. They can also use words with *dis-* and *un-*.
- Definitions. This may be done in teams or pairs. Students find words from the unit, e.g., *submarine, iceberg, drown* and list them. The others have to write or say a definition. They take turns.
- Play any of the word games to practise sequencing events, e.g., writing or telling a story around the class.

Homework

- Students research and make notes on another disaster or another wonder of the world.
- They then write up the notes as a series of paragraphs. They focus on paragraphing and time sequencing.
- They may also use their notes to make a presentation in class.
- Students add the words with negative prefixes *in-* and *im-* to their vocabulary notebooks.

Pairwork

Pairwork Activity pp 107 and 115
Aim: to complete a map and find hidden treasure by means of an information gap activity.

- Students first familiarise themselves with the map, the features on it and the objects they must find.
- They prepare their questions.
- Students A ask first.
- Students B find out where their features are.
- For the second part, they take turns to give their partner their clues.
- The partner asks questions to establish where the hidden treasure is.
- Check with the whole class at the end. You could sketch a map on the board for students to complete.

Answers

The bag of diamonds is in the lighthouse.
The gold statue is on the mountain.
The silver coins are on the beach.

Optional activity

- Students draw their own map and decide where to hide treasure. Then they give their partner a map with features missing, and ask questions as before.

Activity Book Unit 3 Lesson 4, p30-31
Grammar Summary p119-120

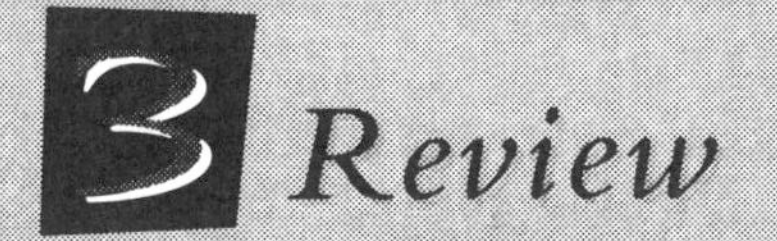

Review

1 Read and complete

- This can be done orally or in writing.
- Check orally.

Answers

1C	*2A*	*3B*	*4B*	*5A*	*6B*
7C	*8A*	*9C*	*10C*	*11B*	*12B*

Optional activity

- Students decide what the topic of each paragraph is.
- They choose one of the three shipwrecks and make notes about it.
- Then they write up their notes or use them to give a short talk about the shipwreck.

2 Complete

Answers

1 must 2 can't 3 must 4 must 5 must 6 can't

Optional activity

- Students work in pairs. They find small objects, e.g., coins, erasers, pencils, and give one to their partner, whose eyes are shut. The partner speculates about what the item is, e.g., *It's long and thin with a point at one end, so it must be a pen or a pencil. It feels like wood so it can't be a pen. It must be a pencil,* etc.

3 Talk about Jack's day

- Students first prepare the sentences, making sure they use linking words like *when* and *after*.
- Then they work in groups, saying a sentence each round the group.

Possible answers

After Jack had met the group at the airport, he went to the harbour with them.

After he had gone to the harbour with them, he took them to the wreck.

When he had taken them to the wreck, he showed them where to dive.

When he had showed them where to dive, he dived with them.

After he had dived with them, he put away the equipment.

When he had put away the equipment, he took them back to his house.

After he had taken them back to his house, he went out to a restaurant.

Optional activity

- Pairs. Students ask each other questions, e.g., *What did Jack do after he had put away the equipment?*

4 Read and choose

Answers

1 been sitting	*2 thought*	*3 travelled*	*4 been moving*
5 reached	*6 killed*	*7 destroyed*	*8 been expecting*

5 Test each other

- Students write sentences or choose sentences from the book.
- They rewrite them out of order.
- Then they give them to their partner to re-order.

Song

- Students pair the rhyming words: *day/pay, find/mind, free/me, funny/money, man/plan.*
- They decide which words go where.
- Play the cassette. Students listen and check.
- Check orally.

Tapescript and answers

I work all night, I work all ***day***

To pay the bills I have to ***pay***

Ain't it sad?

And still there never seems to be

A single penny left for me

That's too bad.

In my dreams I have a ***plan***

If I got me a wealthy ***man***

I wouldn't have to work at all

I'd fool around and have a ball.

Chorus

Money, money, ***money***

Must be ***funny***

In the rich man's world

Money, money, money

Always sunny

In the rich man's world

All the things I could do

If I had a little money

It's a rich man's world

It's a rich man's world

A man like that is hard to ***find***

But I can't get him off my ***mind***

Ain't it sad?

And if he happens to be ***free***

I bet he wouldn't fancy ***me***

That's too bad.

So I must leave, I'll have to go

To Las Vegas or Monaco

And win a fortune in a game

My life will never be the same.

Optional activity

- Listen to the song again. Students sing along.
- Ask the students what the song is about. Is the person singing rich or poor? What does the singer want? Why does she say her life will never be the same if she gets the money?
- Ask the students what they would do if they 'had a little money'. Students discuss in groups and report back to the class.
- In the song the girl wants to marry a man for money. Encourage the class to discuss whether they think money can buy love and happiness.

Activity Book Unit 3 Review, p32-33

Posters p111

- In this unit, students make a poster about news stories.
- Students look back over the texts in the unit to see how news stories are presented.
- They work in groups and brainstorm suitable news events. These may be international, national or local events.
- Encourage each group to choose a different story.
- At home, students research the story, trying to find more information as well as suitable pictures. If they have access to the Internet, this could be a useful source.
- They make notes.
- They should discuss their notes in their group before deciding who writes up what.
- They write their part neatly, check it carefully, and select suitable illustrations.
- They put everything together on a large piece of paper, arranged to look like part of a newspaper, if possible.
- Display the posters or allow groups to look at each other's.

Lesson 1 *He's such an idiot!*

p38

Target language
What ...!
so/such
Result clauses

Vocabulary
Exclamations
Animals

Optional Aids

Bring pictures of something exciting or frightening or beautiful, etc., or amazing architecture, art or fashion, so that students can make exclamations.

Warmer

- Ask students who they like,at ACE, and why?
- Ask students if they have ridden a horse or know anything about horses.

1 Read and Listen

Aim: to present and practise exclamations, *so/such* and result clauses.

- Students then read the dialogue silently and complete the blanks with the given adjectives.
- Now play the cassette. They listen and check.
- Students read the dialogue.

Tapescript and answers 

Holly *I'm having such a **great** time! I've never been pony-trekking before. What an adventure!*
Manuel *Oh, wow! What an **amazing** view!*
Tara *That's Clovelly - isn't it a beautiful village?*
Lucy *Look at all the boats! And what **pretty** houses!*
Tara *There's only one street in the village, and it's very steep. It's called 'Up along' when you go up it and 'Down along' when you go down it! And there are no cars. They use donkeys to carry things.*
Mark *It's just another fishing village. What's so **special** about it?*
Holly *Mark, why are you so **grumpy**?*
Mark *I'm tired and I'm so **hungry** I could eat a horse.*
Manuel *What a **terrible** thing to say!*
Tara *He doesn't really mean it, Manuel, it's just an expression. Cheer up, Mark, we're stopping for lunch soon.*
Mark *But can't we go a bit faster? This is so **slow**, it's boring!*
Holly *It's not boring. It's fun!*
Mark *Well, I want to go faster.*
Tara *Mark, slow down! He's going so **fast** that he'll fall off and hurt himself! Mark!*
Mark *Aaagh!*
Lucy *Oh, he's such an idiot!*

Optional activities

- Students act out the dialogue.
- They speculate about what will happen next.

2 Listen

Aim: to listen for specific information.

- Students decide what happened to Mark.
- They read the sentences.
- Play the cassette.
- They decide whether the sentences are *true* or *false*.
- Check orally.

Tapescript and answers 

Tara *Mark! Mark, are you all right?*
Mark *I think so. Ouch - **I've hurt my hand**.*
Tara *Let me have a look.*
Mark *It's nothing. **Oh, no!***
Tara *What? What's the matter?*
Mark *My jacket! Look, **I've torn my jacket**.*
Tara *Well, at least you're in one piece.*
Mark *But **it's such a shame!** It's my favourite jacket!*

Answers

1 *False. He'd hurt his hand.*
2 *True.*
3 *True.*
4 *False. He'd torn his jacket*
5 *False. It's a shame means sad, not ashamed.*
6 *True.*

Optional activities

- Find out how many students guessed correctly.
- Ask if they sympathise with Mark.
- Students retell the story round the class.

Activity Book p34 Exercise 1

3 Grammar File

Aim: to present and practise making exclamations with *What (a/n)* and *so/such*.

- Students copy and complete the chart.
- Check orally.
- Make sure students realise that if the noun is preceded by an adjective. we still use *such (a/n)*.

Answers

Making exclamations

What ...!

*What **a** terrible thing to say!*

*What **an** amazing view!*

What pretty houses!

so/such

*I'm having **such** a good time!*

*He's **such** an idiot!*

*This is **so** slow!*

*It's **such** a shame!*

*Adjectives come after **so** and nouns and adjectives come after **such**.*

Activity Book p34-35 Exercises 2 and 3

4 Sound File

Aim: to practise correct intonation for exclamations.

- Play the cassette, pausing for students to repeat the exclamations. Pay particular attention to their intonation.

Tapescript 

Manuel *What a terrible thing to say!*
Manuel *What an amazing view!*
Lucy *What pretty houses!*
Holly *I'm having such a great time!*
Lucy *He's such an idiot!*
Mark *This is so slow!*
Mark *It's such a shame!*

Optional activities

- Students pick out other exclamations from the text.
- Show students the pictures you have brought. They exclaim, e.g., *What a beautiful dress!* etc. Pay attention to intonation.

5 Speak

Aim: to practise making exclamations.

- Students first match the exclamations with the three correct topics.
- Check orally.
- Then they make exclamations about other topics. This can be done round the class or in groups, with the others guessing what the topic is.
- Pay attention to intonation. You may wish to chorus the exclamations.

Answers

It's such a difficult language! - Chinese.
They're so tall! - giraffes
What a big city! - London

Optional activity

- Groups, pairs or teams. Students think of other topics, and make exclamations. The others guess the topic.

6 Speak

Aim: to practise result clauses in speaking.

- Students read and match the sentences.
- Check orally.
- Draw attention to the LOOK! box.
- You may point out that *so* can also be used with adverbs, e.g., *so slowly*.

Answers

1b 2f 3e 4c 5a 6d

Optional activity

- Students make up their own sentences with *so/such ... that.*

7 Write

Aim: to practise writing result clauses.

- You may elicit one or two suggestions orally first.
- Students write sentences.
- Check orally, letting several students read their sentences, for variety.
- Check their written work, in case of problems.

Optional activity

- Students think of other similar phrases and give them to a partner to make into sentences.

Activity Book p35 Exercises 4 and 5

8 Read and Speak

Aim: to read a text for specific information.
- Students read the text and find the answers.
- Check orally.
- Discuss the text and the ideas in it. This can be done in groups, and the groups report back to the class.

Answers

1 mammals	*2 mythical*	*3 forehead*
4 transport	*5 essential*	*6 agricultural*

Optional activities

- Ask students if they know of other members of the horse family, e.g., zebras.
- Review names of other facial features, e.g., *cheeks, chin, eyebrows,* etc.

9 Write

Aim: to write a letter telling a story and using result clauses.
- You may first go through this orally. Encourage the students to make notes.
- This is suitable for homework.
- Take the work in for checking.

Consolidation and Extension activities

- Game. This can be played in teams or groups. A student thinks of an adjective and mimes it. The others have to guess what it is.
- Game. Make a list of adjectives that have come up recently, but don't tell students what they are. Then give them two or three letters. They must think of adjectives and nouns beginning with those letters and use them in sentences, e.g., *A: What an amazing animal! E: Is that equipment essential?*

Homework

- Students reread the grammar file and the LOOK! box, making sure they know how to use these forms.
- Students list positive and negative adjectives that can be used in exclamations, e.g., *great, wonderful, amazing,* etc., and *terrible, stupid, boring,* etc. These can be written on opposite pages of their vocabulary notebooks.
- Students write a letter to a friend about a good or bad day out, using exclamations and result clauses.

Activity Book Unit 4 Lesson 1, p34-35
Grammar Summary p120

Lesson 2 *Whales have been hunted...* p40

Target language

Present continuous passive
Present perfect passive

Vocabulary

Whales and turtles
Conservation issues

Warmer

- Find out what students know about whales or dolphins.
- Review adjectives and exclamations from Lesson 1.
- Does anyone know about conservation issues and these creatures?

1 Read

Aim: to present the present continuous passive and present perfect passive.

- Students first look at the picture and try to work out what is happening.
- Use the cassette to present the text.
- Then students answer the comprehension questions. Check orally.

Tapescript

WHALE STRANDED ON DEVON BEACH

An eight-metre-long whale has been washed up on the beach in Shipload Bay, North Devon. The whale is being looked after by lifeguards, who hope they can return it to the sea at high tide later today.

Whale expert Sarah Douglas is at the scene. 'The whale has been covered with wet towels to keep it cool. It's the first time a whale has been seen on this beach, so it's attracting a lot of interest. Perhaps it swam too close to the shore because it was confused and disturbed by passing ships. It hasn't been attacked so we don't think it's been hunted.'

Enemies of the whale.

Whales have been hunted for over 1,000 years. Whale products have been used for fuel, margarine, soap, candles and pet food. Commercial whaling has now been banned, and the whales have been saved from the hunter. These highly intelligent and sensitive giants are now being protected by conservation groups. But whales are being threatened by a new enemy - pollution. Many types of sea creature are being killed by pollution, and whales will die if their food supply is poisoned.

Answers

1. *It's been washed up on the beach.*
2. *Lifeguards.*
3. *To keep it cool.*
4. *Because it's the first time a whale has been seen on this beach.*
5. *No, it hasn't.*
6. *For over 1,000 years.*
7. *Not any more./No, it isn't.*
8. *By pollution.*

Optional activity

- Books closed, students recall the passage.

Activity Book p36 Exercise 1

2 Grammar File

Aim: to present and practise the present continuous passive and present perfect passive.

- Students copy and complete the chart.
- Then they look through the report for other examples of the two structures.

Answers

Present continuous passive: is/are being + past participle

*The whale **is** being looked after by lifeguards.*

*Many types of sea creature **are being** killed.*

***Are** whales **being** threatened by pollution?*

Present perfect passive: has/have been + past participle

*The whale **has** been covered with wet towels.*

*Whales **have been** hunted for over 1,000 years.*

***Has** the whale **been** attacked?*

- You may wish to remind students that the passive is used when we focus on the action rather than the agent, or when we don't know the agent. If we include the agent, it follows the verb, after *by*, e.g., *The whale is being looked after by lifeguards.*

Activity Book p36 Exercise 2

3 Write and Listen

Aim: to practise the present continuous passive and present perfect passive, and to listen for specific information.

- Students write the sentences.
- Check the questions orally.
- Play the cassette. They listen and answer the questions.
- Play it again for them to check.

Tapescript 

Rick	*Hi Sarah. I'm Rick from ACE.*
Sarah	*Hello, Rick. Nice to meet you.*
Rick	*Isn't this incredible!*
Sarah	*Yes, it sure is.*
Rick	*Tell me, what's the music for?*
Sarah	*The whale likes it, so we've got a cassette recorder on the beach.*
Rick	*You're joking!*
Sarah	*Not at all. Whales like listening to music - they like classical music best.*
Rick	*That's amazing! What about food? Is the whale hungry? Has it been fed?*
Sarah	*No, we haven't given it anything to eat. In fact, whales can go for months without food.*
Rick	*Really?*
Sarah	*Yes. But we've given the whale some water to drink.*
Rick	*And is it OK? Has it been injured?*
Sarah	*No, it hasn't. A vet is examining it now. It seems fine, and we're hoping to get it back into the water in the next hour.*
Rick	*And who are all the other people here?*
Sarah	*Well, there are scientists and journalists, and they're taking lots of photos.*
Rick	*I think I'll take a couple of photos myself. I've never seen such an unusual whale!*

Answers

1 *Is music being played? - Yes, it is.*
2 *Has the whale been fed? - No, it hasn't.*
3 *Has it been given water? - Yes, it has.*
4 *Has it been injured? - No, it hasn't.*
5 *Is it being examined by a vet? - Yes, it is.*
6 *Is it being photographed? - Yes, it is.*
7 *Has it been returned to the sea? - No, it hasn't.*

4 Speak and Write

Aim: to practise the present continuous passive and present perfect passive orally and in writing.

- Students ask and answer the questions in pairs or groups.
- Then they write about the whale, following the pattern.
- Check orally or by taking in their work.

Answers

The whale hasn't been fed but it's been given water. It hasn't been injured but it's being examined by a vet. It's being photographed. It hasn't been returned to the sea.

Optional activity

- Ask further comprehension questions about the story, including questions which ask for an explanation.

Activity Book p37 Exercise 3

5 Sound File

Aim: to distinguish between the words *been* and *being*.

- Students first read silently through the chart.
- Play the cassette. They listen and note which phrase they hear.
- Check orally.
- Establish that *It's being = It is being* and *It's been = It has been.*
- You may play the cassette again, pausing to give additional practice.

Tapescript and answers 

1 *They've been hunted.*
2 *It's being killed.*
3 *She's being watched.*
4 *He's been fed.*

Activity Book p37 Exercise 4

6 Listen

Aim: to listen to a narrative for specific information.

- Students read through the sentences.
- Play the cassette. They listen and write *true* or *false*.
- Check orally. Students should correct the false sentences.

Tapescript

Rick: Last year, I had a holiday on the south coast of Australia. One morning, one cold morning, I decided to go snorkelling near the shore. I'd been snorkelling for about half an hour when someone started shouting 'Whale! Whale! You're being followed!' ... I turned round and suddenly there was an enormous whale in front of me - it was about ten metres long! It was such a shock, I've never been so surprised in all my life. And I was quite frightened. At first, we just looked at each other - I looked at the whale, the whale looked at me. But then I moved closer and closer and I started ... to swim next to it and I swam ... and just looked into the whale's eyes, and it looked so kind and gentle, so warm that ... I calmed down completely and I dared to touch it. And its skin was like a baby's skin - incredibly soft. And then I spent the morning swimming with the whale - I swam next to the whale, under the whale, over the whale, and the whale carried me on its back. It was just, just fabulous. I didn't realise how cold I was - after two or three hours I had to leave the water because my hands were frozen. I'll never forget swimming with the whale - it was so amazing.

Answers

1 *False. He was snorkelling.*

2 *True.*

3 *False. It was about 10 metres long.*

4 *False. It looked kind and gentle.*

5 *True.*

6 *False. He says, about two or three hours.*

7 *False. He was very cold.*

Optional activity

- Ask students for their comments on this story. Do they know any stories about people swimming with animals?

7 SPEAK

Aim: to retell a story from notes.
- Students re-order the sentences.
- Play the cassette again if necessary.
- Pairs retell each other the story.
- Let pairs retell the story to the class.
- Ask the class the questions. Let two or three students tell the class an experience.
- Then they work in pairs or small groups and tell each other stories about frightening animals. They may invent a story.

Answers

The correct order is: f d b e a g c

Optional activities

- Students retell the story without the text.
- One student is Rick and the other is a reporter asking him questions about the adventure.
- Groups. Each group decides on their best animal story and presents it to the class.
- Students write about their own or someone else's animal experience.

8 WRITE

Aim: to write a short article given notes using different tenses of the passive.
- Students re-read the newspaper report. They should focus on the use of the passive.
- You may want to go through the notes orally first.
- Students then write a paragraph about leatherback turtles.
- Check their work. This is suitable for homework.

Suggested answer

The 2.5-metre-long leatherback turtle is one of the world's oldest and largest reptiles, but turtles' eggs have been stolen and eaten for thousands of years. The beaches where the turtles always lay their eggs have been destroyed. Now, however, the turtles are being protected by local people and conservation groups. Twenty years ago, 90% of eggs were lost. Since then, hundreds of thousands of turtles have been saved. Now record numbers of turtles are being born.

Consolidation and Extension activities

- Mime game. Pairs of students act out short scenes for the others to guess the situation, e.g., being chased by a dog; a house being broken into; being overtaken in a race, etc.
- Question game. This can be played in pairs or round the class. Student 1 asks, e.g., *Can I have a sweet?* Student 2 answers, e.g., *No, sorry, they've all been eaten.* He/She then asks a question in turn, e.g., *Can I use a computer?* The answer could be *No, sorry, they're all being used.*
- Chain story. Round the class, students each add one or two sentences to a story about an adventure involving animals.

Homework

- Students write up the chain story.
- Students choose another endangered animal, do some research on it if necessary, and then write one or two paragraphs about it. They may illustrate their work and show the class.
- Instead of writing up their article, students write notes and use them to tell the class about their animal in the next lesson.

Activity Book Unit 4 Lesson 2, p36-37
Grammar Summary p120

4 Lesson 3 *You won't be attacked!*

p42

Target language

Future passive

Vocabulary

Geographical features
Holidays
Animals

Optional Aids

Bring in a piece of paper that has been written on and torn, had coffee spilt on it, rained on and dropped in the street; a map of the world.

Warmer

- Show your piece of paper and ask *What's happened to this?* Students guess. They will probably use the active form, e.g., *Did you drop it?* You confirm each time, e.g., *Yes, it's been dropped.*
- Students use the notes they made for homework to tell the class about an adventure with animals.
- They talk about adventure holidays. ACE offers holidays in England in the summer. What can people do in other countries or at other times of year?

1 Read and Speak

Aim: to read for gist and for specific information; to present the future passive.

- Ask students about the photos.
- Use the cassette to present the passage.
- They read the passage and match each picture with its holiday.
- After that they answer the questions.
- Check orally.
- Finally, students decide which holiday they would like to win and why. They discuss this in groups.
- Ask several students to tell the class about their choice.

Tapescript

WIN AN ADVENTURE HOLIDAY!

Enter our competition and you could win the holiday of a lifetime!

ARCTIC ADVENTURE

Find polar bears in the Arctic! You will fly to Churchill - the 'Polar Bear Capital of the World' - on the shores of Hudson Bay, in Canada. The Arctic region takes its name from the Greek word 'arktos' which means bear! The polar bear is one of the largest and most dangerous of all creatures - it's up to three metres tall and weighs as much as 550 kilos. Don't worry - you won't be attacked! You will travel in specially designed vehicles which are high enough to be safe from the bears. The vehicles are heated, and snacks and drinks will be served on board.

TROPICAL SAFARI

See wildlife in Africa! You will be taken on safari to Amboseli National Park in Kenya, where you can see elephants, giraffes, lions and zebras. In the background is snow-capped Mt Kilimanjaro, the highest mountain in Africa. After two days in Amboseli, you will be driven north to Lake Nakuru, home of millions of pink flamingos, and then you will spend two days with leopards and rhinos in Nakuru National Park! The rest of the holiday will be spent on the coast near Mombasa, where you can surf and snorkel in the Indian Ocean.

SNOWBOARDING SCHOOL

Be really cool and ride the slopes on a snowboard! You will be flown to Geneva in Switzerland. You will be met at the airport by your tour guide and taken by minibus to your chalet in the mountains. The days will be spent snowboarding, and you will be given three hours of lessons every day. In the evenings, exciting entertainment will be provided, including discos, treasure hunts and karaoke evenings.

Answers

A Polar bear and big lorry with Arctic Adventure.
B Snowboarder with Snowboarding School.
C Elephants with Tropical Safari.

1 *Snowboarding school*
2 *Arctic adventure*
3 *Snowboarding school*
4 *Tropical safari*
5 *Tropical safari*
6 *Snowboarding school*

Optional activities

- Have a class survey to see how many people prefer which holiday and why.
- Students write the competition entry. This is suitable for homework. Check their work.

Activity Book p38 Exercise 1

2 GRAMMAR FILE

Aim: to present and practise the future passive.
- Students copy and complete the chart.
- Check orally.
- Finally students find other examples of the future passive in the text.

Answers

Future passive: will be + past participle

*You **will** be taken on safari.*

*Snacks and drinks **will be** served.*

*The days **will** be **spent** snowboarding.*

*You **won't be** attacked!*

***Will** you **be** given lessons?*

Activity Book p39 Exercise 2

3 READ AND WRITE

Aim: to practise the future passive.
- Students read through the passage and work out the correct verb forms.
- They write the verbs.
- Check orally.

Answers

1 will be met	*2 will be taken*	*3 will be driven*
4 will be hired	*5 will be flown*	*6 will be spent*

Optional activity

- Students compare this holiday with the other three and see whether their choice would still be the same.

4 LISTEN AND SPEAK

Aim: to listen to instructions for specific information.
- Explain that Lundy is a small island in the Bristol Channel. It's a wild life sanctuary, particularly famous for puffins.
- Students first read the questions.
- They listen to the cassette and note the answers.
- Check orally.

Tapescript

Alison *All right, quiet everyone. Now this is about the wildlife adventure trip to Lundy tomorrow - so all of you who are going to Lundy, listen carefully. You'll be picked up outside the activity centre by minibus at half past seven in the morning. Yes, I know it's early but there's only one boat to Lundy in the morning. You'll be taken to Clovelly and then you have to walk to the post office where you'll be given your boat tickets. The boat to Lundy leaves at nine in the morning so don't miss it! The crossing takes 1 hour and 15 minutes. When you get to Lundy, you'll be met by your guide, David Cook - you'll be taken round the island by him. The boat back leaves Lundy at half past six in the evening - don't miss that one either! The minibus will be waiting for you in the car park in Clovelly, and you'll be brought back to ACE for supper at about 8 o'clock. OK, got that? Are there any questions?*

Mark *What about lunch?*

Alison *You'll be given packed lunches tomorrow morning at breakfast. All right? And there is a shop on Lundy if you want to buy anything.*

Answers

1. *At half past seven (in the morning).*
2. *(They'll be taken) by minibus.*
3. *At Clovelly Post Office.*
4. *On Lundy.*
5. *David Cook.*
6. *At about 8 o'clock.*
7. *They'll be given packed lunches.*

Optional activities

- Ask additional questions about the day on Lundy.
- Ask students if they know of any wildlife sanctuaries in their country.

Activity Book p39 Exercise 3

5 Word File

Aim: to record vocabulary in a word map.

- You may draw the basic word map on the board and let students add to it.
- You could also start with a brainstorming session.
- They could do the word maps directly in their vocabulary notebooks.

Activity Book p39 Exercise 4

6 Write

Aim: to write a paragraph describing a place and encouraging people to visit it.

- You may start with a whole-class session for ideas or students may discuss suitable places in groups.
- If possible, give time for them to do some research and to find some suitable illustrations.
- Students write their brochure entry.
- Collect and check the work.
- If possible, display it, and let all the students see each other's work.

Consolidation and Extension activities

- Students make an animal and bird word map.
- Students work in pairs to create a simple geography crossword. They exchange with another pair and try to solve each other's clues.
- Word game. Say a geographical area, e.g., *Africa* or *the mountains*. Then give students a limited time to think of five climate words, five animals, five activity words and five adjectives to go with it. This can be done as a team game.
- Predictions. Students make predictions about the future using the future passive, e.g., *Everything will be done by computers. Cars will be banned*, etc. This could be used as a team game.

Homework

- Students learn the words in their geography word maps.
- They write predictions, using the future passive.
- Students write about an imaginary adventure holiday in space.
- Students imagine they went on one of the adventure holidays and write a letter about it to a friend.
- Instead, they can make notes and tell the class about their holiday in the next lesson.

Activity Book Unit 4 Lesson 3, p38-39
Grammar Summary p120

Lesson 4 *ACE Advice*

Vocabulary

Personal problems
Advice
Linking words: *either... or, both... and*
Suffixes: *-ness* and *-ity*

Warmer

- Students talk to the class about holidays they wrote brochures for.
- Whose holiday sounds the most interesting/ exciting/fun?
- What kinds of problems can one have on holiday? (e.g., losing things, missing a train, being harmed by a wild animal, not liking the food, not liking the other people.) Give students a short time to see how many they can think of.
- Then give them a short time to come up with suggestions for avoiding the problems or solving them.
- Review the language of giving advice, e.g., *Why don't you...? You should(n't)....*

READING

1 **Aim:** to read for gist.
- Use the cassette to introduce the text.
- Students read the paragraphs and match the topics.
- Check orally.

Tapescript

Boy *I'm Robert. I'm fifteen and I'm from Manchester. I'm on an adventure holiday at the moment. Most things are great but there's one problem and I need your advice.*

I'm the only boy in my group and I'm always being teased by the girls. They make fun of me all of the time and I hate it.

What can I do? I don't want to leave the centre but their teasing is really spoiling it for me.

Agony Aunt *There are two reasons why you are being teased.*

Firstly, the girls can probably see that it makes you angry. Try pretending that you haven't heard what they've said. When I've been teased in the past, I've just ignored it and it's stopped. If one girl is the leader, try and talk to her on her own. Help her with something she's doing and talk to her then. Tell her how much you'll be hurt if they carry on teasing you. Not many people really want to hurt someone once they know how they feel. And if the others see both you and the leader doing things together, they may change their attitude and see that teasing is really stupid.

Secondly, these girls are teasing you because you are different from them. Stop worrying about being a boy and join in with the others. Help when equipment is being cleaned and put away. When everything has been done, the girls will see that you are the same as them - ready for anything!

Girl *I'm Sharon from Southampton. I'm sixteen and I'm really enjoying my holiday. Most of the time that is, because there's a problem and I'd like some help.*

It's our drama classes. We're all fed up with our drama teacher and her favourite pupil. The teacher either tells this girl how good she is all the time or she complains that the rest of us are hopeless. The teacher's pet is always asked to do things first and never seems to do anything wrong. What can we do about this? I don't want to give up drama but it's no fun now

Agony Aunt *I can understand that you're angry that one girl is being given all the teacher's attention. This is a tricky problem. You can either talk to another adult at the centre about it or discuss it with the teacher herself. Be careful though, because the teacher may not know she is doing this, and think she is being criticised unfairly. If you speak to another adult, explain that you love your lessons but that you all want to have a go and that your happiness is important too.*

Once the problem has been discussed it may get better. But don't worry if things don't change. Your drama skills may still improve because the teacher tells you about all your mistakes. While the teacher's pet will think she's perfect because she has never been criticised! So both she and you will be affected by the problem. And the person who is really losing out most here is the teacher's pet!

Answers

1 *Don't listen*

2 *Become part of the group*

3 *A choice you can make*

4 *You're really OK*

Optional activity

- Students reread the text and decide if they agree with the advice given. What would they do?

2 Aim: to focus on the use of *either... or* and *both... and*.

- Students underline the words in the text.
- Then they answer the questions.
- Check orally.
- Students then complete the text.
- Check orally.

Answers

1 ***Both*** *means* ***the two together***.

2 ***Either*** *means* ***one or the other***.

1 either	*2 or*	*3 Both*	*4 and*
5 both	*6 and*	*7 either*	*8 or*
9 Both	*10 and*	*11 Both*	*12 and*

LISTENING

3 Aim: to listen for specific information.

- Students read through each passage before you play the cassette.
- Play each in turn and give time for them to answer the questions.
- Check orally.

Tapescript 

Call 1

Hello. Is that the Ace Advice Hotline? My name's Helen and the reason I'm ringing is that I've got a problem with my best friend. She's called Jane and we've been best friends for years and years. Last year we both started diving together and it was great fun at the beginning. I still love it but Jane is always so afraid. She won't dive for very long or anything. She's really frightened. But at school she tells everyone she's the best diver at the centre. It's all lies - she says she dives very deep and stays down a long time and everything, but the truth is that she doesn't. I don't know what to do. I don't want to lose my best friend but ...

Call 2

Hi I'm Rod. This is a bit difficult because it isn't really about adventure holidays. I'll start at the beginning - it's my girlfriend, you see, she's called Tanya. It's just that, you know, I never see her. She says she likes me but she spends all her time with her pet dog, talking to it and looking after it. I think she likes Tommy, that's the name of the dog, more than me! Please help me. What can I do?

Call 3

Is that the hotline? I'm Wendy and I'm calling about a problem in our group. It's not just me - we're all upset about it and that's why I'm ringing. There's a rich girl in our group called Ella - and when I say rich, I mean very rich indeed. She's got lovely clothes and lots and lots of sports equipment. But she's so spoilt and lazy - she doesn't look after her things at all. And she doesn't help clean the equipment - we all have to clean it but she won't help. She just talks to the boys - boys, boys, boys and has lots of fun while we do all the work. Everyone hates her. We want her to change, so how can we teach her a lesson?

Answers

Call 1: best; this; diving; best; diver; worst

Call 2: has; never; enough; dog

Call 3: rich; has; never; all; lesson

SPEAKING

4 Aim: to give advice about specific problems.

- Students reread the problems.
- Then they work in groups to discuss what advice to give.
- The groups report back to the class.

Optional activities

- Pairs. Students take the part of the caller with a problem and the helper who gives advice.
- Pairs. They think of other such problems and give advice.

Activity Book p 40 Exercise 1

WRITING

5 Aim: to write a letter asking for advice.

- Students first check the correct layout of a personal letter (see page 14).
- Discuss ideas with the class, or they can do this in groups.
- Then they write their letters.
- Take them in to check.

Optional activity

- Students exchange letters and write answers to each other's problems.

Activity Book p 41 Exercise 2

WORD BUILDING

6 Aim: to present and practise the noun suffixes *-ness* and *-ity*.

- Point out that the suffixes *-ness* and *-ity* can be added to certain adjectives to make abstract nouns.
- Students add the correct suffix to each word.
- Then they complete the sentences.
- Check orally.

Answers

1 popularity 2 sadness 3 cleverness 4 similarity

Optional activities

- Students think of other words which use the same two suffixes, e.g., *weak, weakness; kind, kindness; hopeless, hopelessness; special, speciality.*
- You may note that adjectives ending in *-y* often take the suffix *-ness*, and adjectives ending in *-ar* or *-al* often take the suffix *-ity*.

STUDY SKILLS

7 Aim: to discuss and give advice about learning problems.

- Discuss this in class or in groups first. Students share their memories of problem areas.
- They write their letters. Remind them to follow the correct layout style.
- Go round checking the letters.
- Pairs. Students exchange letters and think of helpful advice, which they write as a letter.
- Afterwards students discuss their problems and the advice given in groups.
- Each group reports the best piece of advice back to the class.

Activity Book p 41 Exercises 3 and 4

Consolidation and Extension activities

- Affix Tennis. Play in pairs or teams. Give students a short time to look through their vocabulary notebooks for words made by adding prefixes or suffixes. Then they take turns to say the base word. Their partner says the word with the affix.
- Suggest a situation, e.g., going abroad on holiday for the first time; starting a new school or college; travelling to space, etc. In groups students write a list of dos and don'ts. Each group reports back to the class. This advice can be written up in a small booklet made from a folded sheet of paper and entitled *Advice to travellers to Mars*, etc.

Homework

- Students write up the words with the suffixes *-ness* and *-ity* on a new page in their vocabulary notebook.
- They write a letter to a friend asking for advice about which holiday from this unit to go on. There should be at least one point about each that they are not sure about, e.g., the heat, the animals, etc.
- Students make notes about their dream holiday. They tell the class about it in the next lesson.
- Students prepare a booklet about their dream holiday, with illustrations if possible.

Pairwork

Pairwork Activity p108 and 116

Aim: to revise vocabulary by defining words.

- Students A and B prepare definitions for their words.
- Then students A give students B their clues.
- They change roles.
- Then they check their answers. They should spell out each word.

Answers

Student A	*Student B*
1 forehead	*1 mammal*
2 unicorn	*2 donkey*
3 enemy	*3 candle*
4 snowboard	*4 crocodile*
5 entertainment	*5 margarine*
6 cleverness	*6 happiness*

Optional activity

- Students think of other words and prepare clues for them. They write the gapped words on a sheet of paper and give it to their partner. Then they repeat the activity.

Activity Book Unit 4 Lesson 4, p40-41
Grammar Summary p120

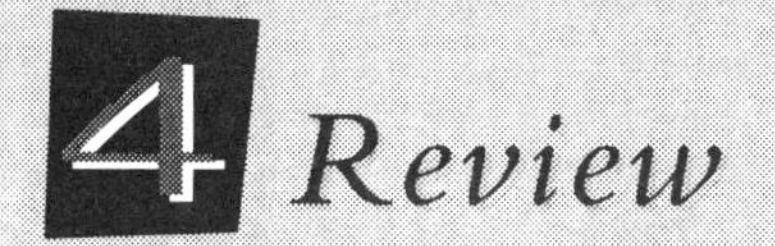

4 Review

1 Read and complete
- Students read and choose the correct words.
- Check orally.

Answers

1 most *2 world* *3 where* *4 brought*
5 an *6 ancient* *7 wave* *8 both*
9 so *10 weighs* *11 favourite* *12 taken*
13 attacked *14 exciting* *15 such* *16 bicycle*
17 be *18 Earth*

2 Listen and exclaim
- Play the cassette. Pause for students to make each exclamation.
- Play the correct exclamation.
- Students should repeat the correct exclamations.
- Pay attention to students' intonation.

Tapescript and answers

Listen and make exclamations, like this:

Narrator *enormous animal*
Voice *What an enormous animal!*

Now you.

1 *enormous animal*
What an enormous animal!
2 *beautiful mountains*
What beautiful mountains!
3 *silly thing to do*
What a silly thing to do!
4 *lovely weather*
What lovely weather!
5 *huge waves*
What huge waves!
6 *horrible thing to say*
What a horrible thing to say!
7 *noisy children*
What noisy children!
8 *steep hill*
What a steep hill!

Optional activity
- Students repeat the above exercise with *so* and *such*, e.g., *It's such an enormous animal.*

3 Make comments and disagree
- This can be done round the class or in pairs.
- Encourage students to speak as if they really mean what they say.

Answers

1 *They're such expensive shoes.*
I don't think they're so expensive.
2 *It's such warm water.*
I don't think it's so warm.
3 *It's such a boring book.*
I don't think it's so boring.
4 *They're such brilliant students.*
I don't think they're so brilliant.
5 *She's such a pretty girl.*
I don't think she's so pretty.
6 *He's such an unfriendly man.*
I don't think he's so unfriendly.

Optional activity
- Students make exclamations with *what* instead.

4 Rewrite

Answers

1 *Rick was so hungry that he had three hamburgers.*
2 *The film was so scary that the audience screamed.*
3 *Mark and Holly were so late that they missed lunch.*
4 *It was so dark/such a dark night that we couldn't see anything.*
5 *Jack is such a good diver that he found the wreck.*
6 *Aliki was so cold that she was shivering.*

5 Write

Answers

1 are being followed *2 is served* *3 are protected*
4 being photographed *5 is being taught* *6 are worn*
7 is expected *8 are being fed*

6 Ask and answer
- Students prepare the questions and answers.
- In pairs taking turns to ask and answer.
- Monitor and if necessary check orally

Answers

1 *Has the food been prepared yet?*
No, but it will be prepared by seven.
2 *Have the drinks been bought yet?*
No, but they will be bought by seven.
3 *Have the glasses been washed yet?*
No, but they will be washed by seven.
4 *Has the music been chosen yet?*
No, but it will be chosen by seven.
5 *Have the tables been laid yet?*
No, but they will be laid by seven.
6 *Have the decorations been put up yet?*
No, but they will be put up by seven.

7 Read and find the word

- You may need to explain this kind of word puzzle to students.
- *My first/second*, etc., means the first, second etc., letter of the mystery word. *My whole* means the whole word.
- Do the first line with the class. The letters in common are *a* and *r*. Students write both.
- Now do the second line. The only common letter is *d*. Students should work out that English words never begin *rd*, so that the first letter must be *a*. Even at this stage they could try to guess at the whole word.
- Let them continue working it out on their own or in pairs. Where there is a choice, they note all the letters, but also note what combinations they make and whether these are possible in English.
- Check orally, making sure students explain how they got any given letter.

Answer

ADVENTURE

Optional activity

- A good class could try to invent their own word puzzles, even if they don't rhyme.

Game: Word Partners

- This could be used as a class quiz.
- Check orally.

Possible answers

treasure hunt	*polar bear*	*horse–riding*	*snowboard*
earthquake	*lighthouse*	*shipwreck*	*pony–trekking*
windsurfing	*life jacket*	*sunrise*	*petshop*
thunderstorm	*raincoat*	*theme park*	

SONG

- Students read the gapped song.
- They decide which words go where.
- Play the cassette. Students listen and check.
- Check orally.

Tapescript and answers

On our block
All of the guys
***Call** her 'Flamingo'.*
'Cause her hair glows like the sun
*And her **eyes** can light the skies.*

*When she **walks***
She moves so fine,
Like a flamingo
*Crimson **dress** that clings so tight*
She's out of reach and out of sight.

*When she **walks** by*
She brightens up the neighbourhood
*Oh, every guy would make her **his***
If he just could, if she just would.

*Some sweet **day** I'll make her mine*
Pretty Flamingo
*Then every guy will envy **me***
'Cause paradise is where I'll be.

Pretty Flamingo
Pretty Flamingo

*When she **walks** by*
She brightens up the neighbourhood
*Oh, every guy would make her **his***
If he just could, if she just would.

*Some sweet **day** I'll make her mine*
Pretty Flamingo
*Then every guy will envy **me***
'Cause paradise is where I'll be.

Optional activity

- Listen to the song again. Students sing along.
- Ask if students have ever seen a flamingo. Ask why the singer describes the girl as a flamingo.
- In groups students discuss what bird or animal they would like to be.
- Students find rhyming words: *tight/sight, neighbourhood/would, me/be, etc.*

Activity Book Unit 4 Review, p42-43

Poster p112

- In this unit, students make a poster about their dream holiday.
- Students reread the text about adventure holidays in Lesson 3, noting what they like about them.
- Then they work in groups, and discuss their dream holiday. They should be able to say why they like each holiday, and what they would do on it. Monitor and give help where necessary.
- Students visit travel agents or look in magazines, for details of holidays. They bring these to class.
- In groups they choose two to four holidays and write a paragraph about each. This may be done for homework.
- Check their work. They write it out neatly and stick it on a large sheet of paper, along with suitable pictures.
- Display the posters if possible and give students a chance to read each other's work.

5 SURPRISE

Lesson 1 *She said she was really upset* p48

Target language
Reported statements
see, hear + object + *-ing*
Vocabulary
Activities
Noises

Optional Aids

Bring pictures showing plenty of activities.

Warmer

• Students close their eyes and listen. Ask *What can you hear?* Make noises e.g., running, writing, etc. Make a list of the sounds on the board.
• Introduce the subject of ghosts. Do students know any ghost stories?

1 READ

Aim: to present and practise reported statements and *see/hear* + object + *-ing*.
• Use the cassette to present the dialogue.
• Students read the dialogue in pairs.
• Then they answer the questions.
• Check orally.

Tapescript

Holly *I saw Lucy at breakfast. She said she'd seen a ghost last night. She said she was really upset.*
Mark *A ghost? I don't believe it!*
Holly *She said she wasn't making it up. It was in the middle of the night. She'd gone downstairs to get something to eat. Then she heard someone moving around in the kitchen. She thought it might be Alison. But then she heard someone singing quietly. It was a boy's voice. It was dark but the fridge was open and she could see someone standing there. So she went in and turned the lights on.*
Mark *Who was it?*
Holly *It was someone she'd never seen before. She said she'd never been so scared in all her life. The boy took one look at her and ran out of the kitchen. She followed him down the corridor. Then something scary happened!*
Mark *What?*
Holly *Lucy said she wasn't sure. The boy seemed to go straight through the wall! One minute she could see him running in front of her and the next minute he'd disappeared!*
Mark *Wow! What happened then?*
Holly *She went upstairs again and told Aliki what she had seen. But Aliki told her she was dreaming. Lucy got annoyed and said she would tell everyone about it in the morning.*
Mark *Do you think it really was a ghost? Or is there someone else living here - someone we don't know about?*

Answers

1 *False. Lucy said she had seen a ghost.*
2 *True.*
3 *False. Lucy said she wasn't making it up.*
4 *False. It was in the middle of the night.*
5 *False. She had heard a boy singing.*
6 *True.*
7 *False. That was what Lucy said.*
8 *True.*
9 *True.*

Optional activity

• Books closed, students retell the story. Make sure they remember who said or saw what.

Activity Book p44 Exercise 1

2 GRAMMAR FILE

Aim: to present and practise reported statements.
• Students copy and complete the chart.
• Check orally, or let students complete the chart on the board.

Answers

Reported statements

Direct speech	*Reported speech*
'I'm really upset.'	*She said she* ***was*** *really upset.*
'I'm not making it up.'	*She said she* ***wasn't*** *making it up.*
'I've never been so scared.'	*She said she* ***had*** *never been so scared.*
'I saw a ghost last night.'	*She said she* ***had*** *seen a ghost last night.*
'I'll tell everyone about it.'	*She said she* ***would*** *tell everyone about it.*

Present simple	***Past simple***
Present continuous	*Past continuous*
Present perfect	***Past perfect***
Past simple	***Past perfect***
will	*would*
can	***could***

Verbs in the present change into the ***past****.*

Verbs in the past change into the ***past perfect****.*

Optional activity

- Students look for examples of reported statements in the dialogue, and note the tenses.

3 SPEAK AND WRITE

Aim: to practise making reported statements.

- Do this orally, round the class.
- Students write the statements down.

Answers

1 *Manuel said he was having fun.*
2 *Holly and Mark said they were ready.*
3 *Mark said he didn't believe in ghosts.*
4 *Aliki said she'd never seen a ghost.*
5 *Lucy said she'd run after the boy.*
6 *Mark said he was going to catch the boy.*
7 *Lucy said she would never get up in the night again.*
8 *Aliki said she couldn't believe it.*

Optional activity

- Groups. Students take turns to whisper statements to one group member, who reports it to the other group members.

Activity Book p44 Exercise 2

4 LISTEN AND SPEAK

Aim: to practise reporting spoken statements.

- Students look at the example.
- Play the cassette, pausing after each sentence for students to report the statements.

Tapescript

1 *There's a ghost in the house.*
2 *I've seen it.*
3 *I heard a noise in the kitchen.*
4 *I saw a strange boy there.*
5 *Then he disappeared.*
6 *I can't sleep because I'm scared.*
7 *I'm going to sleep with the light on.*
8 *I don't care if you believe me or not.*
9 *I'll tell everyone about it in the morning.*

Answers

1 *Lucy said there was a ghost in the house.*
2 *She said she had seen it.*
3 *She said she had heard a noise in the kitchen.*
4 *She said she had seen a strange boy there.*
5 *She said then he had disappeared.*
6 *She said she couldn't sleep because she was scared.*
7 *She said she was going to sleep with the light on.*
8 *She said she didn't care if she believed her or not.*
9 *She said she would tell everyone about it in the morning.*

Optional activity

- Play the cassette again. Students write the reported statements.

Activity Book p44 Exercise 3

5 SPEAK

Aim: to practise *see* + object + *-ing* by describing a photo.

- Students look at the picture.
- Read the speech bubble.
- Students say what they can see.
- Use the LOOK! box to draw students' attention to the structure. Give an explanation if necessary.
- Students complete the box.

Possible answers

I can see...

...someone riding a bicycle	*...someone jogging*
...someone talking on a phone	*...someone climbing*
...two people playing football	*...two people carrying a canoe*

LOOK! box answers

She ***heard*** *someone* ***singing****.*

She could ***see*** *someone* ***standing*** *there.*

Optional activities

- In groups, students talk about the pictures you have brought in.

Activity Book p45 Exercises 4 and 5

6 LISTEN AND SPEAK

Aim: to practise *hear* + object + *-ing* by describing what one can hear.

- Students look at the words and prepare sentences.
- Play the cassette. Students listen and describe what they hear.

Tapescript

1 banging	*2 clapping*	*3 whistling*
4 squeaking	*5 whispering*	*6 sneezing*
7 a vacuum cleaner	*8 splashing*	*9 a guitar*

Answers

1 *I can hear something banging.*
2 *I can hear someone clapping.*
3 *I can hear someone whistling.*
4 *I can hear something squeaking.*
5 *I can hear someone whispering.*
6 *I can hear someone sneezing.*
7 *I can hear someone using a vacuum cleaner.*
8 *I can hear someone splashing.*
9 *I can hear someone playing the guitar.*

Optional activities

- Students write sentences about what they heard.
- Pairs. Student 1 says what they can hear, but quietly; student 2 says *Sorry, I couldn't hear what you said*; student 1 says *I said I could hear. . .* .

Activity Book p45 Exercise 6

7 SOUND FILE

Aim: to distinguish between the sounds /eə/ and /ɪə/.

- Play the cassette. Students listen and repeat.
- Play the next section. Students listen and write.
- Check orally.

Tapescript and answers

/eə/	/ɪə/
scare	*skier*
hair	*hear*
air	*ear*
dare	*dear*
chair	*cheer*

skier hear air dear chair

Activity Book p45 Exercise 7

8 LISTEN AND WRITE

Aim: to practise the target language by creating a story from sounds heard.

- Play the cassette. Students write what sounds or words they hear.
- You may first check what sounds they heard.
- Students then write their story. This may be done in groups or alone. It is suitable for homework.
- Collect the work and check it.

Tapescript

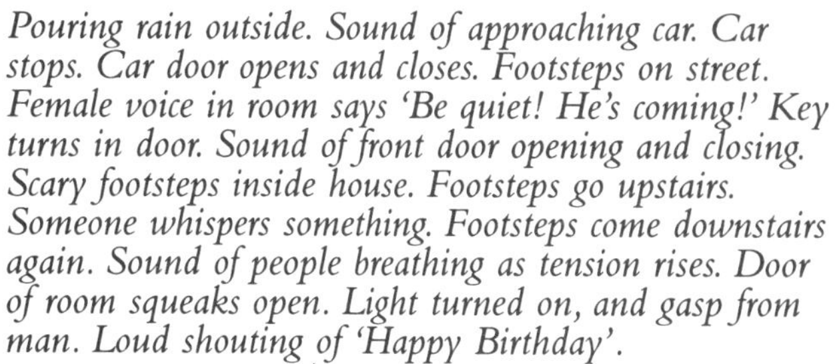

Pouring rain outside. Sound of approaching car. Car stops. Car door opens and closes. Footsteps on street. Female voice in room says 'Be quiet! He's coming!' Key turns in door. Sound of front door opening and closing. Scary footsteps inside house. Footsteps go upstairs. Someone whispers something. Footsteps come downstairs again. Sound of people breathing as tension rises. Door of room squeaks open. Light turned on, and gasp from man. Loud shouting of 'Happy Birthday'.

Possible answer

It was a dark night and it was raining hard. Suddenly we heard a car coming down the road. The car stopped outside the house, and we heard the car door opening and then closing. We heard footsteps on the street, coming towards the house. A woman said 'Be quiet! He's coming!' We heard a key turning in the door. Then we heard the front door opening and closing. After that we heard footsteps inside the house. We heard them going upstairs, then someone whisper something. After that we heard the footsteps coming down the stairs again. We could hear people breathing. Then we heard the door opening and he turned on the light and gasped in surprise. Then we all shouted 'Happy birthday'.

Consolidation and Extension activities

- Game. Students stand in lines of 8. Whisper something to the student at the front of each line, e.g., *It's ten o'clock.* They whisper the message to each other one by one down the line, saying *He/She said it was ten o'clock,* etc. They may not say the message more than once to the same student. The last student says aloud *You said it was ten o'clock* - or whatever message has become.
- Memory chain. Student 1 says, *I saw three boys playing football.* Student 2 reports what the first said and adds what he saw, e.g., *He said he had seen 3 boys playing football and I saw a woman in a car,* etc.
- The game can also be played with the verbs *hear, feel* and *watch.*

Homework

- Students look at the grammar file again.
- Students write a new story where sounds are important.
- Good students could prepare a sound story of their own, using bicycle bells, clattering cups, etc. They sketch the story and note which sounds are used. Then they bring it to class and try it on the others.

Activity Book Unit 5 Lesson 1, p44-45
Grammar Summary p120-121

5 Lesson 2 *She asked if ACE was haunted*

p50

Target language

Reported questions

Vocabulary

Phrasal verbs with *up*

Ghosts

Warmer

- Round the class students make statements, e.g., *It's cold today*. Each time they speak quietly, and you ask the next student *What did he/she say?* They reply *He/She said it was cold today*.
- Next ask students what they can see out of the windows. They will probably start by saying e.g., *I can see a tree/some cars*, etc. Help them say e.g., *I can see some people walking along the road/some children playing in the playground*, etc.
- Then tell them all to close their eyes and listen. Ask *What can you hear?* Encourage replies such as *I can hear birds singing/lorries going past/music playing*, etc. If there are no obvious sounds from outside, make some yourself, e.g., play the *Shine* cassette, play music, open and close the door, etc.
- Finally ask students what other people said they heard and saw. They answer e.g., *Several people said they heard birds singing*.

1 Read

Aim: to present and practise reported questions.

- Use the cassette to present and practise the dialogue.
- Students read it in pairs.
- Then they answer the questions.
- Check orally.

Tapescript

Mark *It's really weird, isn't it? I wonder who it was.*

Holly *Who or what! Lucy is sure she saw a ghost.*

Mark *I don't believe in ghosts! I think it was just someone playing a trick on her.*

Holly *Well, Lucy talked to Rick at breakfast. She asked if ACE was haunted and Rick told her that there was a ghost in the house. He said it was the ghost of a sailor who had drowned in a shipwreck. Then Lucy wanted to know how old the ghost was and Rick said he was a hundred years old! Lucy got angry and told Rick to shut up.*

Mark *Rick was just teasing Lucy.*

Holly *Yes, but she did see someone last night. She isn't making it up.*

Mark *I know! I'll stay up all night tonight and catch whoever it is. Then we'll know if there's a ghost or not. Do you want to come ghost-hunting with me tonight?*

Holly *I don't know about that. But you can do some clothes hunting now! Manuel can't find his jacket anywhere and he asked me if I could help find it.*

Mark *That's funny. Aliki asked me if I knew where her jumper was. And Tara wanted to know where her green rucksack was.*

Holly *Come on then, we'd better hurry up while there are still some clothes left!*

Answers

1. *She asked if ACE/it was haunted.*
2. *She wanted to know how old it was.*
3. *He asked if she wanted to go ghost-hunting with him.*
4. *He asked if she could help him find his jacket.*
5. *She asked if he knew where her jumper was.*
6. *She wanted to know where her green rucksack was.*

Optional activities

- Books closed. Students retell the story, focusing on the questions people asked.
- Students speculate on what is happening. at ACE

Activity Book p46 Exercise 1

2 Grammar File

Aim: to present and practise reported questions.

- Students copy the chart.
- Draw their attention to the different verbs used to report questions, i.e. *want to know* as well as *ask*.

Optional activity

- Students find reported questions in the dialogue.

Activity Book p46-47 Exercises 2 and 3

3 Speak

Aim: to practise reporting questions.
- Do this orally with the whole class.
- Students then write the reported questions.

Answers
1 *Lucy asked Rick if he had seen the ghost. He said he had.*
2 *She wanted to know when he had seen it. He said he had seen it last month.*
3 *She asked if he had been alone. He said he had.*
4 *She wanted to know if anyone else had seen it. He said no one else had seen it.*
5 *She asked what it had been wearing. He said it had been wearing a long white coat.*
6 *She asked if he had spoken to it. He said he had.*
7 *She asked what it had said. He said that it had told him its life story.*
8 *She wanted to know how long he had talked to the ghost. He said he had talked to it for two hours.*
9 *She asked him if he was making this up. He said he was.*

Optional activities
- The activity can also be done in groups of four with one pair asking and answering the direct questions and the others reporting to each other what was said. They should change roles so that all four practise reporting speech.
- Pairs. Students imagine they are Rick and Lucy, but in a very noisy place. So Lucy asks the questions, and each time Rick says *What did you say?* She then says *I asked if you had seen the ghost,* etc. Then she can't hear his replies, so he, too, reports his answers.

Activity Book p47 Exercise 4 and 5

4 Word File

Aim: to focus on phrasal verbs with *up*.
- Students find the meanings of the verbs.
- Check orally.
- Then they find examples in the dialogue and rephrase the sentences using the meanings.

Answers
1 d *2g* *3h* *4c*
5f *6e* *7a* *8b*

Optional activity
- Students make sentences using the phrasal verbs.

Activity Book p47 Exercise 6

5 Write and Speak

Aim: to ask questions about past activities.
- Start by asking a few students some questions, or letting them ask you.
- They write their questions.
- They either work in groups or go round the class asking questions. They write the answers.

6 Speak and Write

Aim: to ask about and report other people's past activities.
- Students work in pairs, with someone they didn't question in the previous activity.
- They first ask each other about their questions and the answers.
- Then they write what the questions and answers were.

Consolidation and Extension activities
- Game. Play the memory game from the end of Lesson 1, but with questions instead of statements, e.g., *What time is it?* The final student reports the question and then answers it, e.g., *You wanted to know what time it was. It's ...*
- Chain story. Students tell an adventure story or a ghost story round the class. Each student says one sentence of the story.

Homework
- Students list the phrasal verbs with *up* on a page in their vocabulary notebooks.
- They learn the phrasal verbs and their explanations.
- Students write up the chain story they told in class.
- Students write a short dialogue and then a report of the dialogue.

Activity Book Unit 5 Lesson 2, p46-47
Grammar Summary p120-121

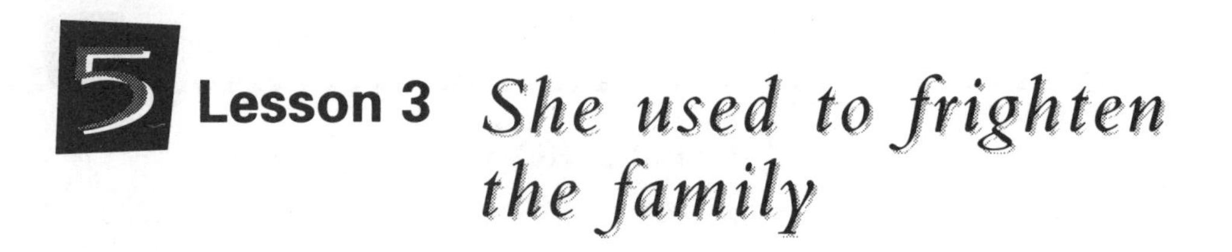

5 Lesson 3 *She used to frighten the family*

p52

> **Target language**
> *used to*
> **Vocabulary**
> Phrasal verbs with *down*
> Inventions

Warmer

- A student asks you a question, quietly, e.g., *What time is it? What is our homework?* Someone else in the class then asks you *What did he/she say?* You say *He/She asked me what time it was.*
- Repeat with other students asking different questions.

1 READ

Aim: to present and practise *used to.*

- Students look at the photo and try to guess where and how old the house is.
- Use the cassette to introduce the passage.
- First ask the students, *Why was the house famous?* and *How many different ghosts are mentioned?*
- Students read through the passage. They answer your pre-reading questions, then reread the text and answer the questions.
- Check orally.

Tapescript

The most haunted house in the world?

In 1863 a new house was built in the village of Borley, about 100 kilometres north-east of London. Soon after the house was finished, strange things began to happen.

The first owner was a man called Henry Bull and he often saw 'The White Lady'. She was a tall white ghost wearing old-fashioned clothes. She used to walk down the garden path at night. She also used to frighten the Bull family by looking in through the window when they were having dinner.

Many other unexplained things happened at this time. Every Monday night a ghostly coach and horses used to race up to the front door. But when the door was opened, the coach disappeared. Plates and glasses used to fly about in the kitchen and the family used to hear strange voices and footsteps. On one occasion, the house became full of strange smells.

In 1930 Mr Foster and his wife Marianne moved in. They didn't use to believe in ghosts but they soon changed their minds! Soon after moving in, they found mysterious messages written on the walls. One message said simply 'Marianne, please help.' The Fosters couldn't settle down in the house.

Harry Price, a famous ghost hunter, spent a year studying the house in 1937. He found a place on the first floor called 'the cold spot' which always used to be six degrees cooler than the rest of the house. On the top floor, doors used to lock and unlock themselves, and furniture used to fall down the stairs. In one bedroom, the Blue Room, people used to be thrown out of their beds at night! Even the bathroom was haunted. A woman going past the door was given a black eye when an invisible hand slapped her face.

In 1939 the house was burnt down in a fire. By then, people had reported seeing over 200 ghosts there. Nothing is left today of what used to be the most haunted house in the world - except ghost stories and a lot of unanswered questions!

Answers

1. *She used to walk down the garden path, and she also used to frighten the family by looking through the window when they were having dinner.*
2. *It used to race up to the front door and disappear.*
3. *Plates and glasses used to fly about, and people used to hear strange voices and footsteps.*
4. *It always used to be six degrees colder than the rest of the house.*
5. *Doors used to lock and unlock themselves, and furniture used to fall down the stairs.*
6. *People used to be thrown out of their beds at night.*
7. *She was slapped in the face and given a black eye.*
8. *The house was burnt down in a fire.*

Optional activities

- Books closed. Students try to remember all the different ghosts that used to haunt the house.
- Ask students if they would like to live in a house like that!

Activity Book p48 Exercise 1

2 GRAMMAR FILE

Aim: to present and practise *used to*.

- Students copy and complete the chart.
- Check orally.
- Point out that we use *used to* for

Answers

She used ***to*** *frighten the Bull family.*
Furniture ***used to*** *fall down the stairs.*
The Foster family ***didn't use to*** *believe in ghosts.*
What ***did*** *the doors on the top floor* ***use to*** *do?*

Optional activities

- Students find examples of *used to* in the text.
- They talk about things they used to do, e.g., a year ago, or before they started school.

Activity Book p48 Exercise 2

3 SPEAK

Aim: to practise *used to* by comparing the present and the past.

- Go through the two lists. Ask questions e.g., *Did they use to have electricity?* Students answer.
- They make sentences referring to the Fact File.
- They can add ideas, e.g., *They didn't use to go to the cinema, but they used to go to the theatre.*

Optional activities

- Students write sentences about the past.
- They look at the Fact File for a short time. Then they ask each other the dates of the inventions.
- Ask students what they think is the greatest invention of the twentieth century.

Activity Book p49 Exercise 3

4 SPEAK

Aim: to personalise the target language by comparing the students' life with their parents'.

- Students read through the topics.
- Students ask their parents questions, if necessary in L1. They write the answers in English.
- In the next lesson, students work in groups and tell each other about their parents' lives.
- Each group then chooses the most interesting information to tell the class.

Optional activities

- Students write a paragraph about their lives compared to their parents'.

Activity Book p49 Exercise 4

5 LISTEN

Aim: to listen to a conversation for specific information.

- Students discuss what has been happening at ACE so far.
- Students first read the questions.
- They listen to the cassette and answer the questions.
- Check orally.

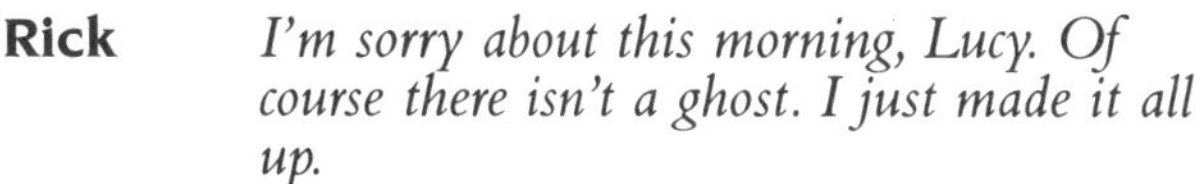

Tapescript

Rick *I'm sorry about this morning, Lucy. Of course there isn't a ghost. I just made it all up.*

Lucy *If there isn't a ghost, who's been taking all the clothes and things? We've looked everywhere and can't find them.*

Rick *There must be a logical explanation. Clothes don't just disappear and ghosts don't walk through walls.*

Lucy *Oh yes they do. I saw it with my own eyes. Look, I'll show you. It was along here in this corridor outside the kitchen. The ghost ran down to the corner there. Then it disappeared. It went straight through the wall.*

Rick *Let's have a look. This used to be an old farmhouse before ACE came here. They knocked some of it down, but this is the old part. The walls are really thick.*

Lucy *You don't believe me, do you? Look the ghost disappeared right here. Oh, look! A door's opening!*

Rick *What did you do?*

Lucy *I just hit the wall here.*

Rick *Come on, let's go inside.*

Lucy *It's dark in here. Look, there are some steps going down.*

Rick *Perhaps there used to be a staircase here when it was a farmhouse.*

Lucy *Come on. Let's go down.*

Rick *Oh no. The door's closed. We're trapped! We can't get out!*

Answers

1 *True.*

2 *True.*

3 *True.*

4 *False. Some of it was knocked down.*

5 *False. A door opens.*

6 *True.*

Optional activities

- Students discuss if there is a ghost at ACE.
- They think about question 6. Are Rick and Lucy really trapped?
- They retell the story round the class.

6 WORD FILE

Aim: to focus on phrasal verbs with *down*.

- Students read and match the verbs.
- Check orally.
- They look for the verbs in Lesson 3.

Answers

1 d *2 c* *3 b* *4 e* *5 f* *6 a*

Optional activity

- Students use the verbs in sentences.

Activity Book p49 Exercise 5 and 6

7 WRITE

Aim: to practise the target language in writing.

- Students may use any notes or sentences they made when they did Activity 3, as well as referring to the Fact File.
- This is suitable for homework.

Consolidation and Extension activities

- Memory chain. Student 1 says *When I was little, I used to live in a big city.* Student 2 says *When I was little, I used to live in a big city and I used to get up late every day,* etc.
- The memory chain can be done using other subjects, e.g., *When my grandmother was young, ...*
- Game. Students work in pairs. One has the book open and refers to the Fact File, making statements, e.g., *There were no railways in 1820.* The other must say *True* or *False*. If they guess correctly, they make the next statement. This could also be used as a team game.

Homework

- Students list the phrasal verbs with *down* on a new page in their vocabulary notebooks, and learn them.
- Students ask an older member of their family, e.g., a grandparent, about things they used to do in the past. They make notes in English and then write a short report, which they can read to the class in the next lesson.
- Students research other inventions and their dates. They write up their facts in a paragraph or short report.
- They could also use their research as the basis for a class quiz.

Activity Book Unit 5 Lesson 3, p48-49
Grammar Summary p120-121

5 Lesson 4 *Helena*

p54

Vocabulary
Adjective suffixes: *-able* and *-y*
Linking words: *and, but, then*
Mystery

Warmer

- Ask students what they remember about the haunted house from Lesson 3.
- Explain the word *mystery* and ask if the students know any mysteries.
- Then tell them that most of this lesson is a mystery story.

Reading

1 **Aim:** to read the first part of a story and predict what will happen.

- Use the cassette to introduce the passage.
- Students read the first part of the story and try to answer the questions at the end of the text.
- Students speculate about what will happen next.

Tapescript 

Helena

I first saw the house two years ago. It was a windy day in November and I was on an enjoyable cycling holiday in the West Country. I was riding down a narrow country road when I saw a large empty house. It was in the middle of a huge wild garden and there was an old sign saying 'For Sale'. I stopped and got off my bike. The gate was open so I walked into the garden.

The house looked as if it had been empty for many years. The walls were cracked and some of the windows were broken. I looked in through one of the dirty windows but all I could see was an empty room. Leaves were blowing off the trees in the strong wind and somewhere I could hear a door banging. There was a strange unhappy feeling about the house and I wondered who had lived there.

I cycled on a few hundred metres to the next village and stopped for a cup of coffee. The old woman in the café complained that no one ever came to the village now. I wondered if she knew who had lived at the old house.

'Have you any idea who used to live at that old house down the road?' I asked.

The woman looked at me strangely. 'It's been empty for as long as I've lived here. Why do you want to know?' she asked.

'I'd like to know why it's for sale,' I went on. 'I don't understand why someone hasn't bought it.'

'Lots of people have been to see it,' said the woman quietly. 'But they don't stay very long and they never come back. They say that terrible things happen in the house. Doors open and close themselves, and you can hear someone crying in one of the rooms. And if you stay there too long, you can hear a voice calling 'Helena! Helena!'.'

'But who is Helena?' I asked. 'Did she use to live there?'

Optional activities

- Books closed. Students retell the story so far.
- They speculate about what will happen next.

Speaking

2 **Aim:** to tell a story from pictures.

- Students look at the pictures and guess what is happening.
- A good way to do this is in groups. Then each group reports back to the class.
- They should note the main ideas of their stories.

Listening

3 **Aim:** to listen to a story for details.

- Play the cassette. Students listen and compare the story with their versions.
- The groups report back again.

Tapescript

'I'll tell you the whole story,' said the woman. 'Forty years ago a man called Truscott lived there with his wife and their beautiful daughter, Helena. Unfortunately Truscott's wife became ill and died suddenly. Two years later Mr Truscott married again. By now, Helena was 16 years old and she looked just like her mother. So the new wife was jealous of Helena - in fact she hated Helena, and she used to get very angry with her. One day she lost her temper and hit Helena on the head. Helena fell to the floor - she was dead! Mr Truscott was afraid to call the police, so he buried the body under a tree in the garden. Mr and Mrs Truscott are both dead now, but Helena returns to the house every night and haunts it!'

'What a terrible story!' I said. 'A beautiful girl, killed by her father's new wife, and buried in the garden by her father!'

When I left the café, I looked back down the road to the empty house and shivered.

Optional activity

- Students guess what will happen next, e.g., Will the narrator go back to the house? Is it haunted?

Activity Book p50 Exercise 1

4 Aim: to use connectors *and, but* and *then* to complete a text.

- Students read and complete the next part of the story.
- Play the cassette. Students listen and check.
- Check orally.
- How many of them guessed this part of the story?

Tapescript and answers

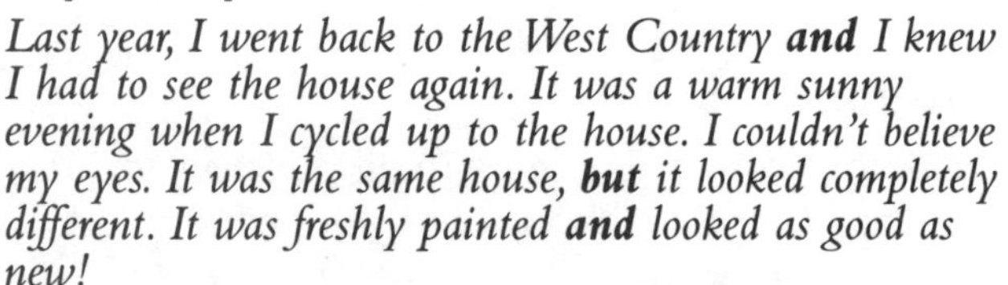

Last year, I went back to the West Country ***and*** *I knew I had to see the house again. It was a warm sunny evening when I cycled up to the house. I couldn't believe my eyes. It was the same house,* ***but*** *it looked completely different. It was freshly painted* ***and*** *looked as good as new!*

I hesitated for a moment. ***Then*** *I walked up to the front door* ***and*** *rang the bell. A servant opened the door* ***and*** *I asked if I could see the owner. The servant asked me to wait in the sitting room.*

I sat down on a comfortable sofa. It was a warm evening, ***but*** *the room felt cold* ***and*** *I started to shiver.*

Suddenly, I heard someone calling 'Helena! Helena!'. ***Then*** *the door opened* ***and*** *a beautiful girl ran into the room! She had long blonde hair* ***and*** *she was wearing a white dress. Again I heard 'Helena! Helena!',* ***and*** *she ran out of the room. I was shaking with fear.*

1 and	*2 but*	*3 and*	*4 Then*
5 and	*6 and*	*7 but*	*8 and*
9 Then	*10 and*	*11 and*	*12 and*

Optional activity

- Students again speculate what will happen next.

5 Aim: to complete a story and then compare that version with the original.

- Students read the next part of the story.
- They decide how it finishes.
- They compare ideas with a partner.
- Some students report back to the class.
- Play the cassette. Students listen and compare with their version of the story.
- Did anyone guess correctly?

Tapescript

'Sorry to keep you waiting,' a voice suddenly said. 'I'm David Moore, the new owner of this house.'

I jumped up from the sofa. A tall man was in the room, and he was smiling. I started to talk at once and told him my story and what I had just seen. He didn't seem surprised.

'Yes, Helena died in this house, but it didn't happen at all as you described it.' he said. 'She wasn't killed - she became ill like her mother with a very high temperature, and she died one night. There was nothing her parents could do and the shock was terrible. After her death, they hated this house and decided never to live here again. I'm Mr Truscott's cousin and I bought the house a few months ago. And I can promise you that we haven't seen any ghosts!'

'But...but...' I said. 'I've just seen Helena, in this room...'

Mr Moore laughed. 'That was my daughter,' he said. 'Her name is Helena too!'

Then he called 'Helena! Helena!' and the beautiful girl ran into the room. She certainly wasn't a ghost!

Optional activity

- Students retell the story.

Writing

6 Aim: to write a summary of a story.

- To do this, students refer back to the whole printed story and to any notes they have made.
- You may replay the cassette.
- They choose their key words.
- They compare with other students.
- They write their summary. This is suitable for homework.
- Take the work in to check.

Possible answer

Two years ago, a man saw a large house for sale. Then he heard that the house was haunted by a girl called Helena, who had been killed there and buried in the garden.

Last year, he went back to the house and asked to see the owner. While he was waiting, someone called 'Helena' and a beautiful girl appeared. Was she the ghost?

Then the owner explained. Helena wasn't killed, but she had become very ill and died. The beautiful girl was the owner's daughter and her name was Helena too. She wasn't a ghost!

Activity Book p51 Exercise 2

Word building

7 Aim: to present and practise adjective suffixes *-able* and *-y*.

- You may first go through the words orally.
- Students complete the sentences.
- Check orally.

Answers

1 windy	*2 comfortable*	*3 dirty*
4 valuable	*5 rainy, suitable*	*6 sunny*

Optional activities

• Students think of other words with the two suffixes. There are a number of weather-related words ending in *-y*, e.g., *foggy, cloudy, icy, snowy.* Draw students' attention to the double letter in *sunny* and *foggy*.
• A number of verbs can add *-able* to make an adjectives, e.g., *drinkable, manageable*, etc. Note the spelling where there is a *g*.

STUDY SKILLS

8 Aim: to improve students' understanding of what they hear.
• Go through the learning tips.
• Students add any ideas of their own.

Activity Book p51 Exercises 3 and 4

Consolidation and Extension activities

• Students list adjectives with the suffixes *-able* and *-y*, six to ten of each. Then they work in pairs, taking turns to give the root word. Their partner must form the adjective and use it in a sentence. This is also suitable as a team game.
• Students tell a story round the class. This time, instead of saying a complete sentence each, they end with *and, but* or *then*.
• Students work in groups to act out the story of Helena.
• Role-play. One student is David Moore, and the other is a reporter who has heard the rumours about the house and Helena. He/She interviews David Moore to find out the true story.

Homework

• Students rewrite the story of Helena as a diary by the writer. This means that they need not write in full sentences, and that they retell part of the story in note form.
• Students write the adjectives in their vocabulary notebooks, with a page for each suffix, and learn them.

Pairwork

Pairwork activities p108 and 116
Aim: to find out what people said.
• Students A ask first and students B report to them.
• Students A complete their speech bubbles.
• Then they change roles.
• Finally they check each other's work.

Optional activity

• Students write a short dialogue. It may be based on the story of Helena, the characters at ACE, or anything else. Then they turn the dialogue into reported speech. Next they draw empty speech bubbles and give them to their partner. Finally they work out the direct speech as before, by asking their partner questions.

Activity Book Unit 5 Lesson 4, p50-51
Grammar Summary p120-121

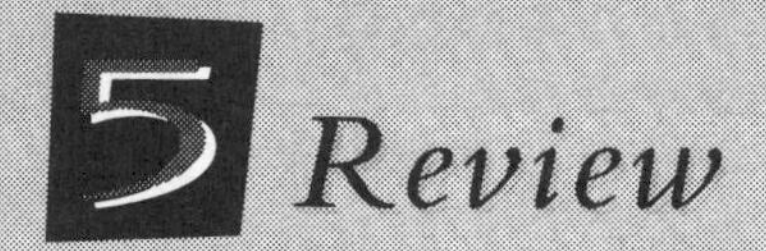

5 Review

1 Read and complete

- Students complete the text.
- Check orally.

Answers

1B 2B 3C 4A 5B 6C 7B 8B
9C 10A 11C 12C 13A 14B 15C 16B

2 Report sentences

- This may be done orally or in writing.
- Check orally.

Answers

1. *Rick said that there wasn't a ghost.*
2. *Lucy said they had looked everywhere for the missing clothes.*
3. *Lucy said she would show Rick where she had seen the ghost.*
4. *Rick said the walls of the old farmhouse were really thick.*
5. *Lucy said he didn't believe her.*
6. *Lucy said a door was opening.*
7. *Rick said the door had closed.*
8. *Rick said they were trapped.*

Optional activity

- If students need more practice with this, they can look back at the dialogues in previous lessons and turn them into reported speech.

3 Choose the verb

- This can be done orally or in writing.

Answers

1 told 2 coming 3 said 4 was
5 told 6 said 7 moving 8 squeaking
9 said 10 was 11 told 12 running

4 Correct the sentences

Answers

1. *Lucy asked what the ghost look**ed** like.*
2. *Mark asked **if** Holly believed in ghosts.*
3. *Mark wondered who **it was**.*
4. *Lucy wanted to know how old **the ghost was**.*
5. *Holly wondered **if the ghost had** taken all the clothes.*
6. *Rick asked what **the ghost was** wearing.*
7. *Manuel asked **if Holly** could help find his jacket.*
8. *Mark asked Holly if she want**ed** to come ghost-hunting with him.*

5 Write sentences

Answers

2. *She used to be afraid of heights.*
3. *She didn't use to speak German.*
4. *She didn't use to like Chinese food.*
5. *She used to go out every night.*
6. *She used to believe in ghosts.*
7. *She didn't use to live in Devon.*
8. *She didn't use to hate TV.*

Optional activity

- Students pretend to be Alison and make statements, e.g., *I ride a motorbike, but I didn't use to ride one.*

6 Test each other

- Students write five to six incorrect sentences in reported speech, following the pattern in Activity 4.
- They read their sentences to their partner, who corrects them.
- Then they change roles.

SONG

- Students read the gapped song.
- They guess what the words might be.
- Play the cassette. Students listen and check.
- Check orally.

Tapescript and answers 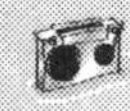

When you're alone and life is making you lonely
*You can always **go** downtown*
When you've got worries, all the noise and the hurry
Seems to help I know downtown

*Just **listen** to the music of the traffic in the city*
*Linger on the sidewalk where the neon signs are **pretty***
How can you lose?
The lights are much brighter there
You can forget all you troubles,
Forget all your cares

So go downtown
Things will be great when you're downtown
No finer place for sure downtown
Everything's waiting for you Downtown

Don't hang around and let your problems surround you
There are movie shows downtown
Maybe you know some little places to go to
Where they never ***close*** *downtown*

Just listen to the rhythm of the gentle bossa nova
You'll be dancing with 'em too before the night is ***over****.*
Happy again
The lights are much brighter there
You can forget all your troubles,
Forget all your cares

So go downtown
Where all the lights are ***bright*** *downtown*
Waiting for you tonight downtown
You're gonna be all ***right*** *now downtown downtown*

And you may ***find*** *somebody kind to help and understand you*
Someone who is just like you and needs a gentle ***hand*** *to guide them along.*
So maybe I'll ***see*** *you there*
We can forget all our troubles, forget all our cares

So go downtown
Things will be great when you're downtown
Don't wait a minute more downtown
Everything's waiting for you

Downtown downtown...

Optional activity

- Listen to the song again. Students sing along.
- Ask students what *downtown* means. (The centre of a town or city where there are lots of shops, cinemas, retaurants, clubs etc.) Where is *downtown* in their city?
- In groups the students discuss where they would go to *forget their troubles*.
- In the song she goes dancing and listens to music to forget her troubles. What kind of music do the students like to dance to? What kind of music makes them happy or sad?

Activity Book Unit 5 Review, p52-53

Poster p112

- In this unit, students make a poster about life in the past.
- Students work in groups. After rereading the questions, they decide which five to choose. They may choose different ones, but do not have to.
- You may brainstorm questions in class. Start by asking students what they think was different in the past. You can also ask what they want to know about the past.
- Students then prepare two questions of their own.
- At home, they ask their questions. They may interview one or more people. They may use L1 to ask questions but should make notes in English.
- They can also try to find photos of their family when they were young.
- The groups compare their notes. Each group chooses seven questions and answers.
- They write them out neatly and check their work carefully before sticking the writing and photos on a sheet of paper.
- Display the posters or let students pass round their work.

Lesson 1 *What would you do?*

p58

Target language
Second conditional
Vocabulary
Phrasal verbs with *away*
Survival

Warmer

- Review the story of Lucy and the ghost so far. This can be done as a chain story or students can work in groups and then compare their versions of the story.

1 READ

Aim: to present and practise the second conditional.
- Use the cassette to present and practise the dialogue.
- Students read the completed dialogue in pairs.
- Then they answer the questions. Check orally.

Tapescript

Rick *Help!*
Lucy *It's no use. No one can hear us. Rick, I was wondering. What would you do if the ghost came back?*
Rick *Nothing! I told you. There isn't a ghost.*
Lucy *OK then. What would you do if someone came up the stairs now?*
Rick *I don't know. I'd try and talk to them, I suppose. I couldn't run away! But I wouldn't worry about that if I were you. No one's going to come up the stairs.*
Lucy *It's so dark in here. If we had a torch, I wouldn't feel so nervous.*
Rick *Hey, what's this? There's a bag or something on the floor. And there are some matches in it! That's better! Look, it's Tara's rucksack! Someone has thrown it away here.*
Lucy *Listen! I can hear someone down there. Come on! Stop! I think I can hear the sea.*
Rick *Look! There's a boy there. He's getting away!*

Answers

1 *False. No one can hear them.*
2 *True.*
3 *False. If someone came up the stairs Rick would try and talk to them.*
4 *True.*
5 *True.*
6 *False. Rick finds some matches in the rucksack.*
7 *True.*
8 *True.*

Optional activities

- Students speculate about what will happen next. Who is the boy?
- Students discuss what they would do in the same situation.

Activity Book p54 Exercise 1

2 GRAMMAR FILE

Aim: to present the second conditional.
- Students copy and complete the chart.
- Check orally.

Answers

Second conditional
If we ***had*** *a torch, I* ***wouldn't*** *feel so nervous.*
What ***would*** *you do if the ghost* ***came*** *back?*

Optional activity

- Students find examples of the second conditional in the dialogue.

Activity Book p54 Exercise 2

3 SPEAK

Aim: to personalise the use of the second conditional by talking about different imaginary situations.
- You may tell students what you would do in two or three of the situations.
- Ask two or three students what they would do in one of the situations.
- Students work through the situations in pairs or groups.
- Ask several of them report back to the class.

Optional activity

- Students write sentences for the situations.

Activity Book p 55 Exercises 3 and 4

4 Read and Speak

Aim: to practise the second conditional and to think about survival.

- Students complete the survival quiz.
- They work in groups and compare answers, saying why they chose a particular answer.
- Groups report back to the class.
- Finally go through the answers on page 124 with the class. Discuss the correct answers.

Answers

1 a) *If it was a bad storm, you would get even more lost.*

b) *A very bad idea. You would quickly get hot and tired.*

c) *An excellent idea. A deep hole in the snow would keep you safe and warm.*

2 a) *You would probably be OK if you ate the fish raw but it wouldn't be good for you.*

b) *You would 'cook' the fish in the lemon juice and then you could eat it safely.*

c) *If the sun was hot, the fish would go bad and you couldn't eat it.*

3 a) *If someone saw the torch, you would be rescued. This is the international signal for someone who needs help.*

b) *If someone saw the torch, and knew Morse Code they would recognise S-O-S and you would be rescued.*

c) *If someone saw this, they would probably think you were playing a trick.*

4 a) *If you waited until sunset, you would have to walk in the dark. A bad idea.*

b) *If you climbed up to the top of the hill or mountain, you would have further to walk to get out of the forest.*

c) *If you followed a river, you would be sure to get out because rivers run downhill.*

5 Word File

Aim: to focus on phrasal verbs with *away*.

- Students match the verbs and meanings.
- Then they find examples in the dialogue, after which they may change their answers.
- Check orally.

Answers

1b 2f 3d 4c 5e 6a

Activity Book p55 Exercise 5

6 Speak and Write

Aim: to use the second conditional to talk and write about imaginary situations.

- You may introduce the topic by asking two or three students about a situation.
- Then they all write their own questions, using the ideas in the book or some of their own.
- If there's space, students go round asking their questions. Otherwise, they ask students near them.
- Finally they write the answers. They may report back to the class.

Consolidation and Extension activities

- Advice chain. Round the class, students give each other advice, e.g., *If I were you, I'd dye my hair green. - No, I wouldn't do that. I'd paint my nails silver,* etc.
- Memory chain. Use the pattern, *If I had a million dollars ...*
- Students work in pairs to write another survival questionnaire. They think of situations they could experience, e.g., a fire in the kitchen, seeing a car crash, an injury on the football field, etc. Then they exchange questionnaires with another pair. Ask several pairs to present their questionnaire to the class. (This may need some research, which could be done for homework.)

Homework

- Students start a new page in their vocabulary notebooks for phrasal verbs with *away*. They learn the verbs from the lesson.
- Imaginative writing. Students use one of the topics from Activity 6, or another one of their choice, and write two or three paragraphs.

Activity Book Unit 6 Lesson 1 p54-55
Grammar Summary p121

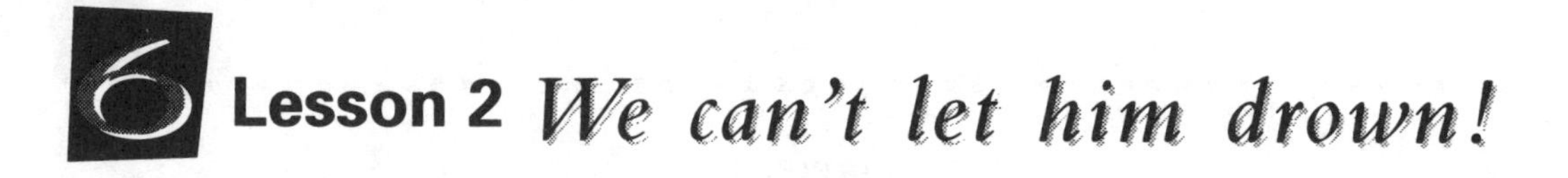

6 Lesson 2 *We can't let him drown!* p60

> **Target language**
> *make/let* + object + infinitive
> *allowed to*
> **Vocabulary**
> Rules and regulations

Warmer

- Groups. Before class, make a list of strange or difficult situations, e.g., you get lost in the countryside; you see a robbery taking place; aliens land in your garden; you are alone in a foreign country, etc. Give one situation to each group and give them a short time to think what they would do in that situation. They note their ideas. Then give each situation to a different group. If time, pass the situations on a third time. Then all the groups report back to the class. Encourage them to be imaginative.
- Review the story about the ghost at ACE.

1 READ

Aim: to present *make/let* followed by object and infinitive, and *allowed to*.

- Use the cassette to present and practise the dialogue.
- Students read the dialogue in pairs.
- Students then read and match the questions and answers.
- Check orally.

Tapescript

Lucy *Look! He's fallen into the water! What are we going to do?*
Voice *Help!*
Rick *We can't let him drown!*
Lucy *I know - I'll climb down the cliff.*
Rick *No, I won't let you climb down. This cliff's very dangerous. We aren't allowed to use it for climbing practice.*
Lucy *Rick, this isn't practice. This is life or death. You can't make me stay up here.*
Rick *Oh, yes I can. I'm in charge. Anyway what's the point? If you climbed down, there would be two of you in the sea! What good would that do?*
Lucy *I'm sorry. You make me feel so stupid!*
Rick *Now let me do the talking. There's no time to waste! We're going back to ACE. You get a life jacket and throw it to the boy. I'll get the boat.*
Voice *Help!*
Lucy *We're coming!*

Answers

1d 2f 3c 4e 5b 6a

Optional activities

- Books closed. Ask students the questions again.
- Students discuss the situation. Do they agree with Rick?
- They speculate about what will happen next. Will they save the boy? Is he badly hurt?

Activity Book p56 Exercise 1

2 GRAMMAR FILE

Aim: to present *make/let* with an object and infinitive and *allowed to*.

- Students copy and complete the chart.
- Check orally.

Answers

make/let + object + infinitive

I won't ***let*** *you climb down.*

You can't ***make*** *me stay up here.*

Let *me do the talking.*

You ***make*** *me feel so stupid.*

Optional activities

- Students find examples of the structure in the dialogue.
- They make up sentences of their own showing the difference between *make* and *let* with an infinitive.

Activity Book p56 Exercise 2

3 Write

Aim: to practise using *make/let* with an infinitive.
- Students complete the exercise.
- Check orally.

Answers
1 let 2 made 3 let 4 made 5 let 6 made 7 make

Activity Book p56-57 Exercises 3 and 4

4 Listen and Speak

Aim: to listen for specific information and to practise *allowed to.*
- Students first read the list of phrases 1–12, and guess what may or may not be allowed.
- Play the cassette. They listen and tick or cross the items on the list.
- Check orally.
- Students talk about what is and is not allowed at ACE. This can be done in pairs or as a whole-class activity.

Tapescript

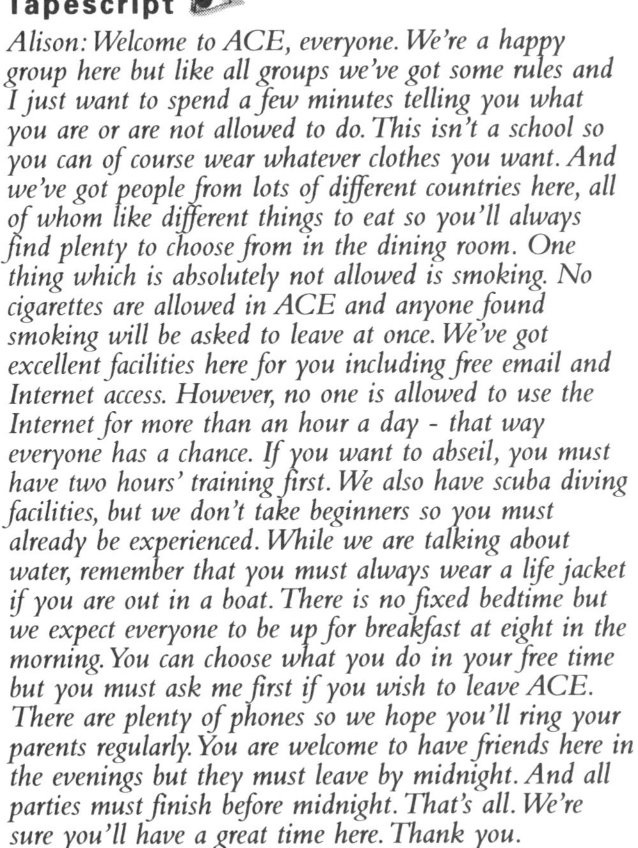
Alison: Welcome to ACE, everyone. We're a happy group here but like all groups we've got some rules and I just want to spend a few minutes telling you what you are or are not allowed to do. This isn't a school so you can of course wear whatever clothes you want. And we've got people from lots of different countries here, all of whom like different things to eat so you'll always find plenty to choose from in the dining room. One thing which is absolutely not allowed is smoking. No cigarettes are allowed in ACE and anyone found smoking will be asked to leave at once. We've got excellent facilities here for you including free email and Internet access. However, no one is allowed to use the Internet for more than an hour a day - that way everyone has a chance. If you want to abseil, you must have two hours' training first. We also have scuba diving facilities, but we don't take beginners so you must already be experienced. While we are talking about water, remember that you must always wear a life jacket if you are out in a boat. There is no fixed bedtime but we expect everyone to be up for breakfast at eight in the morning. You can choose what you do in your free time but you must ask me first if you wish to leave ACE. There are plenty of phones so we hope you'll ring your parents regularly. You are welcome to have friends here in the evenings but they must leave by midnight. And all parties must finish before midnight. That's all. We're sure you'll have a great time here. Thank you.

Answers
Tick 1, 2, 8, 10
Cross 3, 4, 5, 6, 7, 9, 11, 12.

Optional activities
- Pairs. Students take turns to ask and answer questions about what is and is not allowed at ACE.
- Students discuss the rules at ACE. Do they agree with them?

Activity Book p57 Exercises 5 and 6.

5 Write and Speak

Aim: to personalise the target language.
- You may start by brainstorming ideas.
- Students then note down up to six things they are and six things they are not allowed to do at home.
- They write a short questionnaire.
- Then they go round and ask three other students their questions. (If the room is too full for this, they ask those sitting near them.)
- Groups. Students compare their completed questionnaires.
- Then each group reports back to the class.

6 Sound File

Aim: to distinguish between the sounds /tʃ/ and /ʃ/.
- Students first look at the words.
- Play the cassette. They listen and repeat the words.
- Now play the next section. They write what they hear.
- Check orally.
- Give extra pronunciation and recognition practice as necessary.

Tapescript and answers 

/tʃ/	/ʃ/
1 choose	*shoes*
2 chips	*ships*
3 which	*wish*
4 watch	*wash*
5 China	*Shiner*

shoes ships which watch Shiner

7 WRITE

Aim: to personalise the target language by writing about home life.

- Students may make use of their notes for Activity 5. This is suitable for homework.
- Take the work in and check it.

Consolidation and Extension activities

- Students play Pronunciation Tennis with words with the sounds /tʃ/ and /ʃ/.
- Students imagine they are parents. They make a list of what they let and make their children do. Then they work in pairs to find out what other people's ideas are.
- This could be projected into the future, or to life in space, etc.
- Boasting game. Round the class, students say things they are and are not allowed to do. These need not be true e.g., *My parents don't make me do my homework and they let me stay in bed till 10 o'clock. - Well, my parents don't make me help them and they let me drive their car. - Well, my parents don't make me go to bed at all and they let me learn to fly.* etc.
- This can also be done with *(not) allowed to.*
- Students work in groups. They discuss the rules for an imaginary club or holiday organisation. Then they write them out. Finally they present their organisation and its rules to the class.

Homework

- Students learn the spelling of any new words.
- They find out what their parents and grandparents were (not) allowed to do and what they had to do when they were younger. Then they write notes.
- They write the notes up in paragraphs, or use them to prepare a presentation for the next lesson.

Activity Book Unit 6 Lesson 2, p56-57
Grammar Summary p121

Lesson 3 *We'd better tell the others*

p62

Target language

shouldn't and *oughtn't to*
had better

Vocabulary

Safety
Phrasal verbs with *on*

Optional aid

A set of school fire instructions

Warmer

- Remind students of the story so far. What do they think Rick and Lucy will do?

1 READ

Aim: to present *should(n't)* and *ought(n't) to.*

- Students first look at the pictures and discuss what the people should or should not do.
- They read and listen to the text.
- Then they answer the questions.
- Check orally.

Tapescript

ACE EMERGENCY TIPS

If you see someone in trouble in the water, you should always think before you jump in yourself. It's often better to get help by telephoning the police or ambulance first. Remember that you won't be much use to someone if you get into trouble in the water yourself. In fact, you can easily be pulled underwater by the person you are trying to save. So, as far as possible, you ought to try and save someone without going into the water.

Try these three methods:

Stay on land and reach out to the person with a long stick. If possible, you should hold on to something like a tree so you are not pulled into the water yourself.

Stay on land and throw a rope to the person. You should remember to hold on to one end of the rope!

Use a boat. You shouldn't help the person into the boat because it could capsize. Get the person to hold on to the boat and row back to the shore.

Answers

1 *False. You should always think before jumping in yourself.*
2 *True.*
3 *True.*
4 *False. You should try to hold onto something yourself so that you are not pulled in to the water.*
5 *False. You should hold on to it.*
6 *True.*

Activity Book p58 Exercise 1

2 GRAMMAR FILE

Aim: to present and practise *should(n't)* and *ought(n't) to.*

- Students copy and complete the chart.
- Check orally or by letting students complete the chart on the board.

Answers

should(n't) and ought(n't) to

You ***should/ought to*** *try to save someone without going into the water.*

You ***should/ought to*** *hold on to something.*

You ***shouldn't/oughtn't to*** *help the person into the boat.*

Optional activities

- Students note the use of the two verbs in the text.
- Students think of things they should and should not do at home and at school.

Activity Book p58 Exercise 2

3 SPEAK AND WRITE

Aim: to practise *should(n't)* and *ought(n't) to.*

- Students read the text.
- Pairs. They take turns to make statements about water safety. You may tell one student to close his/her book and the other to ask questions about water safety. Then they change roles.
- Students write sentences about safety when swimming or sailing.
- Check orally.

Optional activities

- Students write five sentences about the other watersport.
- Students discuss safety for other watersports, e.g., windsurfing, water-skiing.

4 LISTEN

Aim: to listen for specific information and to practise *had better.*

- Students first look at the photo, and then read the sentences. They try to work out the correct alternatives.
- Play the cassette. Students listen and choose the correct answers.
- Check orally.
- Go through the LOOK! box.

Tapescript

Rick *There. That's it. We're on the beach now, so you can let go. Good. Now let's get your life jacket off. Good. Can you just sit over there while I help Lucy with the boat. You're really cold. Here's my jacket - you'd better put it on.*

Sam *Thanks.*

Rick *Come on Lucy, let's pull it up on the beach.*

Rick *Thanks, that's great.*

Lucy *Where's the boy gone?*

Rick *What do you mean - Oh no, he's gone again! And he's taken my jacket!*

Lucy *Let's go after him!*

Rick *I think we'd better go back to the Centre first and put on some dry clothes.*

Lucy *Yes, you're soaking. And we'd better tell the others what we've been doing. I wonder who the boy is and why he's so scared.*

Answers

1 put on 2 change 3 tell

Optional activities

- Books closed. Students retell the story.
- Pairs act out the story from memory.
- Students speculate about what will happen next.

Activity Book p59 Exercises 3 and 4

5 WORD FILE

Aim: to focus on phrasal verbs with *on.*

- Students match the verbs and meanings.
- They find examples in the texts.
- Then check orally.

Answers

1c 2f 3d 4a 5b 6e

Optional activity

- Students use the phrasal verbs in sentences.

Activity Book p59 Exercises 5 and 6

6 WRITE

Aim: to use the target language to write a set of instructions.

- You may first discuss these.
- Bring a set of school fire instructions.
- Check the vocabulary.
- Students write the instructions.
- They may compare orally, but make sure you also check the work.

Consolidation and Extension activities

- Team game. Students have a short time to prepare a list of phrasal verbs and their meanings. Then they take turns to give the other team a phrasal verb which they must use in a sentence that shows they understand the meaning.
- Agreeing. Pairs. Student 1 makes a statement, e.g., *It's already late.* Student 2 responds e.g., *Yes, we'd better go to bed or we'll be tired tomorrow.* This could also be used as a team game.
- Play a spelling game to test recent vocabulary.
- Students make a word map for emergency and safety vocabulary.

Homework

- Students bring their vocabulary notebooks up to date, especially for phrasal verbs.
- Students produce a set of safety instructions for an activity they enjoy e.g., cycling, skateboarding.
- Students invent a game, write its rules and explain how to play it.
- Students consult an older member of their family and produce a set of advice for a happy life, using *should(n't)* and *ought(n't) to.*

Activity Book Unit 6 Lesson 3, p58-59
Grammar Summary p121

6 Lesson 4 *School bus heroes* p64

Vocabulary
Suffixes: *-ful* and *-less*
Driving

Optional aid

If there has been a heroic rescue of any kind in the national or international news, bring in newspaper cuttings, in English if possible.

Warmer

- Talk about driving. What is public transport like in the students' country? Do many people have their own cars? Is this good or not? Encourage statements using *should(n't)* and *ought(n't) to*.
- Discuss the idea of a *hero*. How do students define the idea? Explain that *heroine* is the feminine form of *hero*, but that *hero* is increasingly used to refer to men and women.
- Talk about the newspaper stories you have brought in.

Reading and Speaking

1 Aim: to predict a story to talk about a hypothetical situation using the second conditional.

- The discussion may be in groups or a whole-class activity.
- Use the illustration to pre-teach some of the driving-related vocabulary that appears in the story, e.g., *windscreen, steering wheel*, etc.
- Use the cassette to introduce the story.
- Students then read the story.
- They discuss the last question.

Tapescript

It was early on Monday morning in a small country town. People were getting ready for the day at work or at school.

'It's half past seven! You'd better hurry or you'll miss the bus!' Tom's mother called up the stairs.

Tom put on a jumper and quickly combed his thick black hair. Then he ran down the stairs two at a time.

'Eat your breakfast,' his mother said. 'I won't let you go to school without any food.'

'I'm 16, Mum, remember,' replied Tom with his mouth full of toast. 'I'm not a child any more.'

His mother smiled. 'Maybe not,' she said.' But you're late again. If you got up earlier, you wouldn't be late every morning.'

2 Aim: to read and discuss a story, using the second conditional.

- Use the cassette to introduce the next part of the story.
- Students read the next part of the story.
- They discuss the questions.

Tapescript

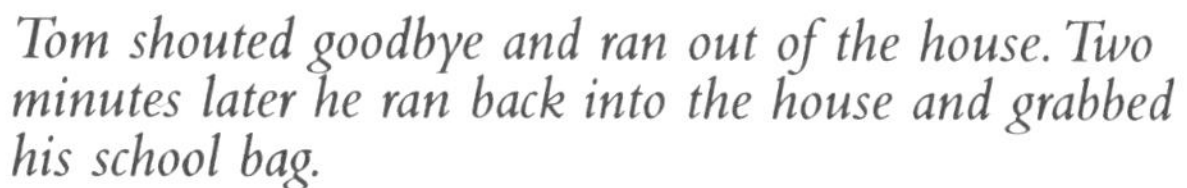

Tom shouted goodbye and ran out of the house. Two minutes later he ran back into the house and grabbed his school bag.

'You'd forget your head if it wasn't on your shoulders,' his mother called after him.

Tom ran down the street. He turned the corner and saw the red and white school bus. He ran up and jumped on.

'Just in time! You ought to get a new alarm clock!' said Jack Dennis, the bus driver, and started the bus. It was nearly full and Tom found a seat near the front. Usually he sat at the back and talked to his friends, but this morning he had to finish his maths homework.

The bus stopped again and Julie, a girl in Tom's class, got on and sat beside him.

'Do we have to do all these exercises?' Tom asked.

'Yes, haven't you done them yet? I've finished mine.' Julie was always top of the class at maths.

'Can you lend me your book, then?' asked Tom in his nicest voice.

'No!' Julie laughed. 'If I lent you my book, you'd just copy the answers.'

'I wouldn't,' said Tom. 'I'd just check to see if I was right.'

'Well, I'm not lending it you anyway, so there,' said Julie, and turned round to talk to a friend.

3 Aim: to predict the next part of the story and to read for confirmation.

- Students discuss what will happen next and then listen and read to check.

Tapescript

The bus was very noisy. 'Please turn on the radio, Mr Dennis,' someone shouted. The bus filled with loud pop music. People sitting at the back of the bus started to sing along with the radio.

Tom couldn't concentrate. He decided to ask the driver to turn the music down. He got up and walked forward to the driver.

'Mr Dennis,' he said. 'I can't work with all this noise. Could you turn the radio down a little please?'

Jack Dennis didn't reply. The bus was near the top of a hill and there was a roundabout ahead.

'Mr Dennis,' Tom said again. He knew you weren't allowed to talk to the driver. 'Please.'

There was no answer. Tom leant forward and looked at the driver. Then he got a terrible shock! Jack Dennis's eyes were closed.

'Julie! Come here quick!' Tom shouted.

LISTENING

4 Aim: to discuss emergency action and to listen for specific information.

- The discussion may be in groups or with the whole class.
- Note down some of the ideas.
- Play the cassette. Students listen and compare their ideas to the story.

Tapescript

'What's the matter with Mr Dennis?' Julie asked when she ran up to the front of the bus.

'I don't know,' Tom replied. 'Perhaps he's had a heart attack or something.'

'We should get him to hospital as quickly as possible,' said Julie. Then she looked through the windscreen at the road ahead. 'But we'd better stop this bus first or else we'll all be in hospital.'

Tom looked up. The bus was almost at the roundabout. Jack's foot was stuck on the accelerator and Tom couldn't move it. He tried to reach the footbrake but Jack's legs were in the way. Where was the handbrake? It was between Jack and the side of the bus and Tom couldn't reach it.

5 Aim: to continue the discussion and to listen for specific information.

- Students predict what will happen next.
- You may wish to go through the situation so far before listening to the next part.

Tapescript

Julie leant forward and pushed Tom out of the way. 'There isn't time to stop the bus,' she shouted. 'We'll have to steer round the roundabout.'

Julie grabbed hold of the steering wheel and turned it left and then right as the bus reached the roundabout. The bus screamed round the roundabout. Two cars had to brake suddenly to get out of the way. But the bus didn't hit anything. Julie held on to the wheel.

'Come and help me!' she shouted to Tom.

When the other students realised what was happening, they stopped singing. Someone at the back started to scream, 'Oh no! We're going to crash!'

6 Aim: to continue the discussion and to read for specific information.

- Continue as before.
- Students then discuss and note what they think will happen next.
- Play the cassette for them to check.
- They predict what will happen next.
- Then they read the last part of the story and check.

Tapescript

A car came up the hill towards them and at the last minute turned off the road to let the bus pass. Further ahead, Tom could see a flat piece of grass by the side of the road.

'We've got to get off the road,' he shouted to Julie. She nodded.

'Right, when I say 'turn', steer left. We'll get the bus onto the grass,' Tom said.

'OK.'

'Turn!'

They turned the wheel together and the bus roared off the road onto the grass. The soft earth slowed the bus down but it was still moving. Then the bus crashed into a hedge and stopped. There was the sound of breaking glass and then silence.

'We did it!' exclaimed Julie.

There was a loud cheer from the students on the bus.

'Mr Dennis is still breathing,' Tom said. 'We'd better get him to hospital at once.'

Optional activities

- Students retell the story.
- They retell the story as if they were one of the other students on the bus, and say what they felt and thought.
- Class discussion. What would your students do in a similar case?

WRITING

7 Aim: to use key points to write a summary.

- Students read and order the key points.
- Then they write their summaries. This is suitable for homework.
- Encourage them to read their work carefully before they hand it in.

Answers

1 Tom late and not done homework
2 bus noisy so Tom couldn't work
3 Tom spoke to driver, no reply
4 Julie and Tom steered
5 safely round roundabout
6 down hill and onto grass
7 everyone alive

Activity Book p60 Exercises 1 and 2

WORD BUILDING

8 Aim: to present and practise adjective suffixes *-ful* and *-less*.
- Students make adjectives and then match them with their definitions.
- Check orally.

Answers

1 colourless	*2 successful*	*3 helpful*
4 painful	*5 truthful*	*6 tasteless*

Optional activities

- Students make other adjectives with the two suffixes, e.g., *beautiful, hopeless.* Note that many adjectives can take either suffix for a positive or a negative meaning, e.g., *thoughtful, thoughtless; careful, careless; helpful, helpless*, etc.
- Students use the adjectives in sentences, orally or written.

STUDY SKILLS

9 Aim: to think about different ways of learning English.
- Give students a short time to think of as many things as possible that will help them learn English.
- Make a class list on the board and encourage students to use the ideas.
- Some other ideas are: watch English language films, trying not just to read the subtitles; listen to the words of English and American pop songs; get English language tourist leaflets for local attractions.

Activity Book p 61 Exercises 3 and 4

Consolidation and Extension activities

- Suffix Tennis. Pairs first list adjectives with the suffixes *-ful* and *-less*. Then they play, going from noun to adjective.
- Role-play. Students take the roles of Tom, Julie, Jack Dennis, other students on the bus and a newspaper or TV reporter. They role-play an interview about the bus incident.
- Team spelling quiz. Teams prepare a list of new words from the unit to test the others on. They may also ask them to use the word correctly in a sentence.

Homework

- Students write the adjectives with suffixes on a new page in their vocabulary notebooks, and learn them.
- Students write up the interview from the role-play.
- Students write two or three paragraphs on why it is useful to know some first aid.

Pairwork

Pairwork Activity p108 and 116

Aim: to listen to a friend's problem and give advice.
- Students first read their problems and pick out key points.
- Then As tell Bs the problems. Bs listen and give advice.
- They change roles.
- Monitor this for correct use of language.

Optional activities

- Students summarise the advice given them, orally or in writing.
- They may decide if they will follow it.

Activity Book Unit 6 Lesson 4 p60-61
Grammar Summary p121

Review

1 Read and choose

- This can be done orally or written.

Answers

1 ago	*2 somewhere*	*3 how*	*4 everything*
5 were	*6 anywhere*	*7 would*	*8 nothing*
9 how	*10 them*	*11 without*	*12 than*
13 only	*14 at*	*15 drink*	*16 make*
17 breathe	*18 has*	*19 than*	*20 make*
21 go			

2 Write

Answers

1 *How would you survive if you were lost in the desert?*
2 *If I knew which way to go, I would walk to the nearest town.*
3 *What would you do if you fell into the sea?*
4 *If I were alone, I would wait for someone to rescue me.*
5 *If you were lost, how would you help people find you?*
6 *If I heard a helicopter, I would write a message on the ground.*
7 *I would wave a flag if I had one.*
8 *If I had matches, I would light a fire.*

Optional activity

- Students discuss the ideas in the completed sentences.
- Students answer the questions in numbers 1, 3 and 5.

3 Order the words

Answers

1 *If you get lost you should not panic.*
2 *You ought to learn how to give first aid to someone.*
3 *You should always take enough food and drink with you.*
4 *You ought to be able to read a map.*
5 *You should always tell someone where you are going.*
6 *You should always be careful with electricity.*
7 *You ought to learn how to swim well.*
8 *If you light a fire you should always stay with it.*

Optional activities

- Students discuss the ideas in the completed sentences.
- They make sentences with *If you panic, ...* etc.

4 Complete

Answers

1 makes people laugh	*2 let him stay*
3 made everyone learn	*4 let her go*
5 made her cry	*6 made everyone tidy*
7 made Lucy get	*8 let Paolo borrow*

5 Complete

Answers

1 had better	*2 is allowed to*	*3 had better*
4 are allowed to	*5 are allowed to*	*6 had better*

6 Complete

Answers

1 on 2 on 3 away 4 on 5 on 6 away 7 away 8 on

7 Test each other

- Students could make a word map for clothes.

Song

- Students read the gapped song.
- They guess what the words might be.
- Play the cassette. Students listen and check.
- Check orally.

Tapescript and answers 

I'd rather be a ***sparrow*** *than a* ***snail****.*
Yes I would, if I could,
I surely would.
I'd rather be a ***hammer*** *than a* ***nail****.*
Yes I would, if I only could,
I surely would.

Away, I'd rather sail away
Like a ***swan*** *that's here and gone.*
A man gets tied up to the ground,
He gives the ***world*** *its saddest sound*
Its saddest sound

I'd rather be a forest than a street
Yes I would, if I could,
I surely would.
I'd rather feel the earth beneath my feet.
Yes I would, if I only could,
I surely would.

Optional activities

• Listen to the song again. Students sing along.
• Ask the students why they think the singer says he'd rather be a sparrow than a snail? A hammer than a nail? A forest than a street? Explain that these can be interpreted as metaphors for freedom, strength and peace.
• In groups the students discuss what they would rather be, using metaphors.
• Students find the rhymes - snail/nail, would/could, ground/sound, street/feet.

Activity Book Unit 6 Review, p62-63

Poster p113

• In this unit students use the ideas from the unit to make a poster about safety.
• Remind students to bring in their work on fire instructions. They reread the texts and look at each other's work.
• Then they discuss fire safety in the school. They may start by brainstorming for sub-topics, e.g., how to avoid fires, what to do if there is a fire, etc.
• When they have chosen their headings they make notes.
• They may do some research for homework, and try to find suitable ilustrations, as well as perhaps drawing a plan of the school with excape routes marked.
• They discuss their work so far, and decide which pictures to use and what to write up neatly.
• When they have written their work, they check it carefully before sticking it and the illustrations on a large sheet of paper.
• Display the posters for the whole class to see.

7 ESCAPE

Lesson 1 *He should have known better!* p68

Target language
should(n't) have
Review of reported statements
Vocabulary
Skydiving and air sports
Compound nouns

Warmer

- Ask students about the story so far.
- Find out if anyone has been skydiving. Would they like to try it? Why? Why not?

1 READ

Aim: to present *should(n't) have* and to review reported statements.
- Use the cassette to present the dialogue.
- Students read the dialogue in groups of four.
- Then they answer the questions.
- Check orally, focusing on the form of the reported statements.

Tapescript

Alison *Now do you all remember what I told you?*
Manuel *You said that the plane would go up to 3000 metres and then we would jump in twos - it's called tandem skydiving.*
Paolo *And you told us that we were going to fall for 40 seconds at 200 kilometres an hour before the parachute opened. And I'm jumping with you!*
Alison *Almost right. You should have paid attention, Paolo. Aliki is jumping with me, and you and Manuel with two instructors.*
Aliki *Alison, what's the matter? You look worried. Is it something to do with Rick and Lucy?*
Alison *Yes, they shouldn't have let the boy escape. They should have brought him back to ACE!*
Aliki *Don't blame Rick and Lucy.*
Alison *It's not Lucy's fault. Rick was in charge. He should have known better!*
Aliki *Alison, can we go right over Stonehenge? I want to take a photograph.*
Alison *We can try. But you should have told me earlier.*
Aliki *Sorry, I forgot. It's for my father, you see - the picture.*

Answers

1 *It's called tandem skydiving.*
2 *She said they were going to fall for 40 seconds at 200 kilometres an hour before the parachute opened.*
3 *Because he didn't know who he was going to jump with.*
4 *They shouldn't have let the boy escape.*
5 *They should have brought him back to ACE.*

Optional activities

- Students recall Alison's instructions.
- Do they agree with her comments?

Activity Book p64 Exercise 1

2 GRAMMAR FILE

Aim: to present and practise *should(n't) have.*
- Students copy and complete the chart.
- Go through it orally.
- Explain that *should(n't) have* is much more common than *ought(n't) to have.*

Answers

should(n't) have
Rick ***should*** *have* ***known*** *better.*
Aliki should ***have told*** *Alison earlier.*
Rick and Lucy ***shouldn't have*** *let the boy escape.*

Optional activities

- Students find examples in the dialogue.
- They rephrase sentences with *ought(n't) to have.*

Activity Book p64 Exercise 2

3 SPEAK AND WRITE

Aim: to practise using *should(n't) have.*
- Students write the sentences.
- Check orally.

Answers

2 *He should have paid attention.*
3 *He shouldn't have ridden so fast.*
4 *He should have worn a helmet.*
5 *He should have written to his parents.*
6 *He shouldn't have pretended that he could swim.*
7 *She shouldn't have left it in the kitchen.*
8 *They should have stayed with the group.*

Activity Book p65 Exercise 3

4 Speak

Aim: to practise *should(n't) have.*
- Go through this orally, or in pairs.

Answers
2 *You shouldn't have picked a fight.*
3 *You should have looked where you were going.*
4 *You should have done your homework earlier.*
5 *You should have seen the lighthouse.*
6 *You should have got up earlier.*

Activity Book p56 Exercise 4

Optional activities
- Students make new sentences using *ought(n't) to have.*

5 Speak

Aim: to practise reporting statements.

Answers
1 *Alison said they were going to fall at 200 kilometres an hour.*
2 *Aliki said she wanted to take a photograph.*
3 *Aliki said the picture was for her father.*
4 *Paolo said he was paying attention.*
5 *Alison said she was worried about the boy.*
6 *Manuel said it was called tandem skydiving.*
7 *Aliki said Rick and Lucy had saved the boy.*
8 *Alison said Aliki was jumping with her.*

Optional activity
- Students write the sentences.

Activity Book p65 Exercise 5

6 Read

Aim: to read a text for specific information.
- Ask if anyone knows about the history of parachutes. Where did the idea come from?
- Students read the text and match the events and countries.
- Check orally.

Answers
1 b) China, c) Italy 2 a) France 3 d) USA

Optional activity
- Books closed. Ask questions to see how much students remember about the history of parachutes and skydiving.

7 Word File

Aim: to make compound nouns.
- Students match the words to make compound nouns.
- Then they find five of them in the lesson.
- Check orally. You may need to draw their attention to the fact that not all compound nouns are one word.

Answers
homework horse power lifejacket lighthouse
motorbike shipwreck skydiving weekend

Compound nouns in lesson
homework, lifejacket, lighthouse, skydiving, weekend.

8 Write

Aim: to personalise the use of *should(n't) have.*
- Students may first work in groups and discuss things they should or shouldn't have done.
- The writing is suitable for homework.

Consolidation and Extension activities
- Team game. Team 1 says a word. Team 2 either makes a compound noun from it or adds the suffix *-ful* or *-less*. Team 1 must then use the new word in a correct sentence.
- Pairs. Students imagine they are from a different planet and they are trying to perform simple actions, e.g., make coffee, brush their teeth. Their partner is on the home planet with a computer giving them instructions, like this:

  Student 1: *I'm thirsty. What should I do?*
  Student 2: *You should make some coffee.* etc.

Homework
- Students make a list of compound nouns and learn them.
- Students write a set of rules for safe skydiving.
- Students write a story using *should(n't) have* and *ought(n't) to have.*

Activity Book Unit 7 Lesson 1, p64-65
Grammar Summary p121

Lesson 2 *I wanted it to go on for ever* p70

Target language
Verb + object + infinitive
Review of reported questions

Vocabulary
Activities
Personal history

Warmer

- Give students a short time to make notes on important events in their lives so far, e.g., date of birth, birth of brothers/sisters, began school, moved house, etc. Then they work in groups and take turns to ask and answer questions about their lives.

1 READ

Aim: to present verbs followed by object and infinitive and to review reported questions.

- Students look at and talk about the main picture. They speculate on what is happening.
- Students read and listen to the text.
- Then they complete the questions on p71 and answer them.
- Listen to the cassette to check the answers.
- Students look at the photo of Stonehenge. Before they read the Fact File, find out if anyone knows what it is.
- Then they read the Fact File.

Tapescript

Aliki screamed as she and Alison fell at 200 kilometres an hour. Then the parachute opened and they suddenly stopped falling. Now they were floating peacefully down towards the ground.

'I wanted it to go on for ever,' said Aliki. 'That was the greatest forty seconds of my life. What an exciting feeling!'

'Get your camera ready,' Alison replied. 'Your father asked you to photograph Stonehenge from the air, didn't he? We'll fly right over it and land close by.'

'There are lots of people near the stones,' said Aliki.

'Yes, there's a fence there,' Alison answered. 'They won't allow people to go right up to the stones.'

'Great. We're right over Stonehenge now. And look, Alison! Quick! See that boy. He's wearing Rick's jacket! It must be the boy who ran away,' Aliki shouted excitedly.

'We'll land next to him,' Alison replied. 'Now let me do the landing.'

The boy in Rick's jacket looked up in surprise as the huge shadow of the parachute passed over him. He was even more surprised when the parachute landed and two people ran up to him. Alison grabbed his arm and asked him who he was and why he had run away from ACE. The boy looked very frightened and didn't reply.

'I can't make you talk to me,' Alison said. 'But I'm worried about you. If you don't say anything, I'm afraid I'll have to call the police.'

'OK,' the boy said. He was about sixteen and had short fair hair. 'It's a long story. You see, I used to live at ACE.'

Answers

1 ***What*** *did Aliki's father ask her to do?*
He asked her to take a photo of Stonehenge from the air.

2 ***Who*** *did Aliki see at Stonehenge?*
She saw the boy who ran away.

3 ***Who*** *said 'Let me do the landing'?*
Alison.

4 *Alison asked two questions.* ***What*** *were here exact words?*
'Who are you?', 'Why did you run away from ACE?'

5 ***What*** *couldn't Alison do?*
She couldn't make him talk to her.

6 ***Who*** *would Alison call?*
The police.

Optional activities

- Groups. Students act out the story as a dialogue.
- They speculate on who the boy is and why he's been taking things from ACE.
- Books closed. What can students remember about Stonehenge?

Activity Book p66 Exercise 1

2 GRAMMAR FILE

Aim: to present verbs followed by object and infinitive.

- Students copy and complete the chart.
- Check orally.

Answers

Verb + object + infinitive

Aliki wanted it ***to*** *go on for ever.*

They won't allow ***people*** *to* ***go*** *right up to the stones.*

I can't make ***you talk*** *to me.*

Optional activity

• Students find examples of verbs followed by object and infinitive in the text.

Activity Book p66 Exercise 2

3 Speak and Write

Aim: to practise verbs followed by object and infinitive.
• Go through this orally first.
• Then students write sentences.
• Check orally by having different students ask questions and choose someone to answer, e.g., *What does Alison want her to do?*

Answers

Her father wants her to take a photo of Stonehenge.
Her mother wants her to phone home every evening.
Paolo wants her to dance with him at the disco.
Tara and Lucy want her to go swimming with them.
Her English teacher wants her to learn lots of English.
Alison wants her to let her do the landing.

Optional activity

• Students work in groups of three or four. One student asks another to do something, e.g., *Please pass me that book/lend me your pencil.* The third student asks the second *What did he/she ask/want you to do?* He/She answers *He/She asked/wanted me to pass him/her that book*, etc.

Activity Book p67 Exercise 3.

4 Listen

Aim: to listen for specific details about someone's life.
• Students first read through the text.
• Play the cassette. They listen and choose the correct words.
• Check orally.
• Play the cassette again. Students listen and tick the questions they hear.
• Finally students report the questions and answers. This can be done orally in pairs.
• Refer to the LOOK! box and give additional practice if they need reminding how to form reported questions.

Tapescript

Alison *Now, tell us, who are you?*
Sam *My name's Sam Palmer. I live in London now but I used to live in Devon. My family used to live in the old farmhouse, you know, where ACE is now.*
Alison *Really! When did you move to London?*
Sam *Five years ago.*
Aliki *Did you want to move to London?*
Sam *No, not at all. I didn't want to say goodbye to all my friends. And I hated London. I still do...*
Alison *I see. So when you left, the farmhouse became ACE.*
Sam *That's right. Then this summer my uncle invited me to come and stay in Devon for a week. It was brilliant! But when the holiday was over I didn't want to go back to London. So I ran away and came to ACE.*
Alison *Where did you live at ACE?*
Sam *On the cliffs. I knew about the secret stairs from when I used to live there.*
Aliki *Did you get hungry?*
Sam *Yes. That's why I used to come into the kitchen at night to get food. I didn't take much so I didn't think anyone would notice.*
Alison *But why did you steal clothes?*
Sam *Because I was cold. I know it was wrong and I'm sorry. I left all my things at my uncle's. And then I fell into the sea. I couldn't stop myself. It was a really frightening feeling. It was lucky those two people helped me.*
Alison *Then why did you run away?.*
Sam *I'm sorry. I was scared. I decided to go back to London but I didn't have any money. I got a lift on a lorry and then I walked. I stopped here to look at Stonehenge and then you two dropped out of the sky.*
Alison *One last question. Are you hungry now?*
Sam *I'm starving!*
Alison *Right - this is what we'll do. We'll take the parachute back and get you a sandwich. Then we'll drive back to ACE and you can phone your parents. All right?*
Sam *Great! Thank you!*

Answers

1 London	*2 Devon*	*3 five*
4 uncle	*5 didn't go home*	*6 used to live there*
7 scared	*8 ACE*	

Tick questions 1, 3, 4, 6, 7, 9, 10, 11.

Possible answer

Alison asked the boy who he was. He said his name was Sam Palmer. She asked when he had moved to London and he said it was five years before. Aliki asked if he had wanted to move to London and he said he hadn't. Alison asked him where he had lived at ACE. He said he had lived on the cliffs. Aliki asked him if he had got hungry. He said he had and that was why he had gone to the kitchen at night. Alison asked him why he had stolen clothes and he said it was because he had been cold. Then she asked him why he had run away. He said it was because he was scared. Finally she asked him if he was hungry and he said that he was starving.

Optional activity

- Pairs. Students ask and answer the questions. The one answering may have his/her book closed.
- Books closed. Students retell the story round the class, reporting what questions were asked and what the answers were.

Activity Book p67 Exercises 4 and 5

5 Write

Aim: to write sentences using verbs followed by object and infinitive and adverbs of frequency.

- Students may refer back to Unit 6, Lesson 2, Activity 4 for the rules at ACE.
- Students make a few sentences orally.
- Then they write the sentences.
- Check orally or take the work in.

Activity Book p67 Exercise 6

Consolidation and Extension activities

- Question chain. Write the four frequency adverbs on the board in order, as in the book. Round the class students ask each other questions which can be answered with an adverb of frequency. These can take the form *Do you ever ...? How often do you ...?* or *Do your parents (ever) let/make you ...?* Students must use the adverbs of frequency in the order on the board, like this: Student 1 to student 2: *Do you ever go swimming alone?* Student 2: *I never go swimming alone.* Student 2 to student 3: *Do you ever get angry?* Student 3: *I sometimes get angry,* etc.
- Role-play. Students work in groups of four. One is an alien. Another asks the alien questions about his/her life. The third asks the fourth what the question was and what the alien said. The fourth reports.
- Write the verbs *allow, ask, expect, let, make, tell, want* on the board. Round the class, students make a sentence each, using the verbs in order, so that student 1 makes a sentence with *allow*, student 2 makes one with *ask*, and so on.

Homework

- Students ask their parents or another older member of their family what they were allowed/made/expected to do, etc. when they were younger. They make notes and then write a paragraph or report to the class in the next lesson.
- Students ask a friend or cousin of their own age the same questions and write a report.
- Students write a letter to a penfriend asking similar questions, and saying what they are/aren't allowed, etc. to do.

Activity Book Unit 7 Lesson 2, p66-67
Grammar Summary p121-122.

Lesson 3 *He couldn't do anything!*

p72

Target language

Past ability: *could(n't), was(n't) able to, managed to*
Purpose: *in order to, so that*

Vocabulary

Safari
Parts of the body

Optional aid

• Bring a map showing the position of the Zambezi River in Central Africa.

Warmer

• Write a few notes to specific students asking them to do certain things, but not to show others the note. Examples: clean the board, give out the books, close the door, etc. At a signal from you, they do the things. Ask the others: *What did I ask him/her to do?*
• Review names of animals. This could be by having an animal alphabet quiz, where students try to think of an animal for each letter of the alphabet. Or they could make word maps with the different animals they know.
• Ask if they remember what a safari is. Where do people go on safari? What kind of animals do they hope to see?

1 READ

Aim: to present past ability and purpose with *in order to, so that,* and to read for specific information.
• Students first look at the picture and the title and try to guess what the story is about.
• Use the cassette to present the text.
• Show students on the map where Philip was working as a safari guide.
• Students then read the text and answer the questions.
• Check orally.
• Finally students discuss what they think happened next.

Tapescript

ESCAPE FROM THE JAWS OF DEATH: PART ONE - THE ATTACK!

In April 1994, Philip Coates Palgrave was working as a safari guide on the Lower Zambezi River in Central Africa. He took groups of about ten people in canoes along the river on safaris so that they could watch the wild animals. Their luggage was all taken by road to the camps where they spent the night so that they could have plenty of room in the canoes. Occasionally the safari stopped in safe places so that the tourists could swim and cool down. But they weren't able to swim very often ... In the Zambezi there are thousands of crocodiles - it's estimated that there is one two-metre long crocodile every ten metres - and there are hippos everywhere.

It was the middle of the last day of a safari and extremely hot. Everyone was holding on to each other's canoes in order to make one big raft - five canoes wide and six metres long - for safety.

Suddenly, Philip's canoe was lifted out of the water and he thought he'd hit a rock or an island. He turned round in order to see what had happened and then he realised his canoe was right on top of a hippo's head! Philip could see one of the hippo's eyes on the left of his canoe and one eye on the right!

He immediately told everyone to paddle to the bank, which was only ten metres away. They all managed to get to the bank except Philip. The hippo tipped Philip's canoe and Philip wasn't able to escape. He couldn't do anything! He just fell into the hippo's mouth! The hippo closed its jaws and took Philip down to the bottom of the river. The animal thrashed about, shaking its head as if Philip was as light as a feather!

Answers

1 *He was working as a safari guide on the Lower Zambezi River in Central Africa.*
2 *So that they could watch the wild animals.*
3 *So that they could have plenty of room in the canoes.*
4 *So that they could swim and cool down.*
5 *Because there are thousands of crocodiles in the Zambezi, and there are also hippos everywhere.*
6 *In order to make one big raft, for safety.*
7 *Because he could see the hippo's eyes, one on each side of his raft.*
8 *Yes, all except for Philip.*
9 *A feather.*

Optional activities

• Books closed, students recall the story.
• Pairs. One student is a reporter and the other is Philip. Philip answers the reporter's questions about the experience. Monitor for use of the first person.

Activity Book p68 Exercise 1

2 GRAMMAR FILE

Aim: to present structures for talking about past ability.
- Students copy and complete the chart.
- Students complete the chart on the board.

Answers

Past ability: could(n't), was(n't) able to, managed to

General ability	*Particular occasion*
Affirmative	
They could swim in safe places.	*They managed to get to the bank.*
*They **were** able **to** swim in safe places.*	*They were **able** to get to the bank.*
Negative	
They couldn't swim everywhere.	*He **couldn't** do anything.*
*They **weren't** able **to** swim everywhere.*	*He **wasn't** able **to** escape.*

Optional activities

- Students look for examples of past ability in the text.
- Where possible, they try using a different verb.

Activity Book p68 Exercise 2

3 SPEAK AND WRITE

Aim: to compare what two people could do in the past.
- Students look at the table and the examples.
- They make sentences comparing Aliki and Manuel, or saying what each could do at different ages.
- They write sentences comparing the two.
- A large number of comparisons are possible.

Answers

Aliki could dive when she was twelve but Manuel couldn't.

Aliki could read when she was six and so could Manuel.

Manuel could ride a bike when he was six but Aliki couldn't.

Manuel could play an instrument when he was six but Aliki couldn't.

Aliki and Manuel couldn't speak English when they were six but they could when they were twelve.

Activity Book p69 Exercise 3

Optional activities

- Students make a chart like that for Aliki and Manuel. They work in pairs and tell each other about what they could do at different ages. Each pair then joins another and they tell each other what their partner could do.
- Students make notes about their partner's past abilities. Then they make comparisons.

4 WRITE

Aim: to practise expressing purpose with *in order to* and *so that.*
- Students may look back at the text first to find examples of *in order to* and *so that.*
- Go through the LOOK! box with the students to explain the difference in use of *in order to* and *so that.*
- Students join the sentences.
- Check orally.
- Point out that in questions 2 and 3, the subject changes.

Answers

1 *People went on canoe safaris **so that they could/ in order to** watch wild animals.*
2 *The luggage was taken by car **so that** there would be plenty of room in the canoes.*
3 *One canoe carried a picnic **so that** the tourists could have lunch.*
4 *They held on to each other's canoes **so that they made/in order to make** a big raft.*
5 *They paddled to the bank **so that they got/ in order to get** away from the hippo.*

Optional activity

- Students look at the text and find examples of purpose structures.

Activity Book p69 Exercise 4

5 LISTEN AND SPEAK

Aim: to listen to a story for specific information.
- Students again speculate about what will happen next in the story.
- Play the cassette. They listen and choose the correct answers.
- Check orally.
- Now ask the students to match the sentences.
- Check orally.
- Play the cassette again for them to check the sequence of events.

Tapescript

Hippos are incredibly strong. I was pulled down under the water. No pain, there was no pain - that was the amazing thing. I didn't panic, I was completely together. I was quite calm. My first idea was to kick the hippo - I kicked it four or five times but then I thought 'What are you doing - you can't fight this animal!' So then I thought if I can't fight the hippo, I'll just relax in order to save energy and try to last it out. But it just went on and on and on. The people on the river bank said they saw me flying out of the water and then down again and then out - they said I came up about three times but I don't remember, I just remember being under the water most of the time. It went on and on, and in the end, I thought right, this is the end of me - still no pain, still very calm. And I had this wonderful rising feeling and the next thing I knew I opened my eyes and I'd reached the surface. I looked around - there was the bank - there were the tourists. I still couldn't feel my leg and I thought the hippo had bitten it off. I thought if my leg's not there I must be bleeding badly and there must be at least ten crocodiles nearby, so I'd better get to my canoe quickly! So I managed to swim to my canoe and I held on to it, and two of the tourists came down in their canoe to pick me up. Still no pain. I was amazed that I was alive, and amazed that I wasn't dead.

Answers

1 wasn't 2 didn't panic 3 didn't manage
4 energy 5 had

1e 2c 3d 4f 5a 6g 7h 8b

Optional activities

- Books closed, students retell the story round the class. Focus on the correct use of the target language.
- They guess what will happen next. Will Philip survive? Has he lost a leg?

Activity Book p69 Exercises 5 and 6

6 Word File

Aim: to review and extend knowledge of words for parts of the body.

- Students make a word map.
- You could have a big one on the board which they all contribute to.
- They check the lesson for suitable words: *head, eye, mouth, jaws, leg.*

Activity Book p69 Exercise 7

7 Write

Aim: to use key words and phrases to write a summary.

- Students may suggest key words and phrases orally.
- Then they choose and note their key words and phrases.
- You may check at this stage.
- Students write their summary. This is suitable for homework.
- Check their work.

Consolidation and Extension activities

- Boasting chain. Round the class students say what they could do at different ages, e.g., *I could walk when I was 18 months. Well I could walk when I was 12 months. Well, I could speak French when I was five,* etc.
- Pairs. Students imagine they went to some amazing place, e.g., the Antarctic, the Sahara Desert, etc. Their partner asks what they did, e.g., *Did you see many penguins? - No, I didn't manage to see any. Were you able to keep warm? Yes, we managed to keep warm enough.* Then they change roles.
- Guess the animal. Team or pair game. A student thinks of an animal. The other has to guess it by asking about parts of the body, e.g., *Does it have a trunk? How many legs has it got?* etc.

Homework

- Students bring their vocabulary notebooks up to date with parts of the body, which they learn.
- Students imagine they are Philip. They write either a diary of his adventure or a letter home, starting with the beginning of the day and describing what they saw and did before the hippo attacked.
- They imagine they are one of the tourists with Philip. They describe the experience of watching him.
- Students imagine they went on a safari and write about it.

Activity Book Unit 7 Lesson 3, p68-69
Grammar Summary p121-122

Lesson 4 *What do we do now?*

p74

Vocabulary
Safari
Narrative connectors
Verb prefix: *re-*

Warmer

• Give them a short time to write down as many animals as they can. Then ask them to sort them into wild and domestic, and sort wild animals by habitat and country.
• Students retell the story of Philip so far. They speculate what will happen next.

Reading

1 **Aim:** to recognise the discourse structure of a story and re-order paragraphs.
• Students read the story.
• They re-order the paragraphs.
• Play the cassette. They listen and check.
• Check orally.

Tapescript and answers 

ESCAPE FROM THE JAWS OF DEATH: PART TWO - THE RESCUE!

[C] Hans and Greta pulled me out of the water into their canoe. I fell into the bottom of the canoe and then I saw my leg. The hippo had bitten my leg three or four times, it had released me, grabbed me again, shaken me around, released me, grabbed me again, and shaken me. What struck me was that the hippo could have taken my head, half of my body, my arms, but every time it was the same leg, which was incredible.

[E] Then the pain started. I couldn't move anything, I couldn't get any message to my foot or below my knee. And I thought 'I'm going to die, within 5 minutes' so I just lay back and closed my eyes. And then Greta turned round and just said, 'Philip, what do we do now?

[A] And those words pulled me back to reality. I just suddenly realised that Hans and Greta had no idea where they were. There were another six tourists somewhere on the river bank and no one knew they were there. And we had no radio.

[D] So I opened my eyes again and I said, 'Right, we have to cross the river - it's our only chance.' I knew that there was a camp on the opposite bank with a radio and a small airfield, and I even knew the people who were working there. I wasn't exactly sure where the camp was, but I knew we were very close to it.

[B] So Hans and Greta paddled as fast as possible. The river there is over four kilometres wide, so it took at least 45 minutes. I lay back in the boat and I closed my eyes. Hans and Greta didn't worry about hippos, they just headed for the opposite bank, and at one point the canoe nearly capsized, and we took in about 100 litres of water! And I looked over the side of the canoe and saw all these hippos! But Hans and Greta just kept paddling, which was the best thing to do.

Optional activity

• Students guess what will happen next.

Listening

2 **Aim:** to listen for specific information.
• Divide the class into two halves, A and B. Students read their instructions carefully.
• Play the cassette. Students listen and note their answers. Students A and B complete the chart together.
• Check orally.

Tapescript 

When we reached the other bank it was about quarter past one. I told Hans to go and find the airfield, which was not more than ten minutes away. Hans ran off - and he was gone for an hour and a half! Greta put a towel over my head and poured water over me and I was just drinking, drinking, I think I drank over 20 litres of water. Where was Hans?

Suddenly he reappeared. He was as white as a sheet, and his eyes were like saucers! He was panicking so much, he couldn't even speak. We calmed him down, and we found out that he had almost jumped on top of a lion! And he couldn't find the airfield. He said he'd seen a car on the bank of the river we had just come from and the next minute he was in the boat and he was pushing off the bank across the river.

So at about three o'clock we started to paddle back across four kilometres of river. Now I was really worried because we had been lucky to cross the river in the first place - to get back again would be a miracle.

Finally at four o'clock we reached the other side of the river again and we found the car that Hans had seen. And then some people came to the bank, and they pulled the canoe out of the water. They put me on a mattress, and put one of the canoe paddles beside my leg. One guy tore up his shirt and he used it to tie my leg to the paddle. Now it was about half past four in the afternoon. I'd been attacked at midday.

But these people had no first aid kit or painkillers, they had nothing, they were camping, they were on holiday. I asked someone to go and find the six tourists who were still waiting on the river bank. Then they picked me up on the mattress, put me in the car, and we drove off back to find an airfield. This was a nightmare - driving along the worst road in Africa in a very old uncomfortable vehicle. It was a five-hour drive to the airfield, and every bump in the road was agony.

By 6pm it was dark and when we finally reached the

airfield it was 10 pm. But I couldn't fly to hospital because there were no airfield lights and the plane wasn't able to land in the dark. So I had to wait in the camp until morning, and still there were no painkillers! One woman stayed with me talking all night in order to keep me awake.

At about 8 the next morning, a plane arrived to pick me up. I finally reached the hospital at about 2 pm on Monday afternoon, 26 hours after I was attacked.

Answers

Time	*Event*
Midday	*Hippo attacked*
1.15	*Reached the other bank*
2.45	*Hans saw a lion and returned*
3pm	*Started to cross the river again*
4pm	*Found people and car*
5pm	*Started to drive to airfield*
6pm	*Dark*
10pm	*Reached airfield*
8am	*Plane arrived*
2pm	*Reached hospital*

SPEAKING

3 Aim: to listen for specific information and to use notes to tell a story.

- Students predict what will happen to Philip in hospital and preteach *surgeon*.
- Play the cassette. Students listen to the end of the story.
- They work in pairs or small groups and tell the story.
- Let two or three pairs or groups tell the class their version. Do they all agree?

Tapescript

I lost part of my left leg. But it's a miracle that I'm alive to tell this story. The surgeons said that I should have died 15 minutes after the attack. No, I don't blame the hippo! And as soon as I could, I went back on the river again with my brother and cousin ... but that's another story!

WRITING

4 Aim: to use key information and connecting words to write a summary.

- You may first ask students to retell the story round the class.
- Then they use their charts and the connectors to write a summary.
- Make sure they check their work carefully.
- Check the work.

Activity Book p70-71 Exercises 1 and 2

WORD BUILDING

5 Aim: to present and practise verb prefix *re-*.

- Students add the prefix to the verbs and complete the sentences.
- Check orally.

Answers

1 repainted 2 redo 3 reopen 4 reread 5 rewrote

Optional activities

- Students think of other verbs that can take the prefix *re-*, e.g., rethink, retell, reuse.
- They use them in sentences.

STUDY SKILLS

6 Aim: to improve one's spoken English.

- Discuss the ideas with the class. Has anyone tried any of them?
- Encourage students to try out some of the ideas and see if they improve. They could keep a diary of what they have done.

Activity Book p 71 Exercises 3 and 4

Consolidation and Extension activities

- Prefix Tennis. The first student says the prefixed verb, e.g., *rewrite*, and the other says the definition, e.g., *write again*.
- Role-play. Groups. Students act out the story of Philip and the tourists. One student could be a reporter; another could be the surgeon who operates on Philip. The others have to explain their story and describe the order of events.
- Students talk about Philip's story saying whether anyone should or shouldn't have done anything different.

Homework

- Students make a list of verbs that can take the prefix *re-* and learn them.
- Students write a diary or a letter about the whole of Philip's adventure. They can be Philip, Hans, Greta or one of the other tourists.
- Students write the story from the Activity Book (p70 Exercise 1) from Terry's point of view.

Pairwork

Pairwork Activity p109 and 117

Aim: to ask questions about a story.

- Students read the story carefully.
- They work out their questions.
- Students take it in turns to ask questions.
- Check orally. Students read the complete story round the class.

Answers

Maurice and Maralyn Bailey were sailing to New Zealand. They were ***in the middle of the Pacific Ocean*** *when there was a sudden crash. An enormous injured* ***whale*** *was thrashing the water with its tail, very near their boat. It dived away* ***after a few minutes****. Then they discovered* ***the damage****.*

There was ***a huge hole*** *in the boat, and water was flooding in. Maralyn was worried. 'I don't know* ***how to swim****!' she thought. They didn't have* ***a radio****, they didn't have* ***any lifejackets****, but they had a small life-raft, which was* ***1.5 metres long****, and they climbed into it before the boat sank. They were now floating* ***1000 kms*** *from land. They had food and water for* ***20 days****.*

They became very hungry. They had ***biscuits and margarine*** *for breakfast, lunch was biscuits, dinner was* ***one tin of meat****. They managed to catch fish to eat, but they were very thirsty. They couldn't drink seawater and although they caught some rainwater, they only had* ***one cup of*** *fresh water a day.*

After ***a week****, they saw a ship but the ship didn't see them. They floated across the ocean* ***for three months*** *and they became* ***very ill****.*

Finally they were rescued by a ***Korean fishing boat****. They had travelled* ***2,500 kms*** *across* ***the Pacific Ocean*** *and survived. What an adventure!*

Activity Book Unit 7 Lesson 4, p70-71
Grammar Summary p121-122

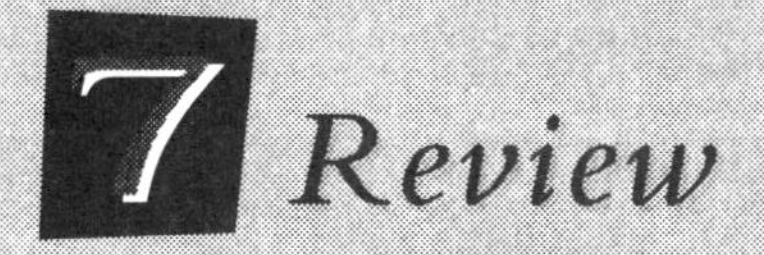

1 Read and choose

Answers

1 have stayed	*2 asked*	*3 told*	*4 to jump*
5 to	*6 couldn't*	*7 already*	*8 if*
9 told	*10 of*	*11 gone*	*12 didn't*
13 my	*14 told*	*15 right*	*16 anything*
17 nothing	*18 at*	*19 to*	*20 able*
21 come	*22 at*	*23 to stay*	*24 the*
25 also	*26 around*	*27 his*	*28 in*

Optional activities

- Students retell the story, in the third person.
- They discuss whether Alison should/shouldn't have done what she said.

2 Rewrite

- You may go through this orally first.

Answers

1 *She should have stayed in bed that morning.*
2 *She shouldn't have gone to the airport.*
3 *He shouldn't have stolen the clothes.*
4 *He should have stayed with Rick and Lucy.*
5 *He should have phoned his parents.*
6 *You shouldn't have picked a fight.*
7 *Rick shouldn't have let Sam escape.*
8 *We shouldn't have missed the last bus.*

Optional activity

- Students rephrase the sentences using *ought(n't) to have*

3 Direct speech

- This could be done orally.

Answers

1 *'What has happened to my parachute?'*
2 *'It was a one in a million accident and it will never happen again.'*
3 *'Are you ready for another jump?'*
4 *'I'll have another go, but I'm a bit scared.'*
5 *'There's nothing to worry about.'*
6 *'Where did you live at ACE and why did you steal clothes?'*
7 *'I left all my things at my uncle's.'*
8 *'We'll get you a sandwich.'*

4 Order the words

Answers

1 *I wanted it to go on for ever.*
2 *Aliki's father asked her to photograph Stonehenge from the air.*
3 *They won't allow people to get close to Stonehenge.*
4 *Alison couldn't make the boy talk to her.*
5 *Sam's uncle invited Sam to stay with him.*
6 *Sam's parents let him go to Devon on holiday.*
7 *Alison wanted the boy to tell her about himself.*
8 *Aliki's brother wants her to bring him a present when she comes home.*

5 Complete

Answers

1 could	*2 couldn't*	*3 managed to*
4 couldn't	*5 could*	*6 managed to*
7 managed to	*8 couldn't*	

6 Test each other

- This could be played as Word Tennis.

Song

- Students read the gapped song.
- They guess what the words might be.
- Play the cassette. Students listen and check.
- Check orally.

Tapescript and answers 

I used to think that I could not go on
And life was nothing but an awful ***song***
But now I know the meaning of true ***love***
I'm leaning on the everlasting arms.

If I can see it, then I can be it
If I just ***believe*** *it, there's nothing to it*

Chorus
I believe I can fly.
I believe I can touch the ***sky***
I think about it every ***night*** *and day*
Spread my wings and ***fly*** *away*
I believe I can soar.
I see me running through that open ***door***
I believe I can fly
I believe I can fly
I believe I can fly

See I was on the verge of breaking down
Sometimes silence can seem so loud
There are miracles in life I must achieve
But ***first*** *I know it starts inside of me*

If I can see it, then I can be it
If I just ***believe*** *it, there's nothing to it*

Chorus
Could I believe in me?
If I can see it, then I can do it
If I just ***believe*** *it, there's nothing to it*

Optional activities

- Listen to the song again. Students sing along.
- Ask the students what they think the song is about. (It's about confidence and belief).
- Ask the students why they think the singer wants to fly. In pairs the students discuss where they would go if they could fly anywhere, and why they would go there.
- Ask students if they believe they could do anything, what would they like to do. Do they agree that a person can do anything if they believe they can?

Activity Book Unit 7 Review p72-73

Poster p113

- In this unit, students make a poster about lucky excapes.
- Students reread the adventure/escape stories in Unit 7, including those in the Activity Book.
- At home they find more stories: in newspapers, on TV, in books or on the Internet. They could also ask friends and neighbours and their family if they have ever had a lucky escape.
- They make notes and try to find suitable pictures.
- They bring all their notes to the group and decide on the two best escape stories.
- Then they write them up neatly, check their work and stick it to a large sheet of paper.
- They illustrate their work with the pictures they found.
- They may decide to do this in the form of a newspaper story.
- Display the posters and make sure they can all see each other's work.

TOMORROW'S WORLD

Lesson 1 *He'll have to behave himself!* p78

Target language

Order of adjectives
Future modals: *will/won't have to* and *will/won't be able to*

Vocabulary

Adjectives
Ecology

Warmer

- Review environmental vocabulary.
- Ask students to talk about what they think life in the future will be like.

1 READ

Aim: to present future modals *will/won't have to* and *will/won't be able to* and to read for specific information.

- Students look at the photo and talk about it. What do they think it is?
- Use the cassette to present the dialogue.
- Then students read the dialogue and they answer the questions.
- Check orally.

Tapescript

Alison *When we go inside, you'll be able to walk through the rainforest without leaving the West Country! In the future, people won't have to travel abroad to see life in the jungle. They'll be able to see it all here.*

Mark *What is this place? Will we have to spend all day here?*

Holly *Why don't you listen and you'll find out? We're just here for the morning. There are two huge round greenhouses full of strange plants. Sam said it was great - he came last week with his uncle.*

Mark *Sam? You mean Sam, the thief.*

Holly *He's not a thief - he's just been badly-behaved, that's all. Anyway Alison hopes he'll be able to stay at ACE until the end of the week.*

Mark *He'll have to behave himself if he does.*

Holly *You're a fine one to talk! Come on, let's go in. I want to see the rainforest.*

Mark *Hang on. You'll be able to see as much rainforest as you want in a minute. There's something I wanted to ask you first.*

Holly *Yes, what? You'll have to be quick - they're going in now.*

Mark *Holly, will we be able to keep in touch? After the holiday, I mean.*

Holly *I don't know. I'll have to see when I get home.*

Alison *Come on, you two. Hurry up or you won't be able to go in with us!*

Answers

1 *True.*
2 *True.*
3 *False. Mark doesn't want to spend all day there.*
4 *False. Sam'll be able to stay at ACE for a few days.*
5 *True.*
6 *False. Holly doesn't think Mark is always well-behaved. 'You're a fine one to talk' means 'You shouldn't criticise him because you don't behave very well yourself.'*
7 *False. Mark wants to hear from Holly after the end of the holiday.*
8 *True.*

Optional activity

- Students discuss whether they agree with Mark or Holly about Sam.

2 READ

Aim: to practise ordering adjectives correctly.

- Students read and complete the Fact File.
- Check orally.
- Then go through the LOOK! box with them. If necessary give or elicit examples of the different types of adjective.
- Students then put the adjectives under the correct headings.
- Check by completing the chart on the board.
- Finally students reread the dialogue and Fact File looking for adjectives and noting their order.

Answers

wonderful brand-new; huge round; fantastic tall

Opinion	*Size*	*Age*	*Shape*	*Colour*
awful	*big*	*brand-new*	*fat*	*black*
beautiful	*huge*	*new*	*narrow*	*blue*
fantastic	*large*	*old*	*round*	*brown*
lovely	*long*	*second-hand*	*square*	*green*
nice	*short*	*young*	*thin*	*red*
strange	*small*		*wide*	*white*
terrible	*tall*			*yellow*
wonderful	*tiny*			

Optional activity

- Students make sentences using as many different types of adjective as they can. (Furniture is a good example to use, e.g., *a beautiful big old round black table*).

3 LISTEN

Aim: to order adjectives correctly and to listen for specific information.

- Students write the sentences correctly.
- Play the cassette. They listen and check.

Tapescript and answers

Holly	*Isn't it amazing?*
Mark	*What's that* ***beautiful tall*** *tree with the* ***big round green*** *leaves?*
Holly	*I'm not sure. I think it's a rubber tree.*
Aliki	*What's that called in English, Holly?*
Holly	*Which tree? The* ***big fat*** *one?*
Aliki	*No, next to it. What's the one with* ***long thin yellow*** *things called? I know the word in Greek but I can't remember it in English.*
Holly	*Bamboo - you can make chairs out of it.*
Aliki	*Yes, of course. Hey, do you know whose this is?*
Holly	*That* ***awful old black*** *rucksack? Yes, I think it's Alison's.*
Alison	*Has anyone seen a* ***nice new black*** *rucksack? I got it for my birthday.*
Holly	*Is this it, Alison?*

Answers

1 beautiful tall; big round green

2 big fat

3 long thin yellow

4 awful old black

5 nice new black

Optional activity

- Guessing game. This can be played in teams or pairs. One student thinks of something, and describes it, e.g., *It's amazing and huge and old and grey*. The others try to guess what it is. (Stonehenge)

Activity Book p75 Exercise 3

4 SOUND FILE

Aim: to recognise and practise the intonation of words in lists.

- Play the cassette. Students listen and repeat.
- Focus on their intonation.

Tapescript

1 *There are two huge round greenhouses.*

2 *It's got lovely big red flowers.*

3 *There's a strange tiny green plant.*

4 *It's a wonderful tall white building.*

5 *I've got a beautiful new blue bag.*

Optional activity

- Pairs. Students make up very imaginative new sentences with lists of adjectives. They tell their partner who comments e.g., *I've got an amazing blue and pink cat! What a strange cat!*

5 GRAMMAR FILE

Aim: to present future modals.

- Students copy and complete the chart.
- Check orally or by letting students complete the chart on the board.
- Then they answer the questions.

Answers

Future modals: will/won't have to and will/won't be able to

Sam ***will*** *have* ***to*** *behave himself.*

Holly ***will*** *be able* ***to*** *see as much rainforest as she wants.*

If they don't hurry, Mark and Holly ***won't*** *be able* ***to*** *go in with the others.*

Will *we* ***have*** *to spend all day here?*

Will *we* ***be able*** *to keep in touch?*

The future of ***must*** *is* ***will have to.***
The future of ***don't have to*** *is* ***won't have to.***
The future of ***can*** *is* ***will be able to.***

Optional activity

• Students find examples of future modals in the text and in the dialogue.

Activity Book p74 Exercises 1 and 2

6 Speak and Write

Aim: to practise using future modals.

• Students complete the questions.
• Check orally.
• Then they write an answer for each question.
• They may discuss their answers in groups.
• Ask several students to tell the class their ideas.

Answers

1 *What **will** we **have** to do to preserve the rainforest?*
2 *What things **will** you **have** to do at home this weekend?*
3 *What **will** you **be able** to do on holiday which you are not able to do now?*
4 *What things **will** computers **be able** to do in ten years' time?*

Activity Book p75 Exercise 4

7 Speak and Write

Aim: to personalise the target language by talking and writing about the next weekend.

• Students first list what they will and won't have to and be able to do.
• They work in small groups, telling each other about their weekend.
• Then they write two paragraphs.
• The writing is suitable for homework.

Activity Book p75 Exercise 5

Consolidation and Extension activities

• Students make a word map of adjectives according to their type.
• Game. Play in groups. Students take turns to add to a description of something, e.g., a favourite thing, like this: Student 1: *My favourite thing is a car.* Student 2: *My favourite thing is a red car.* Student 3: *My favourite thing is a fast red car*, etc.
• Memory chain. Students talk about what they will or won't be able or have to do in the future. This is best played in groups unless you have a small class.

Homework

• Students learn the order of adjectives. They could list adjectives they know by type.
• Students write a short description of a place or object, using as many adjectives as they can.
• Students write about a future holiday or about their career plans, using future modals.

Activity Book Unit 8 Lesson 1, p74-75
Grammar Summary p122

Target language
Future continuous
Vocabulary
Numbers The future

Warmer

- Review numbers. Students count up to 100; up to 1,000 in hundreds; down from 20 to one; up to 20 in even numbers; down from 21 to one in odd numbers, etc.
- Note that in British English a billion used to be a million million (1,000,000,000,000), but in American English a billion is a thousand million (1,000,000,000), and this tends to be the number understood as a billion nowadays in Britain as well.
- Review times in English, including the 24-hour clock, and dates.

1 Read

Aim: to present the future continuous and large numbers.

- Use the cassette to present and practise the dialogue.
- Then students answer the questions. Check orally.

Tapescript

Mark *This is really interesting. It's about the world's population. By 2035, 8½ billion people will be living on Earth. And the temperature will be 2°C higher than it is now.*

Holly *So how are we going to feed all these people?*

Mark *Well, because the weather will be hotter and wetter, plants will be growing in deserts like the Sahara. And people will be farming in places in the north which are frozen all year round now. I'm glad we came here - it's much better than I expected.*

Holly *Yes, I'm so glad I came to ACE. It's been a brilliant holiday.*

Mark *It's nearly over now, and we'll all be going home soon. What will you be doing in a week's time?*

Holly *That's easy. I'll be showing everyone my holiday photos! And what will you be doing?*

Mark *Well, I won't be going canoeing, that's for sure! No - I'll be thinking of everyone at ACE. I'm going to miss you all.*

Holly *But you said you didn't want to come here at first.*

Mark *I know. But I didn't realise I'd meet such great people. I know something else I'll be doing next week.*

Holly *What's that?*

Mark *I'll be waiting for a letter from you!*

Answers

1 *8½ billion.*
2 *Plants will be growing in deserts.*
3 *They'll be going home.*
4 *She'll be showing everyone her holiday photos.*
5 *He'll be thinking of everyone at ACE and waiting for a letter from Holly.*
6 *Because he didn't realise he'd meet such great people.*

Optional activity

- Students discuss the ideas about the future in the dialogue. Do they agree? Will everything in the future be so positive?

Activity Book p76 Exercise 1

2 Grammar File

Aim: to present the future continuous.

- Students copy and complete the chart.
- Check orally.

Answers

Future continuous

By 2035, 8½ billion people ***will be*** *living on Earth.*
Plants ***will*** *be* ***growing*** *in deserts like the Sahara.*
I ***will be*** *waiting for a letter from you.*
I ***won't be*** *going canoeing.*
What ***will*** *you* ***be*** *doing?*

Optional activities

- Students find examples of the future continuous in the dialogue.
- Books closed. Ask questions about the dialogue using the future continuous.

Activity Book p76-77 Exercises 2 and 3

3 Listen

Aim: to listen for specific information about the future.

- Students first read through the choices.
- Play the cassette. They listen and tick Mark's opinions.
- Check orally by asking e.g., *Where does Mark think people will be living in 2035?*

Tapescript

Mark: 2035 isn't very far into the future but people can't agree about what life will be like then. Some people say we'll be living in the same way as we do now while others say that our lives will be completely different. I think that there'll be lots of changes. For a start, I think that people will be living on the Moon. I don't think they'll be living in glasshouses because it will be too hot and I don't think they'll be living underground either. However I expect that some people will be living underwater. What about school? I don't think people will be studying computers or space travel because they will be so complicated then. Farming will all be done by machines. So I think people will be studying poetry because they will have lots of free time. As far as music goes, I think people will be listening to the same kind of music as they do now. I don't think music made by animals or computers will be popular. I said people will have lots of free time but I'm not sure what they will do with it. Travel will be difficult with so many people in the world and only a few people are going to paint. So I think it will be much the same as now. People will be playing sport and watching TV! I don't know about shopping. We can buy electronic pets now so they'll be out of fashion then, and we've got plastic clothes already too. So I think people will be buying space food grown on the Moon and robots! And of course I hope that people will still be going to ACE and I'm sure they'll still be learning English!

Answers

1 underwater; on the Moon
2 poetry
3 the same as now
4 playing sport; watching TV
5 space food; robots

Optional activity

- Groups. Students discuss Mark's ideas and add their own. Each group then reports back to the class.

4 Word File

Aim: to present and practise numbers.

- Students match the words and figures.
- Check orally.
- They look for numbers in the dialogue.

Answers

A million - 1,000,000
Two degrees Celsius - 2°C
Ten million - 10,000,000
Twenty thirty-five - 2035
A hundred million - 100,000,000
Nineteen sixty-seven - 1967
A billion - 1,000,000,000

In the dialogue: *2035, 2°C*

Optional activities

- Team game. Teams say numbers for the others to write correctly on the board.
- This can be played in reverse; one team writes the number on the board for the others to say.

Activity Book p77 Exercise 4

5 Speak

Aim: to perform a role-play about future plans.

- Pairs. Students work through the prompts and the days and engagements given.
- Ask some pairs to act out the role play in front of the class.

Answers

1 *I'm coming home on Sunday.*
2 *I'm sorry, I won't see you because I'll be filming on the beach.*
3 *Will I see you on Monday?*
4 *I won't see you on Monday because I'll be filming in Hollywood.*
5 *What about Tuesday?*
6 *On Tuesday I'll be rehearsing the actors.*
What about Wednesday?
On Wednesday I'll be doing a TV interview.
What about Thursday?
On Thursday I'll be recording the film music.
What about Friday?
On Friday I'll be doing a newspaper interview.
What about Saturday?
On Saturday I'll be watching baseball.
7 *OK. I've decided to stay at ACE for another week.*

Optional activity

• Students talk about what they will be doing tomorrow, next week, next month, next year, in ten years' time and in 25 years' time.

Activity Book p77 Exercises 5 and 6

6 WRITE

Aim: to write about what will be happening at a given time in the future.

• Students may first discuss the questions in groups.
• They write their answers. This is suitable for homework.
• Check their work.

Consolidation and Extension activities

• Memory chain. Groups. Students use the pattern: *In 2020, I will be earning lots of money. In 2020, I will be earning lots of money and living in a big house,* etc.
• Pairs. Students write themselves a diary for the next week, with engagements, like the one in Activity 5. It should have mornings and afternoons, and maybe times as well. There should be a few free slots. Their partner tries to arrange to see them, asking *What will you be doing on Saturday afternoon?* etc.
• Role-play. One student is a famous person and the other is a reporter. The reporter interviews the famous person about what he/she will be doing at certain times, and makes notes.

Homework

• Students write predictions for their own future.
• They write up the interview with the famous person. This can be in the first or third person.

Activity Book Unit 8 Lesson 3, p76-77
Grammar Summary p122

8 Lesson 3 *It will have been worth it*

p82

Target language

Future perfect

Vocabulary

Environment
Compound nouns

Warmer

- Review numbers from Lesson 2.
- Ask students what they know about Everest and if they know anything about the mountain's future.

1 Read

Aim: to present the future perfect.

- Students first look at the picture and talk about it.
- Ask why they think the title is *Cleaning Everest.*
- Then they listen to the text.
- Were they surprised to learn about all the litter?
- Students read the passage and answer the questions.
- Check orally.

Tapescript 

Cleaning Everest

Ten years ago Paul Deegan helped organise the first clean-up expedition to Mount Everest. We spoke to Paul about that trip and the future of the world's highest mountain.

Where did you get the idea?

I saw a TV programme about all the rubbish which climbers had left on Everest. Forty-five people each paid £1000 to join the first clean-up expedition.

What did you find?

All sorts of stuff from empty food packets to used oxygen bottles. Some expeditions had even sprayed their names on rocks with aerosol cans!

What has been done since?

There have been a number of other clean-up expeditions. But the real problem now is not the hundreds of climbers but the tens of thousands of walkers who visit Everest every year. They are the people who bring plastic water bottles and chocolate wrappers. They are the people who will soon have ruined Everest, and all the work of the clean-up expeditions will have been wasted.

What about the future?

Some people think that by 2010, visitors to Everest will have destroyed the thing they have come to see. People will have left so much litter that no one will be able to go there. Perhaps then nature will get a chance to start repairing herself.

So what is the answer?

Make visitors to Everest take responsibility for their own litter! If everyone takes a rubbish bag with them into the mountains and carries home all their litter, we will have made a fantastic start. And it's not just in the mountains - it's on the train on the way to the mountains, it's on the school bus, it's at home. When cleaning up Everest makes people think about cleaning up the world, then we won't have wasted our time.

Answers

1. *False. He saw a programme about all the rubbish that climbers had left on Everest.*
2. *True.*
3. *True.*
4. *False. By 2010, visitors to Everest will have destroyed the thing they have come to see.*
5. *True.*
6. *False. We will have made a fantastic start if everyone takes a rubbish bag with them to the mountains and carries home all their litter.*
7. *True.*

Optional activity

- Students think of other places where there is a surprising litter problem. Examples are the oceans, Antarctica and even Space!

Activity Book p78 Exercise 1

2 Grammar File

Aim: to present the future perfect

- Students copy and complete the chart.
- Check orally.

Answers

Future perfect

*People **will** have **left** so much litter.*

*We **will have** made a fantastic start.*

*We **won't have** wasted our time.*

***Will** people **have** destroyed Everest?*

Optional activity

- Students find examples of the future perfect in the text.

Activity Book p79 Exercise 2

3 SPEAK

Aim: to practise the future perfect.

- Students read through the information.
- Pairs or groups take turns to make sentences.

Answers

In three days' time...

People in Finland ***will have bought*** *a pile of ice cream packets twice as high as Mount Everest.*
A panda ***will have eaten*** *100 kilos of bamboo.*
Two people ***will have escaped*** *from British prisons.*

In three nights' time...
People around the world ***will have seen*** *more than 80 flying saucers.*
People around the world ***will have slept*** *for over seven million years.*
1.3 million Germans ***will have been*** *to the cinema.*

Optional activity

- Students write the sentences.

Activity Book p79 Exercise 3

4 LISTEN AND SPEAK

Aim: to give further practice with the future perfect and to personalise its use.

- Students read through the questionnaire.
- Play the cassette. They listen and complete the questionnaire for Aliki.
- Check orally, by asking questions about Aliki's plans.
- Students next complete the questionnaire for themselves.
- Finally they ask questions and complete it for their partner.

Tapescript

Aliki *Hi, Manuel!*
Manuel *Hi, Aliki, I've got another questionnaire for you!*
Aliki *You know I like questionnaires!*
Manuel *OK, can I ask you some questions about your life in three months' time?*
Aliki *Yes, of course. I hope I can answer them.*
Manuel *Will you have been on holiday? And if so, where?*
Aliki *Yes, we'll have been on our summer holiday. We'll have spent it with my grandparents in the country.*
Manuel *Will you have taken any exams?*
Aliki *Oh yes! I hope I'll have passed.*
Manuel *And will you have started in a new class or school?*
Aliki *Yes. I'll have started in a new class.*
Manuel *How many hours' TV will you have watched?*
Aliki *That's a difficult one. Let me think. Perhaps I watch two hours' TV a day. And there are about 90 days in three months. So that makes 180 hours. It seems an awful lot!*
Manuel *How many games of football will you have played?*
Aliki *I won't have played any. But I'll have played lots of games of volleyball on the beach.*
Manuel *How many hamburgers will you have eaten?*
Aliki *Oh, I don't know. I have one once a week, so three months is twelve weeks and that makes twelve hamburgers.*
Manuel *How many English books will you have read?*
Aliki *That's easy. I read a book a week so that makes twelve books!*
Manuel *And finally, what else will you have done?*
Aliki *I'll have written to all my friends at ACE.*
Manuel *Me too!*

Answers

1 *Yes. With her grandparents in the country.*
2 *Yes.*
3 *Yes. A new class.*
4 *180 hours.*
5 *None.*
6 *Twelve.*
7 *Twelve.*
8 *She will have written to all her friends at ACE.*

Optional activities

- Students report to the class about their own and their partner's plans, e.g., *In three months' time, I will have read two English books but my partner will have read four.*
- Students write sentences about themselves and their partner.

5 WORD FILE

Aim: to learn more compound nouns.

- Students read and match the words. Sometimes more than one combination is possible.
- Check orally.
- Then they look for compound nouns in the lesson.

Answers

aerosol can; ice cream; chocolate wrapper; rubbish bag; flying saucer; school bus; food packet; water bottle; global warming

All these compound nouns can be found in the lesson.

Optional activity

• Students use the compound nouns in sentences.

Activity Book p79 Exercises 4 and 5

6 WRITE

Aim: to personalise the target language in a piece of continuous writing.

• Students may use the questionnaire from Activity 4.
• They may also brainstorm other ideas.
• The task is suitable for homework.

Consolidation and Extension activities

• Team game. One team says a time or date in the future. The others have to say what they will or won't have done by then.
• Students play Compound Noun Tennis. They should first list compound nouns so that they know there is a possible compound noun to be made.
• Students play Hangman with compound nouns.

Homework

• Students make lists of compound nouns with the same word, e.g., *bag* preceded by *shopping/school/paper/plastic/overnight/hand,* or *school* followed by *bus/bag/gate/work/boy/girl/day,* etc.
• Students ask their family or friends to make predictions about what they will have done by a specified time in the future. They make notes for a presentation in class, or write a report.
• If possible students research plans for their local area and write about them, e.g., *By 2020, two new schools will have been built. The hospital will have been extended and modernised. Four new hotels will have been built,* etc.
• If they are interested they could research the environment and its problems, e.g., *If we are not careful ... hectares of fertile land will have become desert. ... species of plants and ... species of insects will have become extinct,* etc. They write this as a report, with illustrations and maps if possible. This could be done by pairs or groups.

Activity Book Unit 8 Lesson 3, p78-79
Grammar Summary p122

Lesson 4 *Predicting the future*

Vocabulary

Technology, computers and robots
Linking words: *however* and *-and*
Suffixes: *-ation* and *-ment*

Warmer

- Students have a short time to think of things that were not in use 50 – 100 years ago, but are now often or occasionally used. They speculate what the situation will be at the beginning of the 22nd century or in 50 years' time. (Think of cars, planes, computers, medicines, etc.)

READING

1 Aim: to read a text to identify topics.
- Students read the text, looking for the topics.
- They note the dates.
- Check orally.

Answers

The start - 1949
Progress - 1999
Things begin to change - 2009
Computers able to do most things - 2019
Computers better than humans - 2029
A new life - 2049
Which is which? - 2099

Activity Book p80 Exercise 1

2 Aim: to focus on linking words *however, and.*
- Students read the text again and underline *however.*
- They complete the passage.
- Check orally.

Answers

1 and *2 However* *3 and*
4 However *5 However* *6 and*

LISTENING

3 Aim: to listen to find out who the speaker is in a conversation about the future.
- Students first read through the statements.
- Play the cassette. They listen and note who says what.

Tapescript

Holly *I think life in the future will be such fun. We'll all be living in palaces with robots who'll do all the work.*

Mark *I'm sure you'll be doing that in California. However, in other parts of the world things won't be so easy. We'll have used up most of the world's resources and lots of people will have to live in poverty.*

Holly *What makes you say that? And anyway we've got lots of poor people in the USA now.*

Mark *That's right and the numbers of poor people in rich countries are growing.*

Holly *So what you're saying is that the poor are getting poorer and the rich are getting richer.*

Mark *That's exactly what I'm saying. For example, in 1976, Switzerland was 52 times richer than Mozambique. Now it is 508 times richer!*

Holly *Where do you get these facts from? I didn't realise you knew so much! That's terrible for poor people, though.*

Mark *There is some good news. In the past fifty years, poverty has fallen more than in the past 500 years. However, one in four of the world's people still lives in severe poverty.*

Holly *More numbers! And big numbers. We'll have to do a lot to change that.*

Mark *Of course we'll be able to if we want to. Did you know that the world's richest 225 people together have over $1 million million? Only 4% of that money, $40 billion, would be enough to give all the people in the world adequate education, healthcare, food and water.*

Holly *I think you're making all these numbers up - you couldn't possibly remember them all.*

Mark *I'm not making anything up. And I do think there's hope for the future for all people. Not just Californians!*

Holly *Oh Mark, don't get angry. I just liked the idea of having my own robot, that's all.*

Answers

Holly; Mark; Mark; Mark; Holly; Holly

Speaking

4 Aim: to use ideas from the book and one's own ideas to discuss the future.
- Students reread the texts and make notes of their own ideas.
- They discuss the ideas in groups.
- Each group then tries to summarise the discussion to report back to the class.

Writing

5 Aim: to introduce mind maps for planning writing.
- You could start with another idea, e.g., 'Life in my country today'. Students think of topics to focus on, e.g., education, health care, entertainment, sports, etc.
- Then brainstorm ideas on these topics on the board.
- Talk students through the mind map in the book, if necessary.
- Students add their own ideas, either as a whole-class activity, or alone.
- Choice of ideas to write on may be made by individuals or discussed by the class or groups.
- They write their paragraphs. This is suitable for homework.

Activity Book p80 Exercise 2

Word building

6 Aim: to focus on noun suffixes *-ation* and *-ment.*
- Students add the appropriate suffix to each verb. (Note that one verb just adds *-ion*. Note also the *-e* is dropped in *argument*.)
- Check orally.
- You may point out that verbs ending in *-ate* often take the suffix *-ation*.

Answers

argument calculation communication education improvement information management population

Optional activities

- Students look for any words with these suffixes in the lesson.
- They use the words in sentences.

Activity Book p81 exercise 3

Study skills

7 Aim: to focus on ways of revising.
- Although many people leave their revision to the last moment, it is useful to review material regularly. This ensures much more thorough, efficient and lasting learning.

Activity Book p81 Exercises 4 and 5

Consolidation and Extension activities

- Suffix Tennis. Students first make a list of nouns ending in the suffixes before they start playing.
- Dates. Pairs or teams. One student says a date in the future. The other makes a statement about what will be happening or will have happened by then.
- Save the world. Pairs or teams. Student 1 says e.g., *By 2050 the polar ice cap will have melted.* Student 2 says what will have to be done, e.g., *Well, we'll have to stop using so many fossil fuels.* The statements could be positive, e.g., *By 2050 we'll be using personal robots. - So, we'll be able to use our free time to save the planet!*

Homework

- Students make a future word map, including technology and computers.
- Students start their revision programme!
- Students ask their parents or grandparents what they think life in the future will be like. They may use the questions in Activity 5. They make notes which they write up as a report or present in the next lesson.

Pairwork

Pairwork Activity p109 and 117
Aim: to practise describing and spelling.
- This activity is useful practice for finding out unknown words in a foreign language.
- This only works well if students describe their items clearly, so they should spend time thinking about this.
- Students A first describe their items in turn.
- Then they change roles.
- Monitor and give help as necessary. Encourage the use of adjectives.

Activity Book Unit 8 Lesson 4, p80-81
Grammar Summary p122

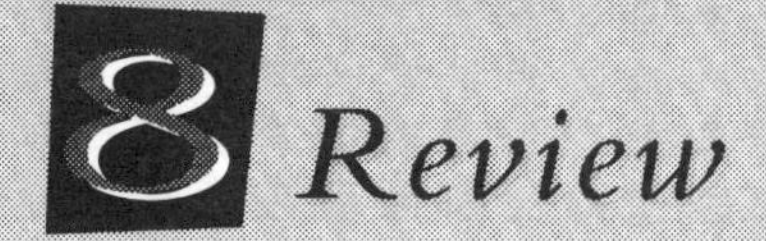 Review

1 Read and complete

Answers

1 because	*2 have*	*3 be able*	*4 using*
5 will	*6 systems*	*7 recognise*	*8 recognition*
9 as	*10 so*	*11 they*	

Optional activity

- Students discuss the idea of eye-recognition.

2 Complete

Answers

1 be able	*2 be able*	*3 be able*	*4 be able*	*5 be able*
6 have	*7 be able*	*8 have*	*9 be able*	*10 have*

3 Complete

Answers

1 will be dancing	*2 will be playing*	*3 will be eating*
4 will be saying	*5 will be wearing*	*6 will be reading*
7 will be singing		

4 Make sentences

- This may be done orally first.
- Students then write the sentences.

Answers

In one year's time, the average person will have...
...slept for 120 days.
...watched 750 hours of TV.
...drunk 1800 litres of water.
...walked 750 kilometres.
...read 250 newspapers.
...made 1000 phone calls.

5 Order

- Students first arrange the adjectives under the correct headings.
- This can be checked on the board.
- Then they order the phrases correctly.

Answers

1 *a boring old grey car*
2 *a small brown chair*
3 *a pretty new pink dress*
4 *an amazing modern painting*
5 *a tall slim model*
6 *a fabulous new restaurant*
7 *an ugly old red box*
8 *an enormous fat cat*

Optional activities

- Students make the phrases into complete sentences.
- They add at least one more adjective to each phrase, in the correct order.

6 Test each other

- This can take the form of Participle Tennis.

SONG

- Students read the gapped song.
- They guess what the words might be.
- Play the cassette. Students listen and check.
- Check orally.

Tapescript and answers 

Call it out around the ***world***
Are you ready for a brand new beat?
Summer's here and the ***time*** *is right*
For dancing in the street

They're dancing in Chicago
Down in New Orleans
In New York City

All we ***need*** *is music, sweet music*
There'll be music everywhere
There'll be swinging and swaying
And ***records*** *playing.*
Dancing in the street
It doesn't matter what you ***wear***
Just as long as you are there
So, come on
Every guy grab a ***girl****,*
everywhere around the world
There'll be dancing
They're dancing in the street

This is an ***invitation*** *across the nation*
A chance for folks to meet
There'll be ***laughing****, singing and music swinging*
Dancing in the street

Philadelphia PA
Baltimore and DC now
Can't forget the motor city

Way down in LA, everyday
They're dancing in the street

Optional activities

- Listen to the song again. Students sing along.
- Ask students if they know where the cities are in America. Look on a map if possible. Explain that the 'motor city' is Detroit because they make so many cars there.
- Ask students if they have ever danced in the street. When and why would there be dancing outside? a wedding? a party? a festival?
- Students find all the happy words in the song, e.g., dancing, swinging, swaying, summer, laughing, singing, music, sweet.
- Students find the rhymes, beat/street, swaying/playing, wear/there, invitation/nation, meet/street, LA/everyday, line/time, blue/you.

Activity Book Unit 8 Review p82-83

Posters p114

- In this unit, students make a poster about life in the future.
- Remind students to bring in their writing on the future.
- The groups discuss the time they wish to choose. Encourage groups to choose different dates. (They can choose dates other than those in the book, e.g., in 25 years, etc.)
- Each group brainstorms predictions and then chooses seven of them.
- They decide how to illustrate the predictions, using their imagination as well as sources such as magazines and the Internet.
- They write their predictions neatly and check them carefully.
- They stick their work on a large sheet of paper with the illustrations.
- Display the posters or let students pass their work round for other groups to see.

Lesson 1 *I'll have them mended*

p88

Target language
have something done
Vocabulary
Household tasks
make or *do*

Warmer

- Students look at the picture and decide what is happening.
- Ask what can go wrong on an assault course.
- Ask what has happened to Aliki.

1 READ

Aim: to present *have something done.*
- Students read and listen to the dialogue.
- Then they answer the questions.
- Check orally.

Tapescript

Alison *Ready everyone! On your marks, get set, go!*
Alison Holly/Paolo *Come on, Aliki!!! You're ahead!!*
Tara/Mark Manuel *Go for it, Lucy! You can do it!*
Aliki *Oh no!*
Tara *Are you all right, Aliki?*
Aliki *Oh! I'm soaking! That water's horrible!*
Holly *You do look dirty!*
Aliki *It's not funny!*
Paolo *What's that smell?*
Aliki *What do you mean? Oh, it's me! Don't be horrible. And look at my trousers. I had them washed yesterday and now they're filthy again. And I'll need to have my hair done before the party.*
Tara *Are these your sunglasses? I'm afraid they're broken.*
Aliki *Oh no! Where can I have them mended?*
Tara *I'll have them mended for you.*
Aliki *Oh, thank you. But I feel awful! What a way to end the holiday!*
Tara *Never mind, Aliki. Give me your clothes after you've changed and I'll have them cleaned. Now let me get you a nice hot cup of tea. Would you like that?*
Aliki *Yes please, and a nice hot shower! I suppose it's quite funny really, isn't it?*

Answers

1 *She is going to ask someone to do it for her.*
2 *Her trousers.*
3 *Her sunglasses.*
4 *Aliki's clothes.*
5 *A nice hot cup of tea.*
6 *The situation.*

Optional activity

- Books closed. Students say what happened. Why is Aliki unhappy?

2 GRAMMAR FILE

Aim: to present *have something done.*
- Students copy and complete the chart.
- Check orally.

Answers

have something done
*I **had** my trousers washed yesterday.*
*Where can I **have** my sunglasses **mended**?*
*Tara will **have** them **cleaned** for her.*

Optional activities

- Students find examples of the structure in the dialogue.
- Ask what things they *have done* and what things they do themselves.

3 SPEAK

Aim: to practise *have something done.*
- Students look at the two pictures and compare them.
- They talk about what Frankie has had done.

Answers

He's had his hair dyed.
He's had his ear pierced.
He's had his beard shaved.
He's had his nose straightened.
He's had his moustache trimmed.

Optional activity

• Students talk about things they, people they know or famous people, have had done to themselves. Does it make them look better?

Activity Book p84 Exercise 1

4 Write

Aim: to give written practice of *have something done*.
• Students may go through this orally first.
• Then they write about Holly.
• Check orally.

Answers

She doesn't polish her shoes. She has them polished.
She doesn't make her bed. She has it made.
She doesn't tidy her room. She has it tidied.
She doesn't wash her hair. She has it washed.
She doesn't do her homework. She has it done.

Optional activity

• Ask students their opinion of Holly. Do they think she really has someone else do her homework for her? Would they like to have so much done for them?

Activity Book p84 Exercise 2

5 Speak

Aim: to personalise the use of *have something done*.
• Students match the nouns and verbs.
• Pairs. They ask questions, e.g., *When did you last have your eyes tested? In June/Four months ago.*

Answers

have your eyes tested
have your hair cut
have some clothes dry-cleaned
have your shoes mended
have your bedroom painted
have your temperature taken
have your height and weight measured

Optional activities

• Pairs join together and compare answers. Each group may then report back to the class, e.g., *I had my eyes tested a month ago, but the others have never had their eyes tested.*

Activity Book p85 Exercise 3

6 Word File

Aim: to practise phrases with *make* and *do*.
• Students complete the phrases.
• Then they look for examples in the lesson.
• Check orally.

Answers

1 do *2 make* *3 make* *4 do* *5 do*
6 make *7 do* *8 make* *9 do* *10 make*
In the lesson: *do hair/homework; make the bed*

Optional activities

• Students use the phrases in sentences.

Activity Book p85 Exercises 4, 5 and 6

7 Write

Aim: to personalise the target language in writing.
• Students may first discuss the ideas in groups, or brainstorm them in class.
• They write the paragraphs for homework.
• Students read each other's work and compare notes.

Consolidation and Extension activities

• Give students two minutes to write as many (short) sentences as they can with *make* (or *do*).
• Pairs. Students write a list of things they need to do or have done, and tick the ones that have been done. They give the same list, but unticked, to their partner, who has to find out what has been done by asking e.g., *Have you done the shopping yet? Have you had your coat dry-cleaned yet?* etc.
• Students imagine they are very rich indeed and say what they would like to have done for them.

Homework

• Students write phrases with *make* and with *do* on opposite pages of their vocabulary notebook. They learn them. (*Do* often has the sense of completing something, and *make* is often creative.)
• Students ask their parents about things they do themselves or have done. They make notes which they write up as a short report.
• Students either draw two 'before and after' pictures of someone, or find suitable pictures in a fashion or other magazine. They write a description of what the person has had done. They may end with a comment on the changes.

Activity Book Unit 9 Lesson 1 p84-85
Grammar Summary p123

Lesson 2 *What would you have done?* p90

Target language
Third conditional
Vocabulary
Personality

Warmer

- Ask students to look at the film strip and say what's happening in the pictures.
- Ask students about the characters in the ACE story. What are their personalities like? Who do we know best? Who do they like or not like?
- Ask students what they think were the most interesting or exciting stories they have read in *Shine* 3.

1 Read and Speak

Aim: to complete a questionnaire, using the third conditional.
- Students read and complete the questionnaire.
- Then they work in groups and discuss their answers.
- They check their answers.
- Have a final class discussion about the questionnaire and the answers.

Activity Book p86 Exercise 1

2 Grammar File

Aim: to present the third conditional.
- Students copy and complete the chart.
- Check orally or by completing the chart on the board.

Answers

Third conditional

*If I **had been** Aliki, I **would have** told the police where the wreck was.*

*If I **had seen** the whale, I **would have** swum to the beach immediately.*

*What **would** you **have** done if you **had seen** the ghost?*

Optional activities

- Students go back over the questionnaire and note the use of the third conditional. In each case, the third conditional is used because the reader was not that person, so the condition is impossible.
- Students think of something else they would or would not have done for the situations in the questionnaire.

Activity Book p87 Exercise 2

3 Sound File

Aim: to recognise and practise unstressed words in third conditionals.
- Play the cassette. Students listen and repeat.
- They listen a second time and underline the stressed words.

Tapescript and answers 

If <u>I</u> had been Aliki, <u>I</u> would have told the police where the <u>wreck</u> was.

If <u>I</u> had met the whale, <u>I</u> would have swum to the beach <u>immediately</u>.

What would <u>you</u> have done if <u>you</u> had seen the ghost?

4 Read and Listen

Aim: to practise the third conditional and to listen for specific information.
- Students read and complete the dialogue.
- Play the cassette. They listen and check.
- Then students find the three questions and say what they would or would not have done.

Tapescript and answers 

Holly *It's a shame that Sam wasn't here for the Team Challenge. He **would have** enjoyed it if he **had been** here.*

Mark *I don't really care. His parents were pleased to see him when they came yesterday. Anyway, what's the point of talking about what would have happened?*

Holly *It's fun. For example, what **would** you **have** done if Celeste **had** asked you to model with her?*

Mark *Don't be silly. I **would have** said no, of course.*

Holly *OK. Now imagine you were hiding at ACE. What **would** you **have done** to get food if you**'d been** hungry?*

Mark *That's easy. I **would have** gone fishing!*

Holly *Oh, yes! Now let's imagine you were parachuting over Stonehenge. What **would** you **have done** if your parachute **hadn't** opened?*

Mark *I would have...*
Holly *What?*
Mark *I would have... I don't know what I* ***would have done****.*
Holly *You* ***would have*** *opened your emergency parachute, silly!*

Answers

1 *would have*	2 *had been*
3 *would you have*	4 *had*
5 *would have*	6 *would you have done*
7 *you'd been*	8 *would have*
9 *would you have done; hadn't*	10 *would have*
11 *would have*	

Activity Book p87 Exercise 3

5 WRITE

Aim: to personalise the use of the third conditional.
• Students first discuss in groups what they would have done if they had been at ACE. They may refer back to see what activities were on offer.
• Then they plan their paragraphs.
• The writing can be done for homework. Ask them to check it carefully themselves before giving it to you.

Activity Book p87 Exercises 4 and 5

Consolidation and Extension activities.

• Groups. Students write three sentences using third conditional. Then they take turns to read half the sentence. They can read either the *if* clause or the main clause. The others complete the sentence. Then they read their new sentences and see how many in the group said the same thing.
• Guessing game. Students describe a well-known personality. The others have to guess who it is.
• Role-play. Do this in groups or pairs. One student is a character from the past. The others talk to him/her about events of that time and say what they would/wouldn't have done then. Then the character from history can say what he/she would/wouldn't have done with hindsight.

Homework

• Students ask older members of their family to think of an incident that marked a turning point in their lives, e.g., meeting someone, going somewhere. What would(n't) have happened if things had been different? They write a short report and tell the class in the next lesson, e.g., *If my mother hadn't gone to the party, she wouldn't have met my father.*
• Remind students to review their work regularly.

Activity Book Unit 9 Lesson 2 p86-87
Grammar Summary p123

9 Lesson 3 *He can't have done!*

p92

Target language
must/can't have for deduction
could/may/might have for speculation

Vocabulary
Presents and souvenirs
Money

Warmer

- Talk about presents. What would students' best present be if money was not a problem?

1 Read and Listen

Aim: to speculate about someone, and to listen for specific information.

- Use the cassette to present the first part of the dialogue.
- Students read and answer the questions. Check orally.
- Then students speculate about where Mark and Holly are.
- Finally play the second part of the story for them to check.

Tapescript 

Part 1

Alison	*OK, everyone, it's nine o'clock and so ... it's time for the Team Challenge Quiz!*
Tara	*Hang on, Alison - Mark isn't here.*
Holly	*What's happened to him?*
Aliki	*He could have gone for a walk!*
Paolo	*He may have gone for a swim in the sea.*
Alison	*He can't have done! It's too cold!*
Manuel	*He might have decided to go to bed.*
Tara	*No, he can't have done - it's far too early! Anyway, he knew it was nearly time for the quiz.*
Rick	*Hey, where's Holly? She's just disappeared!*
Lucy	*She must have run off to look for Mark. Oh, honestly, those two!*

Part 2

Holly	*Mark - what are you doing?*
Mark	*I'm celebrating! I can swim! Why don't you join me?*
Holly	*You must be joking! It's freezing ... Aagh, Mark!*
Mark	*Oh, don't be a spoilsport, Holly. Come for a swim!*
Holly	*Mark, you're crazy. And everyone's waiting for you - please! Come out before you drown!*
Mark	*Only if you promise to write to me.*
Holly	*OK, OK. Now, please, come out of the water!*
Mark	*All right, Holly! Anything you say!*

Answers

1. *He could have gone for a walk. She isn't sure - we know this from* ***could have****.*
2. *He may have gone for a swim in the sea. He isn't sure - we know this from* ***may have****.*
3. *Mark can't have gone for a swim.*
4. *Mark can't have decided to go to bed.*
5. *She thinks Holly must have gone to look for Mark.*
6. *C*

Optional activity

- Game. Hide something in the classroom. Ask the students to close their eyes, or you will have to hide some things at the beginning of the lesson or while they are working and don't notice. They could be things that are needed, such as the board cleaner, or your book, or anything else. Students then speculate where you could have put the things. They should use negatives as well, e.g., *He/She can't have put it on the table, or we would see it.*

Activity Book p88 Exercise 1

2 Grammar File

Aim: to present *must/can't have* for deduction and *could/may/might have* for speculation.

- Students copy and complete the chart.
- Check orally.

Answers

Deductions about the past: must/can't have + past participle

She must have run off to look for Mark.

He can't ***have gone*** *for a swim!*

Speculation about the past:

could/may/might have + past participle

He could have gone for a walk.

He may ***have gone*** *for a swim!*

He might ***have decided*** *to go to bed.*

Optional activities

- Students find examples of deduction and speculation about the past in the dialogue.
- They make other speculations about where Mark could have gone, and agree or disagree. This could be done in pairs or groups.

Activity Book p88 Exercise 2

3 Speak and Write

Aim: to practise deduction and speculation about the past.

- Go through one line of the chart with the whole class.
- Then students continue in pairs or groups.
- Monitor, encouraging them to give reasons, e.g., *It's too early/cold. He/She doesn't like running,* etc.
- They write sentences.
- Check orally.

Answers

Paolo can't have gone to bed. He might have gone for a swim or a walk. He must have gone for a run.

Lucy can't have gone for a swim or for a run. She could have gone to bed. She must have gone for a walk.

Mark can't have gone for a run. He might have gone to bed or for a walk. He must have gone for a swim.

Aliki can't have gone for a walk. She could have gone for a swim or a run. She must have gone to bed.

Optional activity

- Students speculate how Alison must have felt when she found the others missing.

Activity Book p88 Exercise 3

4 Read and Speak

Aim: to practise *must have* and *can't have.*

- Go through the items bought as presents and check students understand the new vocabulary. Point out that *marmalade* is jam made from citrus fruit.
- Students should first read the clues and discuss who they think bought what, and why.
- Then they work together in pairs or groups to complete the chart.
- Check their answers orally. Apart from asking who bought what, you can also ask e.g., *Who didn't buy something to eat? Who bought the least expensive present,* etc.

Answers

Aliki - mug - £3.75

Holly - honey - £2.65

Lucy - scarf - £4.99

Manuel - jigsaw - £4.50

Mark - gloves - £3.50

Paolo - marmalade - £1.99

Optional activity

Students write sentences about what each person bought, e.g., *Lucy bought the .... This was the most expensive present.*

Activity Book p89 Exercise 5

5 Read and Speak

Aim: to deduce the answers to a quiz.

- Students read the quiz. They make guesses at the answers.
- Then they discuss their ideas with their group or partner.
- They come to a decision.
- Go through the answers with the class.

Answers

1c 2b 3a, b 4a 5b 6b 7a 8b 9b 10c

Activity Book p89 Exercise 4

6 Sound File

Aim: to focus on different spellings with the same sounds.

- Students match the words with their rhymes.
- Play the cassette. They listen and check.
- Check orally.

Tapescript and answers 

climb - time

done - run

gone - on

honey - funny

quiz - his

star - far

war - for

wear - where

year - here

Optional activity

- Play the cassette again, pausing for students to repeat the words.

7 Write and Speak

Aim: to prepare and take part in a quiz.

- Students may do this in pairs or groups.
- They should focus on the events at ACE though they could also include the story of Philip and the hippo, or of Helena.
- The quiz may be multiple choice, like the one in Activity 5, or just questions.
- Allow time for all the quizzes to be done.

Activity Book p89 Exercise 5

Consolidation and Extension activities

- Spelling quiz. This can take any form, e.g., Hangman, gapped words, *I'm thinking of a word that begins with ...*, or *My word rhymes with ...*
- Teams or pairs. Student 1 says a word. Student 2 says a word that rhymes with it. They get 2 points if the word has a different spelling from the first, e.g., one/won.

Homework

- Students learn the spelling of any new words from the lesson, especially those with different sound/spelling combinations.
- Students write a general knowledge quiz. It does not have to be multiple choice, but it could, with different dates, etc. given. There are plenty of facts in Shine 3 to base the quiz on. Or they could include well-known local or national facts.

Activity Book Unit 9 Lesson 3 p88-89
Grammar summary p123

Lesson 4 *Mystery*

> **Vocabulary**
> Crime and detection
> Suffixes

Warmer

- Students speculate on what the people at ACE will do next. Will they all keep in touch with each other? What will the next group of holiday-makers there be like? etc.

Reading

1 Aim: to read a mystery and speculate about what happened.

- Use the cassette to introduce the newspaper article.
- Students read the newspaper article and the notes on the suspects.
- They make their first guesses at what happened and discuss their ideas in groups.

Tapescript

ROCK SINGER FOUND DEAD

The famous musician, Rocky Storm, has died at his home in the village of West Witching, near Bristol. He was found in the garage near his silver Rolls Royce by his driver, Jim Wheeler, at 8.30 this morning. Police believe that Storm must have died between 10.30 and 11.30 pm last night, and they are treating the death as suspicious. Storm died as a result of a blow to the head from a blunt instrument. Several people were staying at the musician's home last night and they are being questioned by the police.

2 Aim: to continue to try to solve the mystery, using new information.

- Students will probably find it helpful to have a sheet of paper for each suspect and write the known facts by each. They can now add the detective's notes.
- Have the new facts caused them to change their minds?
- Then they discuss their ideas in groups again.
- They should particularly note any contradictions in the stories, and try to decide who might be lying, and why.

Listening

3 Aim: to speculate about what someone might say and to confirm by listening; to listen for specific information.

- Students work in pairs to speculate about what the detective might ask. They should focus on the contradictions in the stories.
- Play the cassette. They note which of their ideas were correct.
- Play it again, pausing after each section for them to note down any new information. (The important information is highlighted).
- Students again discuss who they now think killed Rocky.

Tapescript

Detective *Now, Mrs Storm, you said you went to bed at about ten o'clock.*

Stella *Yes, I was very tired.*

Detective *I understand that. But* ***Rufus Miles said you didn't go to bed immediately.*** *You went to the kitchen.*

Stella *Er, well, yes, I was feeling quite upset. So* ***we talked for a bit.***

Detective *Why didn't you tell me this before?*

Stella *Because Rufus is in love with me, and I didn't want you to think ...*

Detective *You didn't want me to think that he killed Rocky.*

Stella *No, that's right.*

Detective *Jenny Clarke, you said you went to watch a James Bond movie on TV at about 10.15 last night.*

Jenny *Yes, that's correct.*

Detective *And when did you go to bed?*

Jenny *After the movie finished - soon after, about midnight.*

Detective *But you weren't in the TV room at 11.30, when Colin Banks came back.*

Jenny *Oh, I remember, there was a phone call ...*

Detective *A phone call? Who was it?*

Jenny *Oh - it was a wrong number.*

Detective *A wrong number?*

Jenny *Yes. Listen,* ***I can tell you who killed Rocky - it was Jim Wheeler. I bet you'll find his fingerprints on the hammer.***

Detective *Rufus Miles, where were you between 11pm and 11.30?*

Rufus *I was walking in the garden.*

Detective *At that time? Why?*

Rufus *Because I couldn't sleep.*

Detective *Did anyone see you?*

Rufus *Well, **yes, I saw Colin Banks**. He was coming from the village.*

Detective *And what time was that?*

Rufus *I don't know - soon after 11 o'clock.*

Detective *And what did you talk about?*

Rufus *Oh, this and that - you know.*

Detective *Colin Banks, I understand you left the café at about 10.55.*

Colin *Yes, I did.*

Detective *But the cafe is only five minutes' walk from the Storms' house. What were you doing between 11 and 11.30 last night?*

Colin *If you really want to know, **I was talking to Rufus Miles in the garden.***

Detective *What were you talking about?*

Colin *I told Rufus that I was fed up with working for Rocky, because I wasn't earning enough money. And that I was going to leave.*

Detective *Why didn't you tell me this before?*

Colin *Why do you think? You might have thought that I was Rocky's killer.*

Detective *Right, Jim Wheeler, **you said you were playing pool at the café last night**.*

Jim *Yes, it was a good evening.*

Detective *Did you win?*

Jim *Yes, I did actually.*

Detective *Well, that's very clever of you. Because **they haven't got a pool table at the café any more**. So what were you really doing last night?*

Jim *Aaah.*

4 Aim: to listen for confirmation of guesses.

- Play the last part of the story. Students listen and confirm their guesses.
- Have a final discussion. How many students guessed correctly?

Tapescript

Detective *Jim Wheeler, I am arresting you because we found your fingerprints*

Jenny *I told you he was the murderer!*

Jim *But I didn't kill Rocky!*

Detective *I know that - you had other things to do. We found your fingerprints in a house in the village which was burgled last night.*

Jim *Oh.*

Stella *But then who killed my husband? Rufus, was it you?*

Rufus *Stella, how can you ask that?*

Stella *But it could have been you - you hated Rocky!*

Detective *You needn't worry, Mrs Storm. Rufus has an alibi - from you and Colin Banks.*

Colin *So who did kill Rocky?*

Detective *Jenny Clarke, why don't you tell us what really happened?*

Jenny *Why are you asking me?*

Detective *Because you knew that Rocky was killed with a hammer.*

Jenny *So?*

Detective *No one else knew that, apart from Jim Wheeler. And he didn't kill Rocky.*

Jenny *Oh. I see.*

Stella *Jenny, it can't have been you!*

Jenny *Stella, I'm sorry. You see, Rocky got very angry with me because I said I was going to print the truth about him and Stella. So I said I was leaving, and I went to the garage - to my car. But Rocky followed me, and he was violent, he attacked me - so I picked up the first thing I saw.*

Detective *You picked up the hammer.*

Jenny *Yes, if he hadn't attacked me, I wouldn't have hit him. I really didn't mean to kill him ...*

Detective *No, I don't suppose you did.*

SPEAKING

5 Aim: to practise the language of speculation and deduction in a role-play.

- Students refer to their notes on the story.
- They act out the conversations.
- Ask several groups to act for the class.

WRITING

6 Aim: to learn how to plan and organise a piece of writing.

- Go through the points and discuss them.
- You could put a sample plan on the board. Students may choose a title.
- Then they plan their description.
- Check the plans.
- Students write their descriptions. This is suitable for homework.
- Make sure they check their work carefully before handing it in. They should check against their plan to see that they have included all their key points. They may also exchange work with a partner and check each other's work for accuracy.
- They hand their work to you for checking.

WORD BUILDING

7 Aim: to use different suffixes changing nouns to adjectives and verbs to nouns.

- Students copy and complete the chart.
- Then they try to find the words in Unit 9.
- Check orally.

Answers

Noun	*Adjective*	*Verb*	*Noun*
expense	*expensive*	*appear*	*appearance*
fame	*famous*	*burgle*	*burglary*
hope	*hopeless*	*celebrate*	*celebration*
horror	*horrible*	*detect*	*detective*
sense	*sensitive*	*differ*	*difference*
suspicion	*suspicious*	*inform*	*information*

STUDY SKILLS

8 Aim: to help students continue their learning outside the classroom.

- Go through the ideas with the class. Discuss which might be possible for them.
- Encourage them to continue with their English during the holidays.

Consolidation and Extension activities

- Prefix and suffix game. Teams prepare lists of words with different prefixes and suffixes. They give each other the root and make a new word.
- Prefix and suffix quiz. Students write as many words as they can each with a different prefix or suffix. Then they use them in sentences.
- Alibi. In groups of five to seven. A crime has been committed. Three or four students are the suspects. Together they prepare their story, saying where they were at the relevant times. There are one or two detectives. The detectives question the suspects, alone, so that they do not know exactly what the others have said. The aim is to find contradictions in their story and discover who committed the crime.

Homework

- Students review the language area they have found most difficult.
- Students make a study plan for the holidays.
- Students choose a topic or story they have enjoyed in *Shine* 3 and write about it or write a new story in that style.
- Students make notes on what they have enjoyed most and least about *Shine* 3 and present it to the class, or have a class discussion.

Pairwork

Pairwork Activity p109 and 117

Aim: to help each other complete a crossword, by making clues.

- Student work out clues.
- Then students take turns to ask each other for their words. Make sure they don't say the word.
- Finally they check each other's crosswords.

Possible clues

A *What's 2 down?*
B *It's a small animal. Cats don't like them.*

A *What's 3 down?*
B *It's a verb. It means to come back.*

A *What's 4 down?*
B *It's in your head. You think with it.*

A *What's 6 down?*
B *It's a verb. It means to put a dead body in the earth.*

A *What's 9 down?*
B *It's a beautiful man or woman who shows clothes on a catwalk.*

A *What's 11 down?*
B *It's money but it's not made of paper.*

A *What's 12 across?*
B *It's a verb. It means to make something better when it is broken, like shoes.*

A *What's 15 across?*
B *It's what you get in football when you score.*

B *What's 7 across?*
A *It means badly-behaved.*

B *What's 8 across?*
A *It's something bad that has happened and everyone must be very quick and careful to help.*

B *What's 10 down?*
A *It's the world we live in. It's under our feet.*

B *What's 12 down?*
A *You drink coffee and tea from it.*

B *What's 13 across?*
A *It's an old broken building.*

B *What's 14 across?*
A *It's the opposite of beginning.*

B *What's 16 across?*
A *It's a board game you play with kings and queens.*

Optional activity

- Students work in pairs to make up a simple crossword. They should complete the grid first, then write the clues. Then they give their crossword to another pair to solve.

Activity Book Unit 9 Lesson 4 p90-91
Grammar Summary p123

1 Read and complete

Answers

1B 2C 3B 4A 5A 6B 7C 8A
9C 10C 11B 12A 13B 14A 15C 16A
17C 18B 19C 20B

2 Ask and answer

- Pairs. Students ask and answer the questions.
- Then they write sentences.
- Check orally.

Answers

1 *Did she have her hair cut?*
Yes, she did. She had her hair cut.

2 *Did she have her car washed?*
No, she didn't. She didn't have her car washed.

3 *Did she have her computer repaired?*
Yes, she did. She had her computer repaired.

4 *Did she have her shoes mended?*
Yes, she did. She had her shoes mended.

5 *Did she have her eyes tested?*
No, she didn't. She didn't have her eyes tested.

6 *Did she have her room cleaned?*
No, she didn't. She didn't have her room cleaned.

3 Write

Answers

1 *I'd have made lots of friends.*

2 *I wouldn't have felt lonely.*

3 *I wouldn't have been bored.*

4 *I'd have enjoyed the holiday.*

5 *I'd have spoken lots of English.*

Optional activity

- Students imagine what would have happened if they had stayed in a haunted house, or if they had been Sam, or if they had met Celeste.

4 What would(n't) have happened?

- Students may first do this orally.
- Then they write the sentences.

Answers

1 *Aliki wouldn't have bought the mug if she hadn't liked it.*

2 *Mark wouldn't have learnt to swim if Tara hadn't given him lessons.*

3 *Rick wouldn't have swum with the whale if he had been frightened.*

4 *Sam wouldn't have run away if he had wanted to go home.*

5 *Rick and Lucy would have stopped Sam falling if they had caught him.*

5 Answer the questions

- This can be done orally in pairs.

Answers

1 *She must have travelled by plane.*
She can't have travelled by train.

2 *She must have come by car.*
She can't have come by bike.

3 *They must have been interested.*
They can't have been bored.

4 *He must have felt frightened.*
He can't have felt excited.

5 *They must have been worried.*
They can't have been relieved.

6 Speculate

- Students first speculate in pairs.
- Then they write the sentences.

Answers

1 *They could have forgotten the time.*
Yes, they might have forgotten the time.

2 *They could have fallen asleep.*
Yes, they might have fallen asleep.

3 *They could have had an accident.*
Yes, they might have had an accident.

4 *They could have gone to the wrong cinema.*
Yes, they might have gone to the wrong cinema.

5 *They could have missed the bus.*
Yes, they might have missed the bus.

6 *They could have changed their minds.*
Yes, they might have changed their minds.

7 Test each other

- This works best if students first make a list of questions.
- They work in pairs.

Song

- Students read the song.
- They guess what the words might be.
- Play the cassette. Students listen and check.
- Check orally.

Tapescript and answers

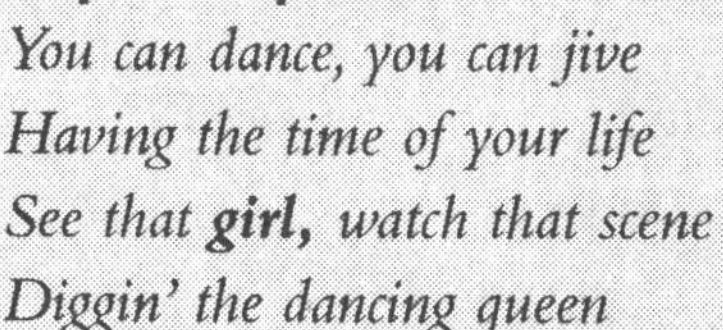

You can dance, you can jive
Having the time of your life
See that ***girl,*** *watch that scene*
Diggin' the dancing queen

Friday night and the lights are ***low***
Looking out for a place to go
Where they play the ***right*** *music*
Getting in the swing
You come to look for a ***king***
Anybody could be that guy
Night *is young and the music's* ***high***
With a bit of rock music
Everything's fine
Your're in the mood for a dance
And when you get the chance

You are the dancing queen
Young *and sweet*
Only 17
Dancing queen
Feel the beat from the tambourine
You can dance, you can jive
Having the time of your life
See that ***girl,*** *watch that scene*
Diggin' the dancing queen.

Optional activities

- Listen to the song again. Students sing along.
- Ask the students if they like dancing; do they know any special dances?
- In groups of four, students use their dictionaries to find different types of dance and music, e.g., jive, swing, rock and roll.
- Explain the meaning of *tambourine* to the students. In the same groups, students make a word map of musical instruments, using their dictionaries.
- Play the song again and sing along.

Activity Book Unit 9 Review p92-93
Activity Book Roundup p94-95

Poster p114

- The final poster is to make a big quiz for the rest of the class to answer.
- Students first reread the Team Challenge Quiz in Lesson 3.
- They also look at the questions they wrote.
- Each group chooses the best of their own questions and writes some more like the ones in the Team Challenge.
- Then they decide how to illustrate their poster.
- They write their work neatly and check it carefully.
- They stick everything to a large sheet of paper.
- Put up the posters around the classroom and allow time for each group to do each other's quizzes.

Aim: to encourage students to read for pleasure, while consolidating language covered in each unit of *Shine 3*. Teachers should decide how many comprehension and other questions they ask.

1 You'll get a great surprise

- Ask students if any of them plays computer games. What would it be like to be inside the game, rather than outside it? Some of them may know the book and the film *Jumanji*, where a player somehow gets inside a board game.
- Students look at the picture and discuss what is happening.
- They speculate what the 'great surprise' of the title is.
- Then they read the story.
- Ask questions about it, e.g., *Whose is the game? What is it called? Who do you sympathise with - Kate or Leo?* etc.
- Then they work in groups and discuss what they think will happen next. Groups present their ideas to the class.

Optional activity

- Books closed. Students retell the story.

2 I can see you're going to lose!

- Books closed. Ask students what happened in the first part of the story.
- What do they think will happen next?
- They look at the picture. What is happening? Who can they see?
- They read the story to see if they were right.
- In groups or pairs they discuss what will happen next.

Optional activity

- Students say which sport they would choose. Which star would they have to compete against? How would they win?

3 That must be it!

- Ask students to retell the story so far.
- What do they think will happen underwater?
- They open their books and look at the picture. What's happening?
- They read the episode and see if they guessed correctly.
- Then they discuss what Leo saw in the captain's cabin, e.g., treasure? a map? a sea monster?
- Finally they predict what will happen in the next episode.

Optional activity

- Books closed. Students retell the story of this episode.

4 I'm being given a lift by a dinosaur!

- Students recall the last episode. What did they think was in the captain's cabin?
- They look at the picture and the title and say what they think Leo found.
- They read the story. Did they guess right?
- They discuss what they think the noise is. What is the castle like? Is it huge? Is it made of rock? Or bones? Is it a maze? What will happen next?

Optional activities

- Books closed, students retell the story round the class, getting the events in the correct order.
- Students imagine they are Leo. What do they do when they realise they are on a dinosaur? Do they use the laser at the same time as he does? What do they do when they reach the castle?

5 Suzy told Leo to hold her hand

- What happened in the last episode? How did Leo get to the castle?
- What do students think the noise was? Why has Leo come to the castle? What will he do next?
- Students look at the picture and talk about it.
- Then they read the story. Did they guess correctly?
- You may ask students to read the story in sections and guess what is going to happen next, e.g., read to the bottom of the left-hand column; then to the part where they hear the dog; then to the part where they see the giant waiting for them.
- Students discuss what will happen to the two. Will the Power Trainers grow wings? Will they fall on a dinosaur? Will they land in a new section of the game?

Optional activity

- Ask who predicted the different events, e.g., did they guess the girl would be Suzy? Did they believe the guitar would work? Did they guess that the giant would take the guitar?

6 You can't escape!

- Students recall the previous episode. How do they think Leo and Suzy will escape from the castle? Where will they land?
- They look at the picture. What is happening? They try to answer the questions.
- They read the story. They may read it in sections and guess what will happen next.
- Did they guess what would happen?
- Students discuss what will happen next.

Optional activity

- Has anyone in the class ever seen or been in a maze? Do they know anything about famous mazes? (There is a famous old one at Hampton Court, just outside London.)

7 You shouldn't have touched the crystal

- Students recall what happened at the end of the last episode. What do they think happened to Leo? Is he all right, or was he hurt in the explosion?
- They look at the picture and try to answer the question.
- Students read the story in sections, speculating as before.
- What does Leo see in the crystal? What could be wrong with the other world?

Optional activity

- Students retell the story, explaining how Leo managed to win. Is this possible?

8 I'll be watching you

- Students remind each other what happened in the last episode. What did Leo see in the crystal? Where is he now?
- They look at the picture. What is different? Where are Leo and Suzy?
- They read the left column only and check their predictions.
- Tell them to look at each puzzle and try first to read it, then to answer it, remembering that this is a negative world.
- Then they read the rest of the story.
- Would they have won the level?
- They discuss the final question - who will win the last game? And what will it be?

Optional activities

- If students have pocket calculators, ask if anyone knows how to make words with them. For example, 577345 upside down looks like ShELLS. Can they make bOb, or OIL, or bELL? They may know words in their own language that they can make.
- Books closed. Ask students what was strange in the story, apart from the questions and answers. What did Leo see?

9 He had to win the race

- Students recall what happened in the last episode. Who does he have to beat this time?
- What game do they think he will have to play?
- Students look at the picture and answer the question.
- Then they read the story in sections, trying to predict what will happen next, as before.
- When they have finished, they discuss the final questions in groups. Each group reports back to the class. Can you come to a class solution?

Optional activities

- Did students expect Leo to win? Why? Why not?
- Is he really out of the game? Was he ever really in the game? Who is the girl?
- Students make up a new episode for the story. This can be put in the middle, or at the end, answering the above questions.
- Students discuss the games in the story. What other games would they have included?

Welcome Unit

1

2 Is he riding a horse?
No, he isn't. He's riding a bicycle.
3 Are they watching TV?
No, they aren't. They're playing computer games.
4 Is he writing a book?
No, he isn't. He's reading a book.
5 Is she sailing?
No, she isn't. She's windsurfing.

2

● • •	• ● •
abseiling	adventure
holiday	excitement
parachute	fantastic
skydiving	instructor
snorkelling	
video	
watersports	
windsurfing	

3

1 teach	2 'm having	3 like	4 speak
5 teach	6 'm learning	7 love	8 speak

4

1 SAILING
2 DANCING
3 WATERSKIING
4 CLIMBING
5 SKYDIVING
6 ABSEILING
7 PONYTREKKING
8 SWIMMING
9 SNORKELLING
10 WINDSURFING

(down: ACTIVITIES)

Unit 1 Lesson 1

1

1 isn't	2 you	3 didn't	4 from
5 What	6 going	7 forward	8 about

2

2 doesn't she	3 can't she	4 is she	5 does she
6 can she	7 hasn't she	8 didn't she	9 has she
10 did she			

3

2 can't she	3 didn't she	4 is she	5 isn't he
6 can he	7 has she	8 does she	

4

1 playing	2 having	3 swimming
4 getting	5 making	6 learning

5

2 Mark doesn't feel like doing anything.
3 Paolo is looking forward to windsurfing.
4 Lucy loves meeting people.
5 Holly can't stand being alone.
6 Manuel feels like dancing.

6

computer games
mountain biking
pony-trekking
scuba diving
skate boarding
water sports
wind surfing

7

1 a lot	2 questions	3 fabulous	4 going
5 wet	6 love	7 borrow	8 far

8

1 alon**e**	arriv**e**	cano**e**ing
2 borr**o**w	forw**a**rd	skateboa**r**ding
3 activi**t**y	fr**i**endly	ques**ti**on
4 c**h**ess	clot**h**es	laug**h**

Unit 1 Lesson 2

1

1 to	2 borrow	3 this	4 problem
5 want	6 lift	7 cycle	8 hear
9 worried	10 talk	11 have	12 teach
13 beach	14 come	15 go	16 cold

2

2 He offered to carry the equipment.
3 She decided to have a cheese sandwich.
4 He refused to go to bed early.
5 She asked to use the phone.
6 He agreed to have swimming lessons.

3

1 canoeing	2 to capsize	3 to be
4 to make	5 having	6 to come

4

with have: fun, a good time, a meal, a shower, a word with someone, a look

with take: an exam, medicine, a photo, a shower, a look, a taxi

5

6

● • •	• ● •
barbecue	canoeing
carefully	capsizing
miserable	completely
practising	decided
excited	
pretending	

Unit 1 Lesson 3

1

1 learn	2 easily	3 easy	4 fast	5 need
6 couple	7 that	8 own	9 first	10 wind
11 trouble	12 land	13 difficult	14 extremely	15 calm

2

1 later 2 more slowly 3 more quickly 4 hardest 5 best

3

2 Aliki can jump higher than Holly, but Mark can jump the highest.
3 Holly can stand on her head longer than Mark, but Aliki can stand on her head the longest.
4 Holly gets up earlier than Mark, but Aliki gets up the earliest.
5 Mark travels further to school than Aliki, but Holly travels the furthest.

4

1 Parascending looks incredibly exciting.
2 Aliki can swim quite fast.
3 Windsurfing is extremely hard work.
4 Lucy is really good at keeping her balance.
5 I think water-skiing is very difficult.

5

1 up 2 up 3 up 4 off 5 up 6 off

6

1 board 2 higher 3 see 4 there 5 wait

7

1 high	sky	✓
2 view	few	✓
3 air	ear	✗
4 float	boat	✓
5 quite	tight	✓
6 water	later	✗
7 early	curly	✓
8 further	brother	✗

Unit 1 Lesson 4

1

1 are looking	2 am writing	3 am having	4 visit
5 live	6 organises	7 draws	8 works
9 go	10 learning	11 stand	12 playing
13 love	14 to go	15 Do you like	16 listening
17 do you like	18 to hearing		

2

Dear Rachel

I read in a magazine that you are looking for a penpal, so I am writing to you.

My name's Paolo Romano and like you, I'm 16. I'm from Milan in Italy, but at the moment I'm having a holiday in England. Milan is in the north of Italy and it's the centre of fashion design.

I live with my parents and brother in a flat in the north of the city. My mother's name is Gina, and she works in a bank. My father is called Giulio, and he's an engineer. He works for Fiat, the car manufacturer. My brother, Carlo, is a student at university.

I go to a school near my home, and I've got lots of friends there. I like art and my favourite subject is music. But I can't stand history - I can't remember anything!

In my free time, I enjoy swimming and I really love taking photos. I want to be a fashion photographer. At the moment I'm learning karate.

What kind of clothes do you like wearing? And what kind of music do you like listening to?

Please write back and tell me all about you and your family.

Looking forward to hearing from you soon,

Best wishes
Paolo

4

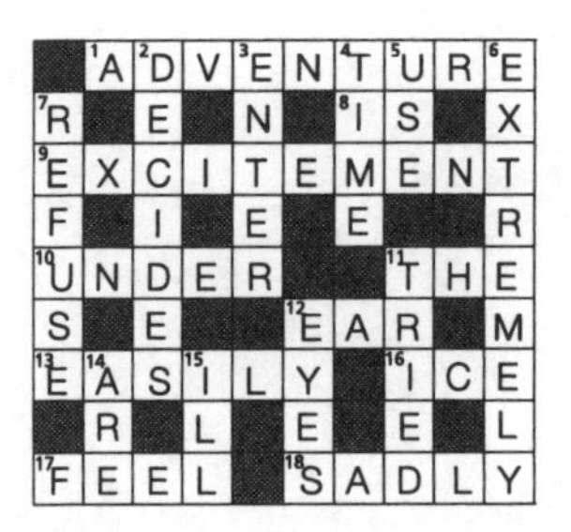

Unit 1 Review

1

1 didn't	2 doing	3 on, getting	4 forward	5 to
6 managed	7 teach	8 falling	9 harder	10 so, but

2

1 relieved (the others are negative)
2 teacher (the others are comparative adverbs)
3 keen (the others are verbs, this is an adjective)
4 listen (the others are to do with saying you will or won't do something)
5 extremely (this adverb modifies adjectives or other adverbs)

3

1 beginner 2 Unfortunately 3 disagree 4 carefully 5 exciting

4

1 Do you feel like water-skiing?
2 Aliki won the holiday in a competition, didn't she?
3 She isn't keen on doing exercises.
4 Mark couldn't swim so he was nervous.
5 Alison gets up earlier than Rick.

5

1C	2A	3B	4C	5A	6D	7D	8C
9B	10A	11D	12C	13D	14B	15B	

Unit 2 Lesson 1

1

2 He's going to ask her for a date.
3 They're going to cross the road.
4 It's going to break the rope.
5 She's going to buy the shoes.
6 He's going to take a photo.

2

2 I'll carry the bag.
3 I won't have another sandwich.
4 We won't be late.
5 I'll have a word with Mark.
6 I'll have a pizza for lunch.

3

1 will	2 is going to	3 are going to	4 is going to
5 is going to	6 won't	7 'll	8 'll
9 are going to	10 won't	1 'll	12 'll

4

1 worn 2 got 3 work 4 die 5 look 6 found

5

2 borrow some money	3 have a rest	4 make a speech
5 pay the bill	6 take a photo	
7 turn down the music	8 wash your hair	

6

/ʌ/	/ɒ/
come	clock
hurry	lost
lovely	model
lunch	promise
money	sorry
one	what

6

1 guess	less	✓
2 one	phone	✗
3 worry	sorry	✗
4 angry	hungry	✗
5 funny	money	✓
6 true	through	✓
7 food	wood	✗
8 climb	time	✓

Unit 2 Lesson 2

1

2 She's been buying presents.
3 He's been making a phone call.
4 She's been painting the ceiling.
5 They've been frying chips.
6 He's been trying to catch a fish.

2

2 She's been driving for three years.
3 She's been modelling for four years.
4 She's been looking for them since half past one.
5 They've been working there for two months.
6 She's been learning English for eight years.

3

How long have you been playing the guitar? Since 1986.
How long have you been writing songs? Since 1991.
How long have you been making records? Since 1993.
How long have you been giving concerts? Since 1994.
How long have you been living in Britain? For four years.

4

1 been meaning	2 met	3 had	4 been
5 been having	6 swum	7 wanted	8 been teaching
9 had	10 been	11 met	12 been having

5

1 bal**l**oon	exp**l**ain	ha**l**f
2 holi**d**ay	bel**i**eve	med**i**cine
3 pe**o**ple	danger**o**us	kil**o**metre
4 wor**r**ied	autog**r**aph	di**r**ection

Unit 2 Lesson 3

1

1 after	2 take	3 once	4 makes	5 every
6 least	7 sessions	8 myself	9 you	10 younger
11 early	12 spend	13 balanced	14 yourself	15 better

2

1 yourselves	2 himself	3 ourselves	4 herself
5 myself	6 themselves	7 itself	8 yourself

3

How often does he eat in restaurants?
He eats in restaurants once a week.

How often does he play tennis?
He plays tennis once a fortnight.

How often does he go swimming?
He goes swimming once a week.

How often does he give concerts?
He gives concerts twice a week.

How often does he go to the cinema?
He goes to the cinema three times a month.

How often does he watch football matches?
He watches football matches once a fortnight.

How often does he have parties?
He has parties once a month.

4

catwalk
changing room
fashion show
junk food
makeup
model agency
mountain air
ski clothes
sunrise

5

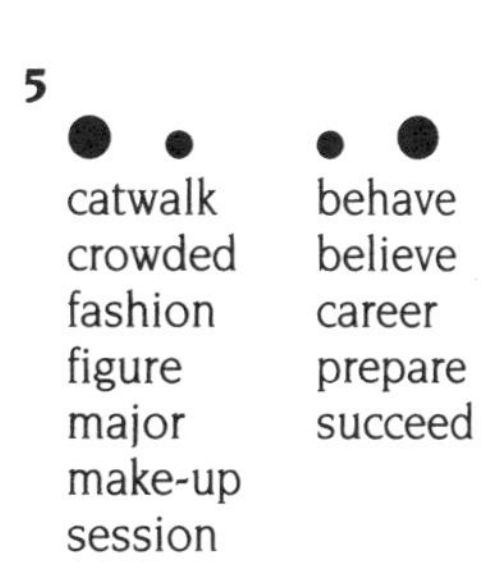

● •	• ●
catwalk	behave
crowded	believe
fashion	career
figure	prepare
major	succeed
make-up	
session	

Unit 2 Lesson 4

1

1 Friends
2 Childhood
3 Starting to perform
4 Career
5 The future

1C 2E 3A 4B 5D

2

1 always wanted to
2 she knew she had to perform the next night.
3 she went to Los Angeles in 1996 and met Stephen Speilberg.
4 he saw her in a TV version of Titanic.
5 starred in The Mask of Zorro.

4

Unit 2 Review

1

1 will catch up	2 going to have
3 will talk to	4 have been missing for
5 has phoned	6 has been living, since
7 themselves	8 every
9 as soon as	10 Until

2

1 photographer	2 exhausting	3 successful
4 unemployed	5 secondary	

3

1 They've never been up in a hot air balloon before.
2 Lucy washes her hair three times a week.
3 If you want to be a successful model, you have to look after yourself.
4 I haven't forgotten to send postcards to my friends.
5 Manuel has been learning English for eight years.

4

1B	2A	3D	4A	5C	6D	7B	8C
9C	10A	11B	12B	13D	14C	15D	

Unit 3 Lesson 1

1

2 He must be bored.	3 She can't be warm.
4 It must be angry.	5 He must be thirsty.

2

2 She can't be very hungry.
3 He can't be serious.
4 He must work hard.
5 He must spend a lot.
6 She can't get much sleep.
7 She must take lots of exercise.
8 He must like taking photos.

3

1 were discovered	2 were found	3 was helped
4 were taken	5 were built	6 were probably sunk
7 were not badly damaged		

4

2 A new roof was put on.
3 All the rooms were painted.
4 New furniture and equipment were bought.
5 A cafe and a swimming pool were built.
6 The centre was advertised in newspapers and on TV.
7 Instructors and helpers were employed.
8 ACE was opened five years ago.

5

1 hard	2 different	3 big	4 discover
5 glad	6 quiet	7 beautiful	8 bells

6

1 drown	known	✗
2 diver	river	✗
3 sail	whale	✓
4 wreck	trek	✓
5 cover	over	✗
6 storm	warm	✓
7 among	long	✗
8 isle	while	✓
9 flood	food	✗

Unit 3 Lesson 2

1

2 Because she had touched a crab.
3 Because she had found a coin.
4 Because she had been in cold water for 30 minutes.
5 Because they had got up early.
6 Because she hadn't had enough practice.

2

2 After Aliki had cleared away some of the sand, she found a coin.
3 After she had stayed underwater for half an hour, she came to the surface.
4 After she had climbed back into the boat, she put a towel round her.
5 After she had changed into warm clothes, the boat returned to the harbour.
6 After they had taken the coins to the museum, they had something to eat.

3

D F B H A E I C G

Yesterday, two young London schoolboys **decided** to go to France. After they **had made** some sandwiches, they **took** a train to Dover on the south-east coast of England. When they **arrived** at Dover harbour, they **found** a small empty speedboat. As soon as it **was** dark, they **started** the engine and the boat **moved** out to sea. But after they **had travelled** a few kilometres, the engine **stopped**. The boys **couldn't** start it, so they **had** something to eat. When they **had eaten**, they **were** very tired so they **went** to sleep. While they **were** asleep, a ship **noticed** the small boat and **contacted** the police. Finally a police boat **reached** the boat and **took** them back to Dover.

4

1 at	2 of	3 for	4 away	5 of	6 with
7 in	8 under	9 After	10 to	11 to	12 out

5

A: Hold my hand. Half an hour

B: Don't just stand there.

C: Was it a coin?

D: I'd touched a crab. I waved to Jack. A piece of eight

It's really cold. The crab had gone.

Unit 3 Lesson 3

1

2 Paolo, because he had been taking lots of photos.
3 Rick, because he had been running.
4 Manuel, because he had been listening to loud music.
5 Alison, because she had been doing some work on her car.
6 Holly, because she had been watching a sad film.

2

2 How long had she been watching TV?
She'd been watching TV for two hours.
3 How long had he been learning to drive?
He'd been learning to drive for three months.
4 How long had she been diving?
She'd been diving for half an hour.
5 How long had they been waiting?
They'd been waiting for 50 minutes.

3

1D 2A 3B 4C
2 and 3 are irregular.

1 raise 2 lay 3 lying 4 rises

4

southern
direction
everyone
discover
surface
afternoon
cargo

5

car + crash, driver, park, drive
bus + driver, station, stop, ticket, catch, drive
ship + captain, harbour, ticket, wreck, sail, sink
plane + captain, crash, pilot, ticket, catch, fly, land, take off

6

2 (lying)	skiing	(buying)
3 our	(pour)	(sure)
4 (year)	(hear)	wear
5 (days)	case	(raise)
6 (go)	(blow)	now

Unit 3 Lesson 4

1

1C 2A 3F 4H 5B 6E 7D 8G

2

Yesterday afternoon, Dan Jones made a fantastic discovery. He had been digging in his garden for some time when he found a metal plate. Dan thought the plate must be valuable as although it was dirty it looked like gold. So he decided to take it to the museum. As soon as he had washed his hands he got on his bike and cycled into town. When he showed the plate to a woman at the museum, she was very excited and she gave Dan £1,000 for the plate. Dan didn't want to carry all that money on him so he cycled to the bank. However by this time it was 5.30 and the bank had closed. Then Dan had a bright idea. He took the money home and he buried it in the place where he had found the plate, but he didn't realise that someone was watching him. As soon as he woke up this morning, he went to dig up the money. and to his horror the money had disappeared because someone had come in the middle of the night and had stolen it! (12 sentences)

4

Unit 3 Review

1

1 can't	2 must	3 were, drowned
4 had, saw	5 had	6 shivering
7 been, got	8 had been telling, hadn't	9 Although

2

1 It must have been difficult to sail among the rocks.
2 Lots of treasure was discovered by divers.
3 After Aliki had spent 30 minutes underwater, she came up.
4 Although she was cold, she wanted to dive again.
5 The sailor hadn't been lying.

3
1 False. He wrote it 14 years before it had sunk.
2 False. It was called the Titan.
3 True.
4 False. 1898 was the date when the book was written.
5 False. They had dreamt that the Titanic would sink.

4
1D 2C 3D 4B 5B 6D 7A 8A 9C 10D 11B 12B

Unit 4 Lesson 1

1
1 such 2 before 3 What 4 been 5 so
6 that 7 so 8 too 9 village 10 what

2
1 such an 2 so 3 so
4 so 5 such 6 such a

3
1 an 2 - 3 a 4 a 5 - 6 a 7 a 8 - 9 -

4
2 It was such a long ride that everyone was exhausted.
3 The weather was so hot that the riders had a rest after lunch.
4 Clovelly was such a beautiful village that Holly didn't want to leave.
5 The village street is so steep that people use donkeys to carry things.
6 It was such a shame that Aliki couldn't see the village.
7 Horses were so important that we still talk about horsepower!

5
1 grumpy 2 scared 3 ashamed
4 upset 5 pretty 6 exhausted

6
2 Slow down or you'll hurt yourself!
3 Be careful or you'll fall off the horse!
4 He had an accident and tore his jacket.
5 Cheer up! It'll stop raining soon.

Unit 4 Lesson 2

1
1 types 2 attacked 3 have 4 been 5 used 6 by
7 banned 8 being 9 easily 10 uses 11 of 12 that

2
1 are being threatened
2 are being caught
3 are being killed
4 are being poisoned
5 are being studied
6 are being taught

3
2 The garden wall hasn't been repaired.
3 The windows have been washed.
4 The abseiling equipment hasn't been tidied up.
5 The video camera has been found.
6 The table tennis table has been put away.
7 The disco hasn't been contacted.
8 The letters haven't been posted.

4
1 has been found
2 is being helped
3 have already been put
4 is being played, is being given
5 is being watched
6 is being returned

5
1 Commercial whaling is no longer allowed.
2 The whale was attracting a lot of interest.
3 Smoking is banned at ACE.
4 Scientists examined the whale.
5 Whales are eating things which poison them.

6

/g/	/dʒ/
agricultural	dangerous
angry	engine
group	giant
grumpy	intelligent
lifeguard	margarine

Unit 4 Lesson 3

1
1 capital 2 taken 3 won't 4 night 5 cooked
6 be 7 flown 8 will 9 taken 10 be
11 or 12 spent 13 lessons 14 provided 15 exciting
16 known 17 will 18 can 19 day 20 animals
21 activities 22 spent 23 meals

2
2 You will be provided with three meals a day.
3 The rest of the holiday will be spent by the sea.
4 Snacks and drinks will be served in the evening.
5 You will be given a questionnaire at the end of the holiday.
6 You will be driven to the airport by minibus.

3
2 Has your hair been washed yet?
No, but it will be washed by the morning.
3 Has your room been tidied yet?
No, but it will be tidied by the morning.
4 Has your computer been turned off yet?
No, but it will be turned off by the morning.
5 Have your sunglasses been repaired yet?
No, but they will be repaired by the morning.
6 Have your shoes been cleaned yet?
No, but they will be cleaned by the morning.

4
minibus
polar bear
packed lunch
post office
snowboarding
treasure hunt

5
● background ● climate ● explore ● flamingo
● karaoke ● leopard ● safari ● vehicle

Unit 4 Lesson 4

1

1 Line 4: it = swimming with whales and dolphins
2 Line 10: them = the whales and dolphins
3 Line 12: them = questions
4 Line 14: it = whale-watching
5 Line 21: these amazing animals = dolphins and whales
6 Line 24: it = swimming with whales
7 Line 26: these = these animals (= whales)
8 Line 29: them = whales
9 Line 36: that = whales being hunted by man
10 Line 37: they = whales
11 Line 42: here = in the Azores
12 Line 46: They = scientists

2

The number of visits to Antarctica has grown enormously, recently. More and more people are going for short trips. These, however, are not enough for some people who want to stay longer. Experts say that snow and whiteness help people to relax, and this is all part of the magic of the empty continent.

However, the Antarctic is a dangerous place with difficult weather. So much rubbish is being left there by visitors that scientists are worried that too many humans in the Antarctic may harm the environment. In the future, visits may be banned so, make your choice and go now, before it's too late!

4

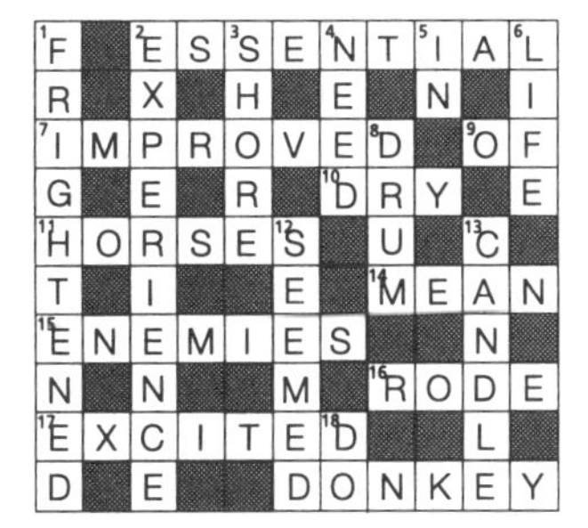

Unit 4 Review

1

1 so, that	2 such	3 being, by	4 have, for	5 been
6 will	7 won't be	8 will, be	9 has been	10 be, by

2

1 unicorn (the others all exist)
2 climate (the others are all types of coastline)
3 vet (the others are all creatures; this is a job)
4 vehicle (the others are all activities)
5 sadness (the others are all positive)

3

1 Mark was being so silly that Holly couldn't help teasing him.
2 We were having such a good time that we forgot the time.
3 Mark is being taught to swim by Tara.
4 Many types of sea creature are being killed by pollution.
5 The whale has been photographed by the journalists.
6 The afternoon will be spent sightseeing.

4

1B	2C	3D	4A	5C	6B	7B	8A
9C	10C	11B	12D	13C	14A	15A	

Unit 5 Lesson 1

1

1 told	2 say	3 heard	4 turned	5 had
6 away	7 been	8 her	9 told	10 would

2

2 Rick and Tara said they were waiting.
3 Aliki said she didn't believe Lucy.
4 Mark said he had never been to the USA.
5 Lucy said the boy had disappeared.
6 Manuel said he was going to talk to Lucy.
7 Holly and Mark said they would help find the ghost.
8 Aliki said she couldn't hear anyone singing.

3

1 said	2 was	3 was	4 said	5 was
6 had	7 told	8 said	9 wanted	10 would
11 said	12 would	13 said	14 was	15 told

4

2 They could hear a car coming.
3 We heard some people singing.
4 He watched the helicopter landing.
5 I can hear someone using a vacuum cleaner.
6 She heard someone whispering.

5

1 I can see a girl sitting on a bench reading a book.
2 I can see two girls and two boys singing.
3 I can see a boy playing a guitar.
4 I can see someone riding a horse.
5 I can see two people riding bicycles.
6 I can see a girl walking with a ball.
7 I can see two boys playing basketball.
8 I can see a boy climbing something.

6

1 annoyed	2 bang	3 clap	4 corridor
5 downstairs	6 squeak	7 turn on	8 vacuum cleaner
9 whisper	10 whistle		

7

/ɪə/	/eə/
appear	bear
career	fair
clear	pair
near	tear
we're	wear
weird	where

Unit 5 Lesson 2

1

1 had	2 if	3 was	4 know	5 what
6 if	7 asked	8 how	9 told	10 tease

2

2 Manuel asked Paolo what the time was.
3 Manuel asked Paolo if he knew what the time was.
4 Lucy asked Aliki if she had ever seen a ghost.
5 Aliki asked Lucy if she had spoken to Rick at breakfast.
6 Lucy asked Rick how old he was.
7 Mark asked Lucy where she had seen the ghost.
8 Holly asked Tara when she had last seen her rucksack.

3
2 Mark asked Holly if she wanted to go ghost-hunting with him tonight.
3 Aliki wanted to know where her jumper was.
4 Tara asked Rick why everyone was laughing at breakfast.
5 Manuel asked Lucy if she wanted to play tennis.
6 Holly asked Tara if there was anything in her rucksack.

4
2 Alison asked Rick **if he knew** where the key was.
3 Aliki asked Lucy **if she was** scared.
4 Everyone wondered who **Lucy had** seen.
5 Mark asked Holly **if she would** like to go to the cinema with him.

5
1 - 2 a 3 a 4 a 5 the 6 a 7 a
8 the 9 - 10 A 11 a 12 a 13 the 14 the

6
1 used 2 get 3 shut 4 growing
5 stay 6 hurry 7 ring 8 making

7

1 tease	knees	✓
2 haunt	can't	✗
3 Rick	trick	✓
4 ghost	most	✓
5 weird	cleared	✓
6 clothes	nose	✓
7 watch	wash	✗

Unit 5 Lesson 3

1
1 to 2 make 3 to 4 eat 5 used
6 were 7 used 8 used 9 called 10 haunt
11 in 12 frighten

2
2 Paolo used to eat fish but he doesn't now.
Mark and Lucy didn't use to eat fish but they do now.
3 Manuel didn't use to enjoy reading but he does now.
Mark and Lucy used to enjoy reading but they don't now.
4 Manuel used to like the Simpsons but he doesn't now.
Mark and Lucy didn't use to like the Simpsons but they do now.

3
2 Manuel used to have fairly short hair but now it is really long.
3 Holly didn't use to play chess but now she is very good at it.
4 'I used to watch a lot of TV when I was younger,' Tara said. 'But here I never have enough time.'
5 'I enjoy speaking English every day,' Aliki said. 'But I used to find it quite difficult.'

4
2 And where did you use to live?
3 And when did you use to get up?
4 What did you use to ride?
5 And what kind of music did you use to listen to?
6 And what did you use to wear?
8 He used to start work at six but now he starts at nine.
9 He used to ride a motorbike but now he rides a bicycle.
10 He used to listen to heavy metal but now he listens to reggae.
11 He used to wear just his swimming things, but now he wears a tracksuit.

5
1 slow 2 knocking 3 settle 4 was burnt 5 broke 6 lie

6

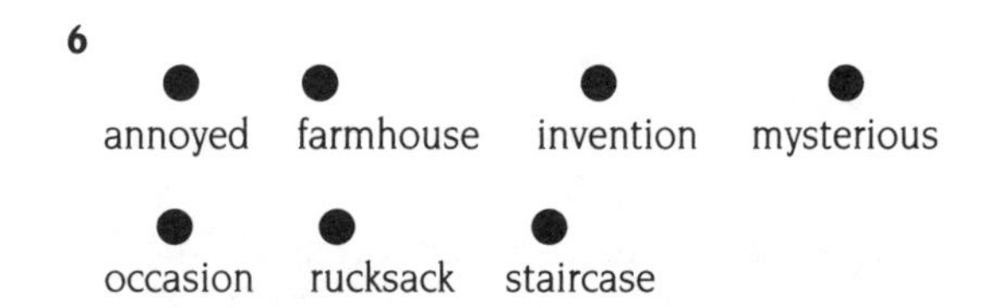

Unit 5 Lesson 4

1
1 and 2 but 3 but 4 Then 5 and 6 and 7 then
8 and 9 Then 10 and 11 and 12 and 13 but 14 but
15 and 16 and 17 Then 18 and 19 and 20 But

2
Helena was so unhappy after her mother's death that, although she liked her father's second wife, she went mad and killed herself. Her father and a servant buried the body under a tree in the garden and then he and his wife went to Italy. After they had died the servant told the police the story. They dug under the tree and found the body. Helena still haunts the house. (70 words)

4

Unit 5 Review

1
1 had, singing 2 told, that 3 asked, if
4 wanted, were 5 asked, had 6 used
7 use, changed 8 used, out 9 said
10 door, asked

2
1 dream (the others are all sounds)
2 vacuum cleaner (the others are all parts of a house)
3 haunt (the others are all actions using hands)
4 mysterious (the others are all adjectives of negative feelings)
5 bury (the others all involve loud noises)

3

1 Lucy said (that) she had never seen anything so strange in all her life.
2 Aliki told Lucy (that) she didn't believe her.
3 Lucy asked Rick what the ghost was called.
4 Aliki wanted to know where her jumper was.
5 Every Monday night a coach and horses used to race up to the front door.

4

1A 2B 3C 4D 5B 6D 7A 8D
9C 10A 11A 12C 13B 14D 15C

Unit 6 Lesson 1

1

1 would 2 if 3 would 4 had 5 to
6 didn't 7 would 8 would 9 would 10 were

2

1 If I met an alien, I'd say hello.
2 If I found some money in the street, I'd take it to the police.
3 If I went out in a boat, I'd wear a lifejacket.
4 If I got lost in the mountains, I'd use my mobile phone.
5 If I won the lottery, I'd give the money away.

3

2 'Who would you talk to if you had a problem?' 'I'd talk to my sister.'
3 'What would you do if you saw a car crash?' 'I'd phone the police.'
4 'Where would you go if you won the lottery?' 'I'd go to China.'
5 'If you wanted to buy something but didn't have enough money, what would you do?' 'I'd ask my parents.'
6 'What would you like best if you went to ACE?' 'I'd probably enjoy everything.'

4

2 If Mark asked her to go to a jazz concert, she would say no.
3 If Lucy asked her to stay with her for a few days after the holiday, she would ask her parents.
4 If Manuel asked her how to play a computer game, she would say she didn't know.
5 If Tara asked her to play tennis, she would say yes.

5

1 throw 2 gave 3 ran 4 got 5 take 6 put

Unit 6 Lesson 2

1

1 someone 2 do 3 Let's 4 let 5 life
6 make 7 charge 8 make 9 I'll 10 I

2

1 let 2 let 3 make 4 make 5 make 6 let 7 makes 8 let

3

1 Rick **didn't let** Lucy **climb** down the cliff.
2 Rick **made** Lucy **stay** with him. 3 Rick **made** Lucy **do** what he wanted because he was in charge.
4 Lucy said that Rick **made** her **feel** stupid.
5 Rick told Lucy to **let** him **speak.**

4

2 You aren't allowed to smoke.
3 I'm not allowed to stay out after midnight.
4 I'm allowed to have friends to stay overnight at the weekend.
5 I'm not allowed to go into the town centre on my own.
6 We're not allowed to wear jeans to school.

5

2 Students aren't allow**ed** to play football in the corridors.
3 The teacher **made** us do some extra work because we didn't listen to her.
4 My mother let me stay the night at my friend's house.
5 Please will you **let** me go to the party on Saturday?
6 We aren't allowed **to** bring food and drink into the classroom.

6

1 overnight 2 permission 3 training
4 experienced 5 plenty 6 practice

Unit 6 Lesson 3

1

1 to 2 should 3 ought 4 up 5 you
6 door 7 should 8 door 9 should 10 should

2

1 should 2 oughtn't 3 should
4 ought 5 oughtn't 6 shouldn't

3

2 You'd better put on a raincoat or you'll get wet.
3 He'd better train or he won't get a place in the team.
4 She'd better practise or she'll never learn to abseil well.
5 They'd better come soon or we'll go without them.
6 You'd better phone home or your parents will be worried.
7 You'd better stop fooling around or you'll get into trouble.

4

2 He'd better get on quick.
3 They'd better pick up the litter.
4 She'd better run away now.

5

1 try 2 got 3 Hold 4 kept 5 put 6 Come

6

ambulance brigade emergency difficulty instructions

lifejacket permission propeller telephone

Unit 6 Lesson 4

1

1 someone 2 shouldn't 3 blood 4 best
5 stop 6 if 7 anything 8 moving
9 anyone 10 this 11 should 12 it

2

Burns

First of all you should cool the burnt area by putting it in cold water or letting cold water run over it for 15-20 minutes. Then you should cover the burn with a clean cloth. However, you shouldn't put anything else on the burn. Finally, you should take the person to a doctor quickly.

Shock

First of all you should stop any bleeding. Then, if the person is conscious, you should ask him or her to lie down and raise his or her legs a little. Next you should undo any tight clothes and keep the person warm. However, you shouldn't let the person get too hot. Finally, you should get a doctor as fast as you can.

4

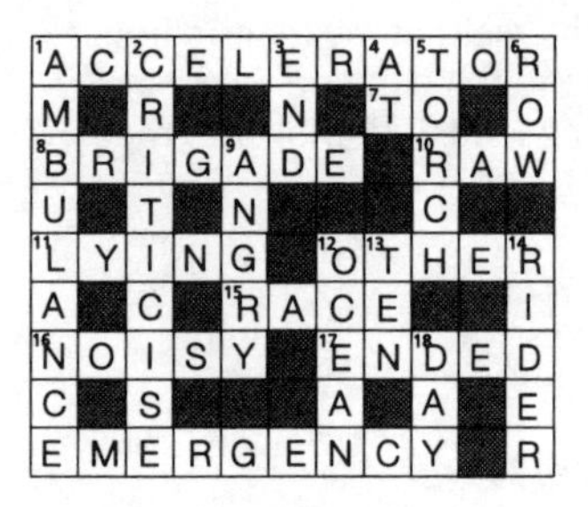

Unit 6 Review

1

1 would, came   2 wouldn't, were   3 allowed
4 make   5 let   6 someone, should
7 ought to   8 shouldn't   9 allowed, to
10 would, came

2

1 roundabout (the others are all to do with the emergency services)
2 snowstorm (the others are all parts of a car)
3 noise (the others are all to do with light)
4 survival (the others are all negative)
5 propeller (the others are all ways of making light)

3

1 If I knew her number, I'd phone her.
2 If I were you I'd go to bed earlier.
3 You're not allowed to stay out so late.
4 You make me feel so silly.
5 You should think before you jump into the water.
6 You'd better hurry up or you'll miss the party.

4

1B   2D   3A   4C   5A   6C   7D
8B   9C   10D   11A   12C   13B   14C

Unit 7 Lesson 1

1

1 have   2 said   3 was   4 should   5 were   6 was
7 were   8 have   9 should   10 said   11 You   12 Who

2

1 should   2 should have   3 shouldn't   4 should
5 should   6 shouldn't have   7 shouldn't have

3

1 Paolo should have paid attention to Alison.
2 Rick should have brought the boy back to ACE.
3 They shouldn't have let the boy escape.
4 Rick was in charge and he should have known better.
5 Aliki should have told Alison about the photograph earlier.

4

1 in   2 up   3 to   4 at   5 for
6 with   7 to   8 at   9 out   10 of

5

2 Alison explained that it was called tandem diving.
3 Paolo thought (that) he was jumping with Alison.
4 Aliki told Alison (that) she looked worried.
5 Aliki said (that) she wanted to take a photograph of Stonehenge.
6 Aliki explained that the picture of Stonehenge was for her father.
7 Alison said (that) they would fall for 40 seconds.
8 Alison told Paolo (that) he should have paid attention.
9 Alison told Paolo and Manuel (that) they were jumping with two instructors.
10 Aliki said (that) Rick and Lucy had saved the boy.
11 Alison told Paolo and Manuel (that) it was time to go.
12 Manuel said (that) he thought he was going to be sick.

Unit 7 Lesson 2

1

1 wanted   2 after   3 to   4 fence   5 them
6 down   7 let   8 grabbed   9 who   10 know
11 how   12 tell   13 make

2

1 Lucy wanted the holiday **to** go on for ever.
2 Rick and Lucy let Sam escape.
3 They won't allow beginners **to** skydive on their own.
4 Alison made Paolo and Manuel check their parachutes.
5 Aliki's family wanted her **to** do lots of things.
6 Aliki asked Alison **to** fly over Stonehenge.

3

2 Alison told Manuel and Paolo to hurry up.
3 Aliki's brother wanted her to bring him a present.
4 Alison made Paolo jump with an instructor.
5 Aliki let Alison talk to the boy first.
6 Sam didn't want Alison to send him back to London.

4

2 'Sam, were you hurt when you fell off the cliff?'
3 'What was the parachute jump like?'
4 'Are you going to call the police, Alison?'
5 'Alison, will you let Sam stay at ACE?'
6 'How much did the parachute jump cost, Manuel?'

5

2 Holly asked what it was like falling without a parachute.
3 Tara wanted to know why Sam had run away.
4 Rick asked if he could have his jacket back.
5 Tara wanted to know where Sam had stayed.
6 Alison asked Sam when he had last had something to eat.

6

2 I asked what the jump had been like.
3 They wanted to know what the time was.
4 He asked what was for supper.
5 The instructor asked what my name was.
6 She asked if she could have another jump.

Unit 7 Lesson 3

1

1 could   2 were able to   3 weren't able to
4 managed to   5 managed to   6 wasn't able to
7 wasn't able to   8 could

2

1C   2A   3C   4B   5B   6A

3

1 was able to   2 couldn't   3 couldn't
4 were able to   5 couldn't   6 was able to

4

2 The tourists took photos in order to remember/so that they could remember their holiday.
3 Philip took the canoes close to the bank so that the tourists could see better.
4 The canoes stopped from time to time so that the tourists could swim.
5 Philip shouted to the tourists so that they could escape from the hippo.
6 The hippo closed its jaws in order to/so that it could pull Philip underwater.

5

1 escape   2 bank   3 estimate   4 feather
5 luggage   6 occasionally   7 picnic

6

1 safe   2 wide   3 cool down
4 rising   5 the surface   6 picked up

7

2 as cold as ice
3 as quiet as a mouse
4 as warm as toast
5 as quick as a flash
6 as black as night
7 as pretty as a picture
8 as safe as houses
9 as old as the hills
10 as strong as a horse
11 as good as gold
12 as fast as lightning
13 as dry as a bone
14 as white as snow

Unit 7 Lesson 4

1

1 remembered   2 well   3 worse   4 lost
5 couldn't   6 laughed   7 agreed   8 dream
9 should   10 shake   11 waited   12 laughing

1 May had a bad dream about a helicopter flight.
2 One day Terry and May took a helicopter flight.
3 Suddenly there was a snowstorm.
4 The pilot said he was lost.
5 The helicopter started to shake.
6 The pilot said he could control it.
7 They came out of the cloud.
8 They landed at the airfield.

2

Possible answer
First May had a bad dream about a helicopter flight. She told Terry about it and they laughed. Then, one day, Terry and May took a helicopter flight to New York. Suddenly there was a snowstorm and the pilot said he was lost, just like in the dream. Next, the helicopter started to shake and then it fell quickly through the air. After that the pilot said he could control it. Later, they came out of the cloud and finally landed at the airfield. Terry and May got a bus to New York.

4

Unit 7 Review

1

1 could, wanted   2 should have   3 asked, to
4 allow, to   5 make, talk   6 so, could
7 weren't able   8 managed   9 sure, close
10 should have

2

1 exciting   2 frightened   3 confused
4 disturbing   5 tiring   6 amazed
7 boring   8 surprised   9 interested

3

1 You should have paid attention.
2 Aliki asked if it was something to do with Rick and Lucy.
3 Aliki's father asked her to take a photograph of Stonehenge for him.
4 Alison asked what his name was and where he was from.
5 The tourists were able to see the animals because they went by canoe.
6 Philip turned round in order to see what had happened.

4

1A   2D   3C   4C   5B   6B   7A   8B
9D   10B   11D   12C   13D   14B   15D

Unit 8 Lesson 1

1

1 will   2 be   3 have   4 won't   5 to
6 able   7 will   8 able   9 be   10 have

2

2 You'll have to be lucky and win a lottery.
3 You won't have to get special training?
4 Will you have to wear special clothes?
5 We won't have to wait long for cheap travel?
6 Will everyone have to travel in space?

3

Opinion	Size	Age	Shape	Colour
amazing	huge	ancient	narrow	black
difficult	tiny	brand-new	round	colourless
glamorous		modern	square	grey
pretty		second-hand	wide	pink
		young		white

4

2 It will be called virtual travel and you will be able to go wherever you want.
3 You will be able to choose everything about your holiday except for two things.
4 What won't you be able to choose? You won't be able to decide who else is on holiday at the same time.
5 And what else won't you be able to choose? You won't be able to control the weather!
6 Will you be able to choose a holiday on the moon? Yes, but you won't be able to take Buzz Aldrin with you.

5

badly behaved
best-known
brand-new
broken-down
full-time
mid-air
non-stop
second-hand

Unit 8 Lesson 2

1

1 going 2 will 3 be 4 be 5 showing
6 be 7 won't 8 sure 9 will 10 writing

2

2 Tara won't be having breakfast at nine o'clock tomorrow. She'll be taking off in a plane.
3 Tara won't be having lunch at one o'clock tomorrow. She'll be arriving at Izmir.
4 Tara won't be out canoeing at three o'clock tomorrow. She'll be checking into her hotel.
5 Tara won't be teaching Mark to swim at half past three tomorrow. She'll be going for a walk on the beach.
6 Tara won't be watching TV at eight o'clock tomorrow. She'll be going to a disco.

3

2 At half past seven I'll be... .
3 At eleven o'clock I'll be... .
4 At four o'clock I'll be... .
5 At eight o'clock I'll be... .
6 At quarter to twelve I'll be... .

4

2 nineteen eighty-six
3 twenty-eight degrees Celsius
4 ten thousand
5 three hundred thousand
6 twenty ten

5

1 underground 2 frozen 3 a billion
4 desert 5 farm 6 robot

6

2 summer holiday — holiday photos
3 horror film — film director
4 glasshouse — housework
5 underwater — water sports
6 underground — ground floor
7 space ship — shipwreck

Unit 8 Lesson 3

1

1 will 2 human 3 have 4 at 5 If
6 damaged 7 rises 8 dies 9 temperature 10 have
11 should 12 them 13 will 14 left 15 have

2

2 He won't have taken any exams.
3 He will have watched TV for 250 hours.
4 He will have played 12 games of football.
5 He won't have eaten any hamburgers.
6 He will have read 12 English books.

3

2 By how many degrees will the ocean temperature have risen in five years' time? Five.
3 How much TV / How many hours TV will Paolo have watched in six weeks' time? Ninety hours.
4 How many showers will Aliki have had in ten days' time? Twenty.
5 How many cokes will Rick have drunk in seven days' time? Twenty-one.
6 How many kilometres will Tara have swum in five days' time? Fifteen.

4

2 oxygen tank
3 aerosol can
4 bottle of water
5 chocolate wrapper

5

aerosol, agricultural, chocolate, definition, expedition, nature, organise, oxygen, popularity, similarity, situation, wrapper

Unit 8 Lesson 4

1

1 lives 2 working 3 able 4 home 5 smaller
6 changing 7 talk 8 have 9 time 10 change

2

Future cars will have to be flexible. We will be able to move seats in the car and we will have to be able to change the size of the car. The cars will have to be able to use either petrol or electricity because there won't be enough petrol for everyone.

In thirty years' time we will be driving intelligent cars. We will be able to talk to our cars and discuss with them the best way to go somewhere. When we tell them where we want to go, they will be able to tell us the best road. We won't have to do much driving - the car will be able to do it for us.

The cars of the future will be personal. We will be able to change the colour of the car and the seats easily. Each car will have a name like a person. The only thing we won't be able to do very often is buy a new car - it will be too expensive.

3

1 calculations 2 population 3 management
4 discussion 5 improvement 6 education

5

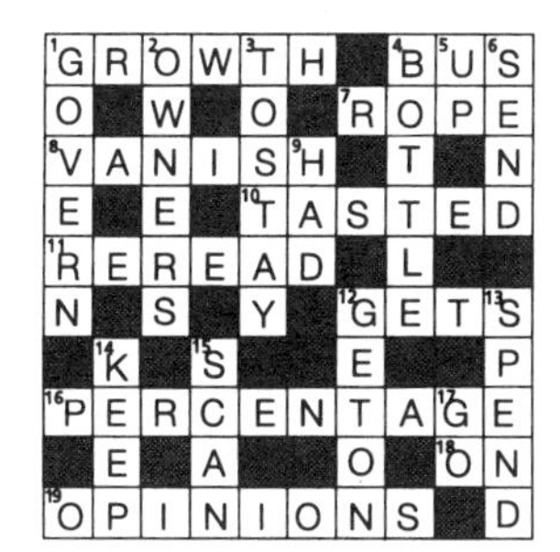

Unit 8 Review

1

1 won't have, be able
2 huge round
3 will be
4 growing
5 will, be doing
6 will have, will have been
7 will have destroyed
8 will have left
9 be able
10 will have become

2

1 oxygen (the others are to do with numbers)
2 expedition (the others are geographical regions)
3 poverty (the others are ways of talking)
4 repair (the others are about spoiling things)
5 accuracy (the others are to do with movement)

3

1 You will be able to visit the rainforest without going abroad.
2 You won't have to do any housework.
3 What will you be doing next weekend?
4 I'll be having a picnic in the garden next Saturday.
5 By Friday I will have spoken to them.
6 By four o'clock she will have finished the book.

4

1C 2D 3A 4B 5C 6D 7A 8C 9B 10C 11D 12C

Unit 9 Lesson 1

1

2 He's had the walls painted.
3 He's had the windows cleaned.
4 He's had the front door replaced.
5 He's had the grass cut.
6 He's had a swimming pool built.
7 He's had some trees planted.
8 He's had the hedge trimmed.
9 He's had the fence mended.
10 He's had a sign put up.

2

2 Has Alison had her bike repaired? No, but she's going to have it repaired.
3 Has Paolo had his photos printed? No, but he's going to have them printed.
4 Has Mark had his jacket mended? No, but he's going to have it mended.
5 Has Holly had her ears pierced? No, but she's going to have them pierced.

3

2 You need to have your car repaired.
3 You need to have your hair cut.
4 You need to have your teeth checked.
5 You need to have the wheel straightened.

4

sunglasses	mistake	housework	shopping
dry-clean	straighten	yesterday	bedroom

5

1 treasure - measure
2 joking - soaking
3 daughter - water
4 choose - shoes
5 bite - right
6 date - weight
7 woken - broken
8 scene - clean
9 lion - iron

6

A: You're ahead. What's that smell? Oh, it's me! Never mind.

B: You can do it. Would you like that?

C: Are you all right? What do you mean?

Unit 9 Lesson 2

1

2 I'd have travelled to Scotland with my parents.
I wouldn't have had so much fun.
3 I'd have worked in a shop in London.
I wouldn't have met Sam.
4 I'd have stayed in Barcelona.
I wouldn't have gone skydiving.
5 I'd have gone to a summer camp in the USA.
I wouldn't have had a ride in a hot air balloon.
6 I'd have been very lazy.
I wouldn't have taken so much exercise.

2

2 he would have had holidays in Devon.
3 he wouldn't have bought a private jet.
4 he would have had to work hard.
5 he wouldn't have become famous.
6 he would have seen his old friends.
7 he wouldn't have talked with an American accent.

3

2 If he hadn't found it difficult, he'd have enjoyed it.
3 If she'd had a map, she wouldn't have got lost.
4 If she hadn't heard the noise, she wouldn't have phoned the police.
5 If he hadn't been hungry and cold, he wouldn't have stolen the food and clothing.

4
2 immediately
3 capsizing
4 imagine
5 emergency
6 parachute
7 responsible
8 challenge

5

1 danger	anger	✗
2 ghost	lost	✗
3 steer	fear	✓
4 daring	wearing	✓
5 touch	such	✓
6 would	food	✗
7 done	gone	✗

Unit 9 Lesson 3

1

1 have	2 can't	3 have	4 on	5 done
6 had	7 have	8 have	9 must	10 many

2
2 Yes, they must have enjoyed skydiving.
3 No, she can't have seen a ghost.
4 Yes, he must have been hungry.
5 Yes, they must have been worried.
6 No, she can't have wanted to call the police.

3
2 She must have lost something.
3 He must have broken his leg.
4 They can't have seen the sign.

4
2 He may have lost his memory.
3 He might have taken a holiday.
4 He could have gone to stay with his parents.
5 He may have had a car accident.
6 Someone might have attacked him.

5

Unit 9 Lesson 4

1

1 A6	B3	C8	D2	E5	F7	G1	H4

The order is A G D F C E B H

2
1 saw a yellow car coming up fast behind him.
2 walked up to the desk and noticed a piece of paper lying by the telephone.
3 his car hadn't been badly damaged.
4 he hadn't tried to miss the dog.
5 look for the doorman.
6 their car was badly damaged at the front.
7 the yellow car was getting closer and closer.
8 the number of the night club, Las Cabanas.

4

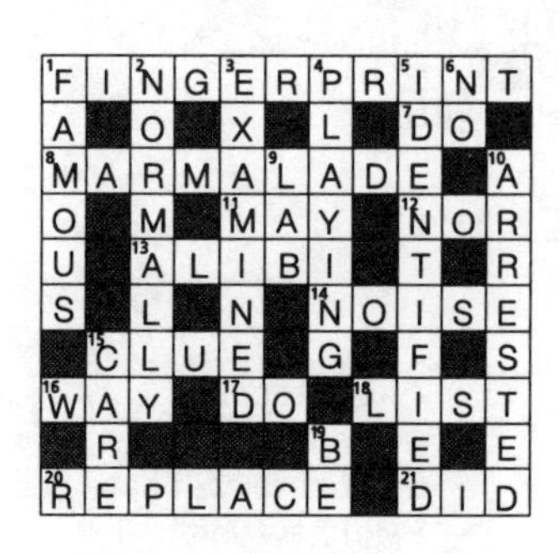

Unit 9 Review

1

1 had	2 have, mended	3 to, done
4 would, had	5 would have	6 had, have opened
7 have gone	8 can't, done	9 must, to, for
10 might have		

2
1 break (the others are to do with cleaning and tidying)
2 knife (the others are for drinks)
3 towel (the others are clothing)
4 burglar (the others are legal professions)
5 success (the others are adjectives)

3
1 detective 2 Information 3 sensible 4 burglary 5 horrible

4
1 I'd have phoned you if I'd had your number.
2 Stella can't have killed Rocky.
3 Alison had her car repaired.
4 Someone might have found my wallet.
5 If Mark hadn't gone to ACE, he wouldn't have learnt to swim.

5

1D	2C	3D	4B	5A	6C	7B	8C
9A	10C	11A	12D	13C	14B	15B	

ROUND-UP

Possible answers

1 This evening I feel like dancing.
2 Recently, I've promised to write to my brother.
3 I get up the earliest in my family and my brother gets up the latest.
4 At the weekend, I'm going to go to a football match.
5 If it rains, I'll watch the match on TV.
6 I've been living in my town for 9 years.
7 I've been at my school for one year.
8 I go to the cinema once a week.
9 She must be in her English class.
10 After I had breakfast this morning I came to school.
11 I felt very tired last Saturday because I had been shopping with my mother all day.
12 What a brilliant film!
13 It had been mended.
14 It will be closed.
15 I said that I was hungry.
16 He/she asked me to open the window.
17 I can see my friend writing and I can hear a bird singing.
18 People used to walk a lot, they didn't use to go by bus.
19 If I saw a flying saucer I would scream.
20 He/she'll let me read my English book in class. He/She won't let me listen to music in class.
21 You should stay away from boats. You shouldn't swim in the dark.
22 You'd better look in all your pockets.
23 I should have read my English book. I shouldn't have played basketball all afternoon.
24 When I was six I could sing but I couldn't read music.
25 I will be able to drive a car. I won't have to go by bus.
26 I'll be talking to my friends.
27 I'll have finished my English homework.
28 I have it cut.
29 If I'd been with the group at ACE I would have liked Mark best.
30 I might have left it at my friend's house.